Gender and Education

Gender and Education

Edited by
Dr.S.K.PANNEER SELVAM
Assistant Professor, Department of Education
Bharathidasan University, Tamil Nadu
and
Mrs.R.DEVI
Assistant Professor,Merit College of Education
Ariyalur, Tamil Nadu

RANDOM PUBLICATIONS
NEW DELHI (INDIA)

Gender and Education

ISBN 978-93-5111-356-0

Published in 2014 in India by
RANDOM PUBLICATIONS
4376-A/4B, Gali Murari Lal, Ansari Road
NewDelhi-110 002
Phone : +9111-43580356, 011-23289044
e-mail : sales@randompublications.com
info@randompublications.com

Reprinted 2025

Type Setting by : Shah Computer Graphics, Delhi-110094
Printed at : Replika Press Pvt. Ltd.

Contents

1

Human Rights Education in India: Needs and Future Actions

Indian textbooks barely mention human rights. Indirect references to human rights are included in the Directive Principles of the Constitution of India and in civics and history textbooks. In Maharashtra, supposedly among the most socially aware states in India, the 9th standard (high school) civics book reproduces the Universal Declaration of Human Rights. Most universities do not offer human rights education, although some have three-month to one-year postgraduate courses on human rights.

The Need for Peace Education

The United Nations was created to protect future generations from the curse of war and to reiterate the belief in fundamental human rights, in the dignity and value of the human being, and in the equality of men and women. The end of the Cold War leads us to a single global conception of human rights.

The UN's message is: Know your human rights. People who know their rights stand the best chance of realizing them. Knowledge of human rights is the best defense against their violation. Learning about one's rights builds respect for the rights of others and points the way to more tolerant and peaceful societies.

Vast numbers of people are still unaware of their rights. While laws and institutions could in many cases defend them, people must first know where they may turn for help.

The Universal Declaration of Human Rights confirms the nations' commitment to the UN Charter on the promotion and protection of human rights. It is now recognized as one of the most important documents in the history of humankind and can be found in the constitutions of countries that became independent after World War II.

The UN General Assembly recommends that the text be distributed in schools. NGOs are asked to bring it to the attention of their members.

How many people have actually read this short, epoch-making declaration? How many know of the International Bill of Human Rights, which consists of the declaration; the International Covenant on Economic, Social and Cultural Rights; and the International Covenant on Civil and Political Rights?

The answer is: very few. NGOs are often the first to bring human rights problems to the attention of the UN and the international community. Schools offer an important means of fashioning a human rights culture, as do research institutions, as they provide in-depth information on specific human rights issues.

Public Campaign

The National Human Rights Commission of India; the Indian Institute for Peace, Disarmament and Environmental Protection (IIPDEP); and many NGOs have launched a countrywide public information campaign for human rights. It aims to make everyone more conscious of human rights and fundamental freedoms and better equipped to stand up for them. At the same time, the campaign spreads knowledge of the means which exist at the international and national levels to promote and protect human rights and fundamental freedoms.

IIPDEP and many NGOs work to make school authorities and the general public aware of civic education. They focus on developing knowledge, skills and attitudes needed to apply fundamental human rights and freedom and, consequently, the nonviolent resolution of conflict.

Campaign activities include the following:

- production and dissemination of information and reference materials;
- workshops, seminars and training courses;
- fellowships and internship;
- special human rights observance;
- media and promotional activities.

A school system based on competition, and therefore failure, cannot promote the ideas of equality, tolerance and peace. The principles of civic education are the following:

- The school exists to serve humanity.
- The school promotes worldwide mutual understanding.
- The school teaches respect for life and for human beings.
- The school teaches tolerance toward attitudes and behavior different from our own.
- The school develops a sense of mutual responsibility. Greater responsibility carries increased responsibility to others and to the planet.
- The school teaches children to overcome egoism. It helps them understand that humanity can only progress through personal efforts and active collaboration.

The IIPDEP and many NGOs are expanding their human rights education (HRE) activities by drawing public attention to the role schools should play.

HRE promotes the application of these rights in the classroom and, by extension, in the daily lives of young people. The IIPDEP and NGOs can make government aware of the necessity of HRE and propose changes in the textbooks and programs.

Objectives

Civic education aims to promote human rights, particularly nonviolent resolution of conflict, and equality and justice. HRE's mission is to encourage personal growth and acceptance of others, and to foster cooperation and peace among individuals and countries. To achieve this, a wide variety of activities in schools and collaboration with teachers and students are essential.

IIPDEP Program on Human Rights Education in Schools

The IIPDEP is a nonpolitical, nonprofit NGO whose activities are mainly research and education of the public. It believes that human rights are a prerequisite for peace, security, development and democracy. If human rights are violated in India, the biggest democracy in the world will be in danger. For the sake of democracy and sustainable development in India, HRE is essential.

The IIPDEP holds seminars and lectures on human rights. It stresses HRE in schools. Materials on human rights using ordinary language are distributed to schools, NGOs and government departments.

The IIPDEP recently organized a regional seminar for teachers from the primary to university level, who, strangely, were not aware of human rights. However, after the discussions and debates on HRE, the participants concluded that respect for human rights is essential for the individual, society and country. The teachers promised to teach their students about the importance of human rights. They suggested that HRE be included in secondary-school subjects, such as history, geography, social studies, moral and religious education, language and literature, current affairs, economics and civics.

The teachers were unanimous on the following:

- Human rights should be taught as a special subject or a part of a special subject in civic education.
- Human rights should be included in all subjects.
- Extracurricular activities and clubs such as an Amnesty International Groups should be formed in schools.

- Schools should adopt the following goals:
  - Teachers should apply human rights to school life and the curriculum.
  - Human rights should be the basis of relationships in the classroom.
  - Human rights concepts should be taught systematically.
  - School rules and disciplinary procedures should be based on fair treatment and due process.
  - Schools should promote equality and avoid discrimination on the basis of gender, race or disability.
  - Teachers should be encouraged to develop a global perspective.

Activities in schools should include the following:

- Pre-school. The idea of human rights can and should be acquired at an early stage. For example, the nonviolent resolution of conflict and respect for other people can be demonstrated in class.
- Primary and high schools. Human rights provide the values guiding the school community. The teacher should be a role model in teaching children to be receptive to others and to diversity in society. Stories, games, poems, songs (from several cultures); shared meals and food; celebrations and festivals; visits to markets, museums, temples, churches, mosques and other cultural places; and inviting parents to school should be employed in teaching human rights.

HRE should teach children that all are equal before the law and that all should have equal opportunities. It should promote respect for the rights of children and the development of their personalities. It is governed by certain principles such as the following:

- Every right is matched by a duty toward other individuals and the community as a whole.
- HRE is not just about teaching rights, but about living them.

- It is about acquisition of habits and attitudes respectful of human rights.
- The school administration should be democratic. Excessively hierarchical structures, inflexibility in teaching, and autocratic head teachers are obstacles to HRE.

The process of learning about human rights can have the following elements:

- Teachers invite students to express their views.
- Students ask each other questions and exchange views
- Teachers ask students to consider sympathetically views they do not hold.
- Teachers and students ask questions which invite further exploration.

At the heart of democratic method is discussion, which is best done in small groups, the results of which are then reported to the class.

The principles for conducting discussions should be:

- reasonableness;
- peaceableness and orderliness;
- truthfulness;
- freedom;
- equality; and
- respect for the person.

Social education based on human rights helps students

- develop a positive self-image;
- develop sensitivity to their environment;
- learn to accept differences while recognizing essential similarities among people;
- develop skills in resolving and preventing conflicts;
- combat bullying.

Principles of nonviolent conflict resolution include

- self-respect and respect for others;

- communication;
- assertiveness;
- open-mindness;
- cooperation;
- conflict resolution;
- taking responsibility.

Even young students learn responsibility through, for example,

- caring for the animals;
- watering plants;
- tidying the book corner;
- choosing a story.

Older students can help younger students by

- reading to them or listening to them read;
- performing plays or providing other entertainment;
- organizing special celebrations or parties;
- helping with craft work;
- working as a responsible member of a group.

The more abstract notions of human rights—philosophical, political and legal concepts—can be introduced in secondary-school subjects such as history, geography, social studies, moral and religious education, language and literature, current affairs, economics and civics.

Problems

We noticed that headmasters and teachers very much favor HRE. However, textbooks are produced and printed by the government and it is very difficult to convince government officials to include HRE in the school curriculum. They must be convinced through a public-information campaign, for instance, or by pressure from international organizations such as the UN, UNESCO, etc.

Lack of money is one of the main troubles faced by IIPDEP and other NGOs. It is difficult to get funding from government or the private sector for HRE. It is also difficult to convince high-level government officials and policy makers of the need for HRE as they are cut off from the hardships of the person on the street.

2

Human Resource Development in Globalization

The pressures on traditional IR models are not all due to globalization, as we shall see, but many of the changes taking place can be traced to globalization. it is not always easy to disentangle the causes and effects of globalization. However, it would probably be true to say that globalization is represented by the opening up of markets due, in large measure, to foreign direct investment consequent upon the lowering of investment barriers in practically all countries; by the liberalization of trade, and by the deregulation of financial markets in consequence of which governments increasingly have little control over the flow of capital across borders. All this implies the dominance of the market system, facilitated by the collapse of alternative economic (and in many cases political) systems. There is also a direct link between globalization and information technology (IT). Rapid technological change and reduction in communication costs have facilitated the globalization of production and financial markets. At the same time globalization stimulates technology through increased competition; it diffuses technology through foreign direct investment. As aptly observed:

"Together, globalization and IT crush time and space." These developments have had further effects such as: democratization and pressures for more labour rights in countries where such rights have been restricted more liberalization and deregulation competition for investment increased economic independence of nations capital, information and technology flows are on the increase internationalization of enterprises and creation of mergers and alliances customer-driven (and not product-driven) global and local markets, but at the same time segmented markets competitiveness increasingly based (not on low wages or natural resources) on knowledge/innovation, skills and productivity. The success of global companies is to a large extent dependent on their ability to organize (within and between organizations) across national boundaries information, money, people and other resources. Employer Responses and Implications for Industrial Relations

Among the responses of employers are the following: Moving production overseas to reduce costs and to facilitate sensitivity to local and regional market requirements. Contracting out and out-sourcing. It is an important rationale of out-sourcing that it, on the one hand, enables an enterprise to concentrate on its core competencies, and on the other hand, it makes service work more productive. For example, in the USA, outsourcing of functions in hospitals not directly related to the work of doctors and nurses (care of patients) has substantially increased the productivity of the hospitals, and provided new opportunities for service employees. "Outsourcing is needed not just because of the economics involved. It is required equally because it gives opportunities, income and dignity to service work and service workers." More part-time and temporary work (especially among women, the elderly and students) Introduction of new technology Pushing for a more deregulated and flexible labour market More emphasis on productivity and quality Greater employee involvement in the design and execution of work Shifting the focus of collective bargaining from the nation/industry level to the enterprise level. Employers are of the view that issues relevant to the employment relationship such as work re-organization, flexible working hours and contractual arrangements, and pay for performance and skills, are increasingly workplace-related, and should therefore be addressed at the enterprise level. In the USA collective bargaining has, with some exceptions, been very much at the enterprise level; in the UK there is a marked shift towards enterprise bargaining; and the trends in Continental Europe are also in that direction. In many Asian countries outside Australia and New Zealand, the relatively little collective bargaining has been mostly at the enterprise level. In New Zealand negotiation has in the 1990s been almost entirely decentralized, and in Australia the trend is in the direction of decentralization. Exceptionally (in the USA) employers have reduced terms of employment through 'concession bargaining' when firms have been in financial difficulties. Downsizing the workforce. One important response has been the introduction of flexibility in the employment relationship to increase the capacity of enterprises to adapt rapidly to market changes. This has involved measures such as flexible working hours part-time work different types of employment contracts to the standard ones familiar to collective IR flexibility in functions, so that employees who are multi-skilled are not confined to the performance of only one task. They can cover up for absenteeism, and make some jobs redundant. flexible pay which involves some component of pay being dependent on performance, whether of the company, a group or the individual. Globalization has, through technology diffusion, substantially increased the introduction of new technology. This, as well as the need for flexible adaptation to market changes, has led to the re-organization of production systems and methods of work, such as the following: Reduction of narrow job classifications and demarcation lines between managers and workers, accompanied by skills enhancement needed to perform jobs with a broader range of tasks. Increasing areas for worker involvement in the conception, execution and control of work. A greater focus on workplace relations and policies and practices conducive to better motivation and performance such as information-sharing and two-way communication. These responses have increased the necessity for employers to make more investments in skills training, to offer incentives to employees to improve their skills, and for workers to take upon themselves some responsibility for their own development. The competition generated by globalization and rapid technological changes accompanied by shorter product life have, while destroying countless jobs in industrialized countries, created opportunities for multi-skilled and easily trainable workers, and for the most significant group of emerging employees - the knowledge worker. Knowledge and skills have become the most important determinants of investment, employment opportunities, productivity and quality and of flexibility.

The impact globalization and information technology have had on each other has made work more mobile, capable of being performed in different parts of the world without the need to actually set up physical facilities in other countries. Other changes in the nature of work and workers are being brought about partly by globalization, but not entirely because of it. For instance, it is arguable whether globalization is solely responsible for the growing service sector, and it does not account for the rapid influx of women into the workforce. Be that as it may, some of the changes which have a fundamental impact on traditional IR include the following:

The expanding service sector at the expense of the manufacturing sector in industrialized and rapidly industrializing countries more advanced and skilled workforces The rapid influx into the workforce of women who will, in some countries, occupy more than half the emerging jobs an increasing number of people who will not be working in an organization, though they will be working for an organization. The decreasing number of people working under 'permanent' contracts of employment, and the proliferation of other types of work arrangements such as part-time and temporary work, home work and contract work. Thus traditional IR has been challenged to accommodate different types of employment contracts, and different types of pay systems to reward performance and skills.

3

Human Rights and Cultural Values

Caste in India

One-seventh of the world's people are Indian. India's population is larger than that of United States and Western Europe, or Latin America and Africa, combined, and the diversity of the Indian people is perhaps even more staking than their numbers. India is the birthplace of two major world religions (Hinduism and Buddhism) has more Muslims than any country in the Middle East of North Africa, and has many other religions of local or regional importance (e.g., Sikhs in the Punjab). Differences between city and countryside (where almost three-fourths of all Indian still live) are striking, and a relatively prosperous modern industrial economy sits loosely and uncomfortably on a largely traditional agricultural economy. Furthermore, this contemporary diversity is matched by a long, complex, rich and varied history, as invader, from the Aryans to the British, periodically injected major new elements into and then was gradually absorbed by an increasingly complex culture.

To talk of "India," therefore, requires reducing this complex diversity to manageable proportions, typically by selecting a single place or a single part to stand, however imperfectly, for the whole, I follow the second course, taking Hinduism as the locus of traditional Indian values.

1. "HUMAN RIGHTS' AND TRADITIONAL INDIAN SOCIETY

The dominant tendency in the literature is to argue that human rights ideas have been present is all society at all times, but India is a partial exception to this tendency.

But a surprising number of authors argue that human right ideas are present in traditional Indian (Hindu) ideas and practice. Yougindra Khushalani claims that "Hindu civilization had a well-developed system which guaranteed both civil and political as well as the economic, social and cultural rights of the human being"

Taking if for granted that there is a Hindu concept of human rights. And S.K.Sajsena, although not explicitly using the language of human rights, speaks of "Hinduism, with its basic principle of equality of opportunity" and argues that pre-feudal Indian society was based on "standards of equality and of the freedom of the individual as an individual"(1967:367,360-61)

In fact, though, social structures and the underplaying social visions of human dignity in traditional India, as in other traditional societies, rest not on human rights but on social duties and status hierarchies: "Indians....base their social structure on duties and obligation rather than on rights." Persons are seen first and by nature as bearers of duties, not right, and whatever rights one does have rest on the discharge of duties or one'status2. and in traditional Indian (Hindu) society, "people's duties and rights are specified not in terms of their humanity but in terms of specific casts, age and Sex" (Mitra 1982:79), while the caste system made the ascriptive hierarchy so rigid that for all intents and purposes one's duties and rights were almost completely defined by birth.

2. Caste, status and purity

Caste may be defined as a small and named group of persons characterized by endogamy, hereditary membership, and a specific style of life which sometimes includes the pursuit by tradition of a particular occupation and is usually associated with a more or less distinct ritual status in a hierarchical system (Beteille 1965:46)

The case system divides the whole society into a large number of hereditary groups, distinguished from one another and connected by three characteristics separation in matters of marriage and contact, whether direct or indirect (food); division of labor, each group having, in theory or by tradition, a profession from which their members can depart only within certain limits; and finally hierarchy, which ranks the groups as relatively superior or inferior to one another. (Dumont 1980:46)

The caste systems divides the whole society into a large number of hereditary groups, distinguished from one another and connected by three characteristics separation in matters of marriage and contact, whether direct or indirect (food); division of labor, each group having, in theory or by tradition, a profession from which their members can depart only within certain limits, and finally hierarchy, which ranks the groups as relatively superior or inferior to one another. (Dumont 1980:21, summarizing Bougle)

Individual elements of the caste system are common elsewhere: all societies have social hierarchies, with a tendency of different group to separate from one another, and hereditary occupational specialization has usually been the norm, even in the west until very recently. But the combination of these three of separation, division, and hierarchy in the intensity characteristic of India makes the caste system largely unique to south Asia and the division of society into an extremely large number of endogamous groups kept separate by extradinarilly powerful and detailed rules of ritual purity is particularly characteristic of Hindu India.

The most ancient Indian formulas recognizes four casts, or varnas (colors): Brahman, Kshatriya, Vasishya, and shudra (symbolized by the colors white, red, yellow, and black), which roughly correspond to priests, warriors/rulers, the landed and mercantile classes, and the servile classes. Below these four varnas were Candelas, "untouchables," It is unclear whether this fourfold (or rather fivefold) division ever accurately desired Indian society.4 but by the third or fourth century A.D. a much more comples system of caste segmentation existed, based on the jati, an endo famous decent group traditionally linked to a particular occupation. Today "there are so many (castes) that is virtually impossible to determine their exact number," the boundaries between casts are maintained by exquisitely detailed rules of ritual purity: contact with, in some instances even sight of, lower casts is viewed as polluting; intimate contact, especially in marriage or at meals, is especially defiling. "Scruples concerning purity are the keystone, or better the foundation stone, or all Hindu construction, and /....the parts are only ordered and kept in place by sentiments of pious respect and sacred horror" the fear of pollution is so intense that it not merely separates, but actually repels, castes from one another

None of this is intended to suggest that questions of power and class cab be ignored, let alone that purity is causally prior. Traditionally, however, purity, wealth and power have largely coincided. Purity offers the clearest entry into the philosophical and cultural logic of the casts system and allows us to treat the practice of casts according to its own terms of self justification. Furthermore, whether we adopt the Weber and notion of legitimacy or the Gramscian idea of hegemony, the ideological structure of in-justification must be a central part of the analysis of such a long lived and deeply ingrained social structure. Nevertheless. I do try to link ideas of purity directly to issues of power by considering rational values as they were embedded and embodied in the actual practice of Hindu-dominated were embedded and embodied in the actual practice of Hindu- dominated India.

3. The ontology of caste

In the traditional Hindu world, all reality is one: Brahma, the absolute. 'Hinduism is a monistic religion which....Believes in one ultimate spiritual reality or existence which reveals itself as this and many other worlds and is present everywhere in the universe and beyond it, and which dwells in every living being" Physical existence however, clouds one's recognition of this reality.

Hinduism is "a unique life style concerned primarily with developing....the paradigmatic self aware man" and having achieved such awareness attaining ultimate and complete reunion with divine reality.

Everything is made of three basic guans, three radical "substance" sattva, rajas, and tamas. Very roughly, sattva, the substance of purity resides in the mind, provides true knowledge of all reality as simply manifestations of Brahma, and is symbolized by the color white; rajas, the substance of virility, resides in life itself, is associated with egoism, selfishness, and virulence, and is symbolized by the color red; and tamas, the substance of dullness, resides in the bosy, gives rise to ignorance, and is symbolized by the color black. Everything –deities, human beings, demons, animals, plants objects- is composed of these three substances but in different proportions: sattva predominates. In deities, rajas predominate in demons and animals, and teams predominate in plants and objects.6 the cosmic hierarchy is replicated at the level of human society. Creating a fundamental "paralleism" between cosmic and social orders

Hindu regards the nature and the cultural as non- dualistic features. Each is imminent in the other; each is inseparable from the other: each is a reflection of and realization of the other....

The entire....Cosmos is ordered by a premise of ranked inequalities; all life forms within the cosmos are defined by the same radical material substances (gun) and the behavioural code dharma appropriate to those gun. The same is also, true, significantly....Of human society of ordered ranks. And these birth-groups are detained according to the internal physical nature and the behavioral code held appropriate to that nature, which are viewed as a dupolex criterion of rank.

Placement in this social hierarchy, or caste system is by birth. Which according to the Hindu theory of reincarnation is not an accident or an arbitrary fact of nature, bur a reflection of moral justice and order? 'One is born where one belongs by reason of his actions over many incarnations" (Organ 1974:194) "The body or family in which a person is born, the society in which he lives, and the position or station in life which he occupies, are all determined by his past conduct and behavior" (Chatter- Rebirht is an essential mechanism in the law of karma or punishment and reward for one's deeds7

Caste hierarchy thus "is the expression of a secret justice" "In a just and stable society a correspondence was presumed between a person's qualities and his social position" caste division and hierarchy are seen not as a matter of social convention but as part of the fabric of the universe. Caste reset on natural distinctions, not on social action; its justification is ontological and metaphysical, not functional. Both the hierarchical structure itself and the placement of each person within that structure rest on a divinely oriented natural order.

Thus, the very ideas if human nature is radically different in traditional Indian and in modern western though. In traditional India, human nature is not viewed as a common possession of all people. Rather, "Human nature." If we can even use that term without gross anachronism, differs from person to person – or rather, from group to group. 'In Indian Thought, the caste is a species of making"

Birth and blood set only the upper limits of purity, however. Even for those born (relatively) Pure, pollution can easily come from one's own acts, even the most pure remain subject to the temptation of selfishness and physical desire, and even the most scrupulous remain vulnerable to violation by the others. Even mere contact with those less pure is polluting impurity is, as it were, contagious.

Caste and purity also serve as the basis of a functionally specialized division of labor, as seen in the frequent correspondence of caste and profession names. Anything connected with the body, especially with its wastes, is polluting; thus the low ranking of washers, sweepers, and scavengers'. In fact, manual labor in any form is considered an inferior form of activity, and thus artisans and agricultural labors are ranked below those, such as Brahman, who do not depends on labour. Occupation, life style and birth are therefore mutually reinforcing parts of a hierarchic social order of purity.

With a passion for the most subtle distinctions, traditional; India elaborated an incredibly varied and complex structure of castes and sub castes for example, we find intricate graduations among crafts; some artisans have relatively high status, while others lie at or near the bottom of the social hierarchy 9particularly leather workers, who are untouchables because of the special religious significance of cattle), In agricultural as well tasks have differential ritual status or purity; plowing is especially degrading, in part because it is likely to involve killing insects and other lower life-forms, which have religion-moral value as bodily forms into which souls are born.

The "Secret justice" of caste, the intimate link between and mutual reinforcement of the type of life one leads and one's natural worth, gives social inequality a special moral significance. One's station has its duties (dharma) which are held to be perfectly suited to one's nature and the discharge of those duties; whatever they may be gives one a place in society and a certain personal dignity. Both the Bhagavadgita (3.35) and the laws of Mamu (10.97) emphasize that it is better to perform one's own duties poorly. Even to die doing so, than to perform another's well and the proper discharge of the duties of one's station will be rewarded in the next life.

In practice, ht "inherited defilement" of member ship in the lower casts has been the central social fact, but caste theoretically assures that each person is treated according to his or her desert and therefore can achieved a sort of contextual dignity. Therefore, the inequality and group repulsion of the social and ritual hierarchy maybe partially mitigated by the fact that all are bound together in to an intricately articulated social and natural order. Each group is in part defined in part relation to the others and requires them Brahmans, for example, could not even survive without the services of other casts. the caste system in India represents an extreme form of Dukheiman organic solidarity, a social solidarity based on bringing together qualitatively different social groups, Brahma, the divine unity of all existence, provides an ontological and metaphysical point of reference toward which all reality aspires (to take extend that it is self aware) Likewise, the Brahman caste provides not merely a social point of reference purity in its broad outlines in perhaps most easily measured by the nature and extend of a caste's permissible contact with Brahmans- but the point towards which all social structures are directed and ultimately converge.

4. Flexibility, mobility, and equality

The caste system of traditional India wan an extraordinarily rigid social structure, but it was by means static. The proliferation of castes, which occurred principally through the fission of existing castes, involved considerable change. Regional variations, not only in particular details but even if fairly substantial ways, such as the paucity of intermediate castes between Brahman and Shudra in southern India also suggest openness to evolutionary change.

Because purity rests on a combination of birth and act, downward mobility is a very real possibility; there are even jatis of "degraded Brahmans" who are shunned by the most other castes upward mobility is more problematic, however, special individual merit, though particularly dedicated performance of the duties of one's station or by becoming a religious ascetic, would be rewarded by a higher rebirth, but there was almost no way an individual could move to a higher caste in a single lifetime " Individual upward mobility, with the partial exception of hypergamous marriages, was virtually impossible.10

Upward group mobility was also theoretically impossible, but in practice upward caste mobility, especially the local rise of a wealthy or powerful jati, has been a rare but real phenomenon throughout Indian history. "The reigning, ideal principle is that of social competition among those close to each other in rank,"

David mandelbaum presents a particularly though analytical account of the process of upward Jati mobility. The jati orginmyuth is typically revised, usually to claim membership in ahiher varna. This also provides a new behavioural model for the group. Srinivas refers to this process of lifestyle change as "Sankritization" In addition, social contacts are revised to reflect the new, aspired-to status. On its own, a jati can try to cut its contacts with groups that it now considers beneath itself. Much more important, thought, is acceptance into the new reference group: ultimately, one's children will have to acceptable as marriage partners or the "mobility drive" will fail.

Building alliances and patron client linkages- for example, by lending money or purchasing services over an extended period – can also be important. Securing the services, and thus tacit recognition, of Brahmans or even lower superior casts is often a crucial step. For the mobility drive to success, wealth is necessary but " wealth alone....is no guarantee of higher rank? Jati members must use it property so that the jati's rank may be elevated for their children". In effect a materially successful jati can attempt to achieve "closer parity between a jati's secular powers and material resources". With some luck and considerable political skill, the jati can raise its status over the course of a few generations.

Such change, however, involve only relatively minor and local rearrangements of the parts; they leave the caste system untouched. The rising caste typically couches its claims almost entirely in reference to the traditional ideology, and once it has successfully raised it adopt the way of life of its new station and defends the immutability of caste divisions. This is a classic example of system maintenance by selective co-operation. Traditional India society could be remarkably flexible about particulars, but it was exceedingly unyielding about basis structures.

Even religious movement that began as hostile of Hinduism, either in general or in its "standard" Brahmanism version, typically have fallen Victim to reabsorption. Mandelbaum discusses one common pattern; a charismatic leader teaching ideas of personal purity largely distinct from notions of caste and ritual becomes the leader of a social movement, which then is reabsorbed into dominant society as a new caste. This pattern is so common that s standard complaint about such bhakti 9devotinal) movements is that "in historical retrospect, their function appears to have been to reinforce the existing social order by channeling discontent into a negative form rather than bring about structural change" because no matter how spiritually egalitarian they are' theory tend to get organized and function within the existing socio – cultural order" and accept the existing hierarchy in secular contexts

The absorptive power of Hinduaste society can also be seen in the penetration of caste ideas and practices into introduced religions, such as Islam and Christianity. Even more striking is the fact that Buffhism, a radically egalitarian religion that began in India, largely died out there and never seriously challenged the caste system. In fact, in some areas of southern Nepal there is even a Buddhist caste system.

Nonetheless, religious opposition to caste inequality, and the underlying social discount on which it must have flourished, should not be denigrated. "The burden on which its oppressive gradations, generated its own antithesis on the ideological plane, and the question of equality was insistently raised in a succession of religious movements that go back to the beginnings of recorded history" There would even seem to be at least some religious resources for reform within traditional Indian Hinduism for example, the doctrine of reincarnation impels a divine essence in each person doctrine that might be transformed in ways that are compatible with the idea of human right. Organ suggests that the notion of varnas should be read simply as an appropriate recognition of moral differences and that efforts at reform should focus on making it possible to move through the entire circuit and become a Brahman in a single life many reformers, including Gandhi, have seen the fourfold varnascheme as a remedy for the jati based caste system. Swami Nikhilanandra among many others has presented Hindu spiritualism as a remedy for many of the ills of modernity. And more examples could be added. In order words, in the contemporary struggle for human rights there may be important traditional cultural resources on which India can draw, but these resources lie at the fringes of a tradition dominated by the remarkably resilient caste system. If the practice of Human rights is to be realized in India, a radical break with tradition is required.

The radical incompatibility between caste and human rights is obvious, we, have already noted the social primary of duties over right in Indian, India also shares with other traditional societies a group orientation that is in contrast to the inherent individualism of viewing each person as possessing natural and inalienable right that ordinarily trace precedence even over the claims of society and the state, “Hindu society is organized around the concept of dharma (the duties of one’s station) in a way roughly similar to modern society around that of the individual”

Perhaps even more important is the difference between the egalitarianism of human rights and the status orientation of the caste system that reflects a fundamentally different understanding of the moral significance of being human. Human rights “ derive from the inherent dignity and worth that arise simply from being human, and thus each person has the same basic dignity; human rights are held equally by all. No less important, human worth and dignity is radically distinguished form the worth and dignity of the rest of creation human rights are radically different from the worth and dignity of the rights of all other beings.

The caste system, by contrast, denies the equal worth of all human beings. If draws sharp, qualitative moral distinctions between human beings other parts of creation. The human soul is not qualitatively different from that of beasts and even plants; it is only a somewhat more evolved 9self-aware) incarnation. In fact, in many ways the distance between high casts and low castes is greater than that between lower castes and animals for example, the law of Manu prescribes the same penance whether a Brahman kills a cat, a mongoose, a blue jay, a frog, dog, iguana, owl crow, and considerably more attention is devoted to the crime of killed a cow, and considerably more attention is devoted to the crime of killing a cow than to killing a Shudra. “Dying without the expectation of a reward, for the sake of Brahmans and cows” will secure beatitude for Chandalas. In a following life, "the slay of a Brahman enters the womb of a dog, a pid, an ass, a camel, a cow, a goat, a sheep, a deer, a bird, a chandala...."

Given the traditional Hindu understanding of what it means to be a human being, the idea of human rights is a moral outrage, an affront to and attack on natural order and justice. Caste, the principal social expression of this understanding of human nature, must be forever antithetical to human rights.

A defender of caste point out that I have yet to shoe why we should not resolve the conflict by dismissing human as an alien incursion. Although human rights purport to be universal, the simple claim of universality provides no reason for those in another cultural to accept it. Therefore, we must pause to consider the counterclaims of cultural relativism, applying the general argument of Chapter 6 to the case of caste.

All Indian governments wince independence has rejected the caste system. Untouchability- which presents the most serious human rights problems that arise from the caste system. Those involving the grossest exploitation of roughly the bottom fifth of Indian society, the poorest of the poor in every poor country – is central government and the separate states have long pursued a variety of relatively aggressive remedial legal, social, and economic programs. Such official government policies, however, might be held to represent only the efforts of largely Westernized elite, In fact, the persistence of caste endogamy and caste- based patterns of social deference – especially in the country side, where most Indian live –might suggest that the rational caste system better reflect popular" human rights' value. But even if we were to grant that this is true, there are good reasons for pressing universal human rights arguments against caste.

We have already seen that the external human rights judgement of caste is in all respects negative. Should we abandon this external judgment just because caste has a long history and is deeply ingrained in Indian society? if the right violations inherent in the practice are of great external importance, it may be appropriate to press a negative external evaluation of even a very important a long –established culture practice. We should of cores, be wary of external moral judgemtns that contradict very important internal moral precepts, but when a large group of people are classified and traded as less than fully human, as they are in the caste system, we have crossed the boundaries of appropriate respect for ersity and self-determination.

In the case of India, the dangers of moral imperialism that may seem to lurk beneath pressing such as external evaluation are greatly reduced by the strong cross-cultural international consensus on the indefensibility of the caste system, the external judgment is not simply a 'western judgment, but one widely shared throughout the Third World as well. Furthermore, caste stands externally condemned not on the basis of a controversial interpretation of human rights or even the violation of just a few right, the Indian caste system violates virtually the full range of internationally recognized human tights, under all plausible interpretations of those rights.11 and this international consensus has considerable internal support, not only in the policies of Indian governments but also in the political activity of the victims of caste.

Caste is no longer 'hegemonic," no longer accepted as legitimate especially but those at the bottom of the system, who increasingly see themselves as victims of oppression and exploitation. In such circumstances, cultural relativist arguments against international human rights standards must be decisively rejected as misguided at best and as little more than upper caste/class ideological subterfuge at worst. It may be necessary and even desirable to take persisting caste attitudes and practices into account when implementing internationally recognized human rights in India, but we must insist that the caste system and caste based domination give way to the demands of human rights, as the victims of caste are themselves increasingly demanding in contemporary India.

Caste and the contemporary struggle for Human rights the preceding account of traditional Indian values is not merely of historical interest; attitudes and practices rotted in the ideas and institutions of the caste system remain of central importance in the struggle of human rights in contemporary India, especially in the countryside. But the caste system, the hedonic complex of caste ideas and practices, has eroded significantly.

Although caste still has great social, economic, and political relevance especially for rural untouchables the traditional coincidence of caste, class, and power is increasingly under attack, both indirect through the processes of economic modernization and political democracy, and directly through political action by and on behalf of untouchables and other "backward" or "depressed" communities. In fact, the struggle for the human rights of lower caste Indians can in many ways be seen as a struggle against the increasingly violent efforts of dominant castes, classes, and political elites to maintain the traditional correlation of caste, class, and power.

The principle challenge to the caste system has been and will continue tube economic change. In the countryside, the development of a money economy – and with it, increased opportunities for upward mobility by delinking wealth and traditional status – ahs weakened the relative power of Brahman castes and radically altered traditional patron-client relations.14 In the citi4s, new jobs (filled in significant measure on the basis of merit, or at least of qualifications), new residential patterns, greater educational opportunities, and the missing of largely anonymous people on the streets, in buses, and in government offices have created important opportunities for at least some individuals to escape many of the burdens of caste.

Such tendencies have often been supported and strengthened by direct intervention by central and state governments. Untouchables is outlawed by Article 17 of the constitution, and the protection of Civil Rights Act (the 1976 successor to the unsociability gives special legal backing and enforcement to this prohibition. Bonded labor is similarly prohibited both by the constitution and by subsequent laws. Further-more, there are relatively aggressive programs of what in the united States would be called "affirmative action," reserving places in educational institutions, jobs in the public sector, and even legislative seats for Untouchables, others Scheduled Castes, Scheduled Tribes, and other Backward classes.15 Special measures intended to benefit these depressed groups are also a regular feature of economic development and social service programs. Land reform and minimum-wage measures as well have often been intended to benefit the lower castes. The efficacy of such political interventions and the vigor of state functionaries in applying the law are frequently open to questions, but the general tendency has been to hasten the erosion of the caste system.

The institutions and practices of political democracy which probably are as deeply rooted in India as in any other country in Asia, Africa, Latin In the gram panchayats (village councils0 and other local political bodies. non- Braman caste- Hindus usually have predominant power because of their iconic, numerical, and political power, Representatives of the untouchables usually do not exercise substantial power, but simply their presences is often of social and psychological significance. The electoral power of non-bran groups at both the state level and the federal level has also been an important source of power and social change, especially as government grants and services play an ever-larger role in the economic and social life of both rural and urban communities. And electoral and local political activity has provided political skills, knowledge, and models for organizing and strengthening caste associations and grassroots political pressure groups.

It might be argued that in rural areas untouchables and other lower castes have to date been harmed at least as much as they have benefited from changes in both rural relations of production and the forms of elite political domination. Michie (19810 argues that the breakdown of traditional parton-client relations in India has been associated with an increasing concentration of resources and the denial of the benefits of traditional clientage, without the slack having been taken up by either the state or the market. S a result, the landless in particular tend to end up even more excluded and more oppressed.

This isrticulaly true given the widespread and flagrant disregard for such protective programs as rural minimum wages. In traveling with a government labor officer in South Gujarat, Bremen was not able to find a single work earning the statutory minimum wage; he computers the typical underpayment as equivalent to between one-forth and one-there of the laborer'a annual income. But in 1983 and 1984, out of more than 27,000 inspections 9virtually all of which must have tuned up violates of the law) only 82 cases(0.003percent) were investigated and prosecuted to a conclusion. When Bremen questioned the responsible officials, it became clear that they had little interest in acting against offending employers. In fact, the chief of the load office plausibly claimed in his own defense that he was powerless to act because tough enforcement would be met by landlord violence against his officers

The rise of private rural violence often with the acquiescence, collusion, or active support of the police, if a chilling and reality recent development. Traditional forms of rural social control, especially the caste system, are losing their efficacy. Feeling challenged and threatened by economic change, government policies, and the growing assertiveness of depressed groups, rural elites have increasingly tended to work to overcome traditional (caste) divisions among themselves in the interest of maintaining a united front against the lower castes and classes, especially the landless (among whom untouchables are disproportionately represented0 and super ordinate groups have increasingly tuned to direct violence against per ordinate groups have increasingly turned to direct overt violence against depressed groups in order to maintain their control; "the landowners control the landless with intimidation and, when this fails, with outright terrorization"

In Bihar, terror campaigns have been carries out against peasants who have attempted to organize to protect their rights and interests. Three major caste-based ' senas' (private armies) - Bhumi sena (used by kurmi land lords), Bramharsi Sena (Bhaumihars), and Larik Sena (Jadavs)- in collaboration with local dets (bandit gangs), have been used by landlords, often with the collusion of local authorities. Gujarat has as analogous problem with zim rakhas, "field guards, " usually hired by local landowners from urban gangs to keep the lower castes / classes in line. Other areas have similar organization and even where the violence is less. Organized, it is a regular feature of rural economic and political relations.16 and, of course, such caste /class violence is only the most visible and dramatic evidence of an intense and multi-face human rights struggle.

In the short run medium run, this new combination of more class like economic and political oppression probably leaves most of the traditional victims of the caste system little or no better off.17 Economic demographic, legal, and political changes have dramatically increased the social and economic opportunities available to some individual members of traditionally low status groups. These changes have also opened new opportunities for them to act politically to better their condition. Btu caste identification remains a central social reality; the struggle of traditionally oppressed groups for equality is being met by strong opposition from both ole and new elites, and the groups traditionally at the bottom of the social hierarchy still remain, for the most part, at the bottom.

The struggle against caste and its legacies remains at the center of the struggle for human rights in India, but we must be careful not to equate the two, particularly to the extent that caste, class, and political power have become separate based of domination. Difficult and momentous as it is, the struggle against caste will not be the end of the struggle for human rights in India. It may not even be the decisive phase. To free landless untouchable India. It may not even be the decisive phase. To free landless untouchable agricultural laborers, for example, from the stigma of untouchability –to truly, not just legally, free them, so that they not others would identify them as untouchables – would be a major victory, a decisive break with a grossly oppressive traditional practice. But unless these laborers are able to obtain ownership of land, a fair wage and good working conditions, or access to a decent urban or industrial job, unless they are able to organize, economically and politically without fear of official and unofficial violence and harassment; and unless their human rights will continue to be violated – in a new form, but no less surely. Class oppression is different from caste oppression but it is no less oppression.

The real human rights question in s not whether caste domination is to be replaced, but what is to replace it. Although still powerful, the caste system, in its traditional form, is on the decline. This significant advance must be purchased further with all possible speed and energy, but overthrowing the caste system is not enough, nay more than overthrowing imperialism sufficed. The struggle against caste in India must be evaluated both by how far India has moved away from the caste system and by how close it has moved toward implementing human rights –two important and perhaps even related, but distinct, directions of social change.

4

Human Rights Education and Dalit Children

In the broadest sense Human Rights is the right of every citizen in this country to be treated with dignity regardless of caste, community, gender and thereby realize their own capabilities and capacities. Access to education is but a part to this right to a life of dignity.

There can be two ways in which the question of human rights can be dealt with in the context of education. One is to state that the education system should facilitate the spreading of an awareness of the importance of human rights and an awareness of the importance of human rights and an understanding of the premises on which they are based as well as the safeguards that are available for the protection of these rights. This can be broadly referred to as Human Rights Education (HRE), and NCERT and UGC documents broadly refer to this. The second is to critically look at the practice of human rights within the education system.

There can be no quarrel with the objective of wanting to strengthen the subject content in relation to human rights wherever it is appropriate in subject areas such as social studies, civics as on. In this context it is probably adequate to integrate the teaching of human rights within the content of what is already being taught rather than introduce an additional subject at the school stage and thereby increase and lad of an already burdened school curriculum. There is considerable potential within existing content areas to do so and it is a matter of how effectively and sensitively this is done.

Of crucial importance to the issue of human rights in relation to education is the practice of human rights within the education system itself. In other words we probably need to first understand the concrete practice of human rights within the education system (and the manner in which the experience of different social groups varies in this context), before we can speak in general of Human Rights Education, the content of this education, whom it should focus upon and so on.

Anyone who looks at the schooling statistics in any government document will be struck by the extent to which certain social groups lack even the minimal access to opportunities where they can acquire basic skills of literacy and numeracy, i.e., to the primary stage of education. I am specifically referring to the relatively low enrolment and high drop-out rates from school of children from Dalit communities, officially called the scheduled Castes. What is however important is that these are social groups that have also been traditionally denied a life of dignity in society. Today when we are discussing the role of education in human rights literacy it becomes important to see whether children from communities whose human rights continue to be trampled upon are able to receive education with dignity from schools. The school is of particular importance as these are institutions that occupy public space and profess aims of equity ensuring equality of educational opportunity with social justice.

There are two points of importance that need to be remembered in the context of the education of Dalit children. One is that these children come from communities that have been traditionally denied opportunities for education. The lack of exposure of generations to skills of literacy, numeracy, literature and other forms of knowledge considered desirable is likely to put them at a disadvantage where access to school knowledge is concerned. This would imply that such children are likely to require specific pedagogic supp9rt from the school system. This is integral to their right of education. The other point is that Dalit communities have been denied learning in the past specifically because of the caste to which they belong. There is hence need for special vigilance to see that they do no continue to face social discrimination within the school.

As mentioned earlier the majority of Dalit Children in both rural and urban areas do not attend schools. Though education documents assure us that schools are available within walking distance to all children in rural areas, this does not even hold if one looks more closely at official statistics. Further, given the spatial segregation of Dalit communities in villages and among them specially those who traditionally remove night soil and the fact that schools are located within the upper caste areas, the question of how socially accessible schools are is also relevant.

Coming to the schools themselves what needs to be seen is the qualit6y of facilities that are available to Dalit children. One knows that the general quality of primary schools in rural areas is poor. What is the condition of schools that cater primarily to Dalit children by virtue of being located in their habitations? Passing references in a few studies and reports give rise to the suspicion that schools where Dalit children predominate may be in poorer conditions than the average rural schools-the minimal facilities may not be available to ensure that education is received in conditions that maintain the dignity of the individual child. Inadequate inputs in schooling, the poor quality of teaching, and as on-likely to be particularly detrimental to the education of children from this communities-are relatively less exposed to the kind of skills required in the classroom.

Equally important particularly for Dalit communities are the social processes within school and classroom that influence the learning environment provided for children. There is not much research evidence on what it means to be a Dalit child within the Indian classroom especially in the rural areas where the majority of Dalit school children are to be found. Scattered references in a number of studies do indicate that the education of Scheduled castes may still not be looked upon with favour by upper and dominant castes in many parts of India.

Within the school it appears that Dalit students continue to experience social discrimination and this can be seen both in the official curriculum, i.e., in the approved content of education and the hidden curriculum of schooling. Scheduled caste communities and the experience of untouchability rarely form part of school knowledge. Textbooks are silent about Dalit communities, even in states where these communities form a significant section of the population. Though untouchability and the maintenance of social distance from certain communities still persists in most parts of India such practices are rarely mentioned in school books or discussed in the classroom.

Dalits who look back upon their often painful experiences in school refer not to their invisibility in textbooks but to the distinct message of social inferiority that is conveyed to them by their teachers (the majority of teachers continue to come from middle and upper castes) and peers. Personal experiences of Dalits educated in the post independence period mention instances of Dalit children being asked to sit separately from their classmates, of being refused drinking water and served in broken teacups, made to dine separately and so on. A number of observers have noted the fact that teachers refuse to touch their slates or copies, or even resort to physical punishment for fear of pollution. Discouragement from teachers (who by and large still belong to the middle and upper castes in rural India) and indifference on their part to the academic needs to Dalit students is also reported in a few studies. Passing reference is also made to friendship patterns tending to remain within caste boundaries in schools.

The point being made here is that children belonging to communities that belong to the lowest of castes in the social hierarchy continue to be discriminated within the school and classroom. While blatant practices of untouchability may be less common than in the past, discrimination continues to exist in school practices particularly in the attitudes of teachers and school authorities as well as in peer behaviour. The inadequate academic support given to dalit children, the prevailing attitudes regarding these communities and the stereotypes that teachers and other members of the school community hold regarding their educability and their destiny impinges on the right of the child to education with dignity.

Given the scenario that exists regarding social groups that suffer from the backlash of caste in society at large, it is unlikely that human rights education in the abstract will bring about any significant change in the education environment provided for children belonging to these communities. What is required is that school practices in relation to discrimination, or the need for social justice within schools, is directly addressed. How this needs to be done is a matter of democratic debate and discussion but one can point to a few areas of intervention.

One is the official content of school education where a conscious effort should be made to critically analyze the manner in which school text books portray socially vulnerable communities both in terms of their visibility as well as the kind of roles they are seen to play if represented. In the context of what is called the hidden curriculum there is need for a multipronged strategy. One is the need to ensure that all children (specially in the rural areas) are entitled to equal access to facilities within educational institutions and the meeting of stringent punishment where there is any form of discrimination. The other is in the context of programmes to sensitize and create awareness among teacher educators, teachers and school administrators not only of human rights where these children are concerned but also of the deleterious consequences that social discrimination can have for the development of children and the realizing of their full potential. The special role that the schools can play in reinforcing academic inputs for these children need to be stressed. Similarly within the classroom the raising of awareness of human rights requires that such awareness is linked to critical consciousness of school practices including peer group behaviour in as sensitive a manner as possible. For both teachers and students this can be done more effectively through dialogue and discussion rather than in a didactic manner. Group projects can offer opportunities both for the recognition of underlying attitudes and critically looking at them.

Children especially those from Dalit and Minority communities are in an extremely vulnerable position in the classroom. Protection and support to children in order that they can exercise their rights will be important in efforts to create an educational environment conductive to learning with dignity. In this context the links that democratic and civil liberties organisations forge with schools will be critical.

5

Poverty, Literacy & Development Challenges for The 21st Century

Poverty and illiteracy are closely linked which go together everywhere in the world. Both poverty and illiteracy are part of the complex system of deprivation and discrimination. Research studies and experiences around the World show that literacy affects human resource development dramatically increasing children participation in primary education reducing infant mortality, accelerating success in child care, immunisation, better health, better hygiene, better nutrition, small family norm, empowerment of women so on and so forth. There is a definite relationship between literacy and development. Literacy strengthens and sustains the process of development. Literacy is both the cause and effect of development. Literacy is one of the most important indicators of the socio-economic and political development of a society.

Poverty & literacy

In the nation's 50 years of planned growth, more than half of the total population in India are still illiterate and continue to live under the poverty line. As per Human Development Report 1997, rural poverty declined from 40% to 33% during 1997 to 1981. By 1994 rural poverty in India was 39% and urban poverty 30%. As for the future, the ninth five year plan (1997-2002) calls for eradicating income poverty by the year 2005. The Planning Commission interprets this goal as reducing income poverty to around 5%. In the same way The National Literacy Mission, is also striving to meet the dead line of 'literacy for all' by the year 2005. Increasing literacy rate, it is hoped, will definitely improve the economic growth of our country.

The analysis of the present situation in India shows that the food production increased four times between 1951 and 1995. Famines were virtually eliminated; yet 53% of children under the age of four years remain under-nourished.

The rate of literacy has more than doubled between 1961 and 1991; yet half of the population is still illiterate. The school dropout rate is almost 50% and is more in case of females. The life expectancy almost doubled to 61 years between 1961 and 1992. We are still facing the threat of population growth. The growth of population is directly affecting the socio-economic growth of our country. Analyzing the present situation it goes without saying that, the importance of literacy and awareness for socio-economic development is highly essential.

Literacy & alleviation of poverty

Literacy can be used as an instrument for increasing production and efficiency through the promotion of training and vocational skills. This is the only way to inter-link literacy and alleviation of poverty. When literacy programme is linked with schemes aiming at the eradication of poverty, the poor people will definitely have a genuine interest in literacy programme. Their interest in literacy can be aroused only by ensuring that literacy will enable them to lead a better life. It can break the nexus between ignorance and poverty which, according to Swami Vivekananda, are the two basic sin in life. Therefore literacy work must be made life centered and poverty must be eliminated with the help of literacy. Poverty alleviating programmes in the country are the first level of response to overcome the problem.

The Government has initiated several income generating programmes with the goal to improve the standard of living of the people. Many of these schemes area for vocational training to develop and upgrade existing skills. Literacy is an essential pre-requisite for vocational training. In today's World of advanced technology, vocational skills are essential for employment. Vocational training like TRYSEM, Jawahar Rozgar Yojana, Integrated Rural Development Programme (IRDP) etc. cannot be successful with illiterate trainees. The literacy programme combined with other developmental programme should be a lifelong process which is otherwise known as continuing education for a truly sustainable development. The continuing education emerges as Post Literacy Programmes (PLP). Quality of Life Improvement Programmes (QLIP), Equivalency Programmes (EP) Income Generating Programmes (IGP), Individual Interest Programmes (IIP) and Future oriented programmes.

The literacy programme and continuing education programme linked with vocational training programmes will have significant impact in the level of living of various strata of poverty stricken masses. Poverty must be eliminated with the help of literacy and proper implementation of different policies and programmes of the Government from time to time.

As Josef Muller rightly pointed out that "Illiteracy has no future but it will, like poverty - be a feature in most developing countries for the foreseeable future. The struggle for literacy is a struggle against poverty and hence simultaneously for social and economic development, justice, equality, respect for traditional cultures & recognition of the dignity of every human being".

Literacy & development

Development refers to qualitative and structural changes in the state of an economy for the betterment of social and economic conditions of the people. This requires, people to acquire new knowledge, information and skills, which provide an impetus for development. Development is not merely growth in the economic sense but is closely related to the notion of quality of life which essentially ought to ensure fulfillment of basic needs properly and with dignity.

1. Over the past fifty years numerous operational and philosophical definitions of literacy and development have emerged keeping in view the changing priorities of Indian developmental goals and influences of international bodies like the United Nations and the World Bank. The concept of literacy and development has undergone tremendous transformation. During 1950's it remained as an integral part of the community development programme. In 1960's, when a direct correlation emerged between education and economic growth, the emphasis of literacy programme shifted from civic to functional literacy. It was argued that one of the reasons for the failure of many developmental schemes like agriculture production, family planning, co-operatives, Panchayat institutions was the lack of functional literacy among the rural masses. During 1970's, Functional Literacy for Adult Women project was implemented with a view to accelerating the participation of adult women in the development efforts of local community and bringing about attitudinal change among them. In 1978 the Janata Government put more emphasis on re-distributive justice and eradication of illiteracy. Through the National Adult Education Programme (NAEP) the Government put equal emphasis on literacy, functionality and social awareness. In 1980's the emphasis was given on people's right to literacy as component of development itself. Importance of literacy was reiterated by the National Policy of Education (1986) which envisaged that adult education would be a means for reducing economic, social and gender disparities; and the nation as a whole would assume the responsibility for providing a resource support. Subsequently when promotion of literacy became an important national mission, the National Literacy Mission was launched in 1988 with an objective to impart functional literacy to 80 million illiterates in 15-35 age groups by 1995 with the involvement of all sections of the society. Subsequently the concept of functional

literacy envisaged under NLM was much broader than the earlier and included the following four aspects.

(i) Achieving self-reliance in reading, writing and basic numeracy

(ii) Becoming aware of the cause of one's deprivation and moving towards amelioration of conditions through organisation and participation in the process of development.

(iii) Acquiring skills to improve the economic status and general well being

(iv) Imbibing the values of national integration, conservation of the environment, women's equality, observance of small family norms etc. With the change of concept, the operational strategies were also modified to make it a mass movement through total literacy campaigns.

It was the Ernakulum district Total literacy campaign in 1989 which created a mass upsurge for literacy. Moduled on the Ernakulum experience, over 370 districts have taken up the literacy programme.

Literacy programmes primarily aim at improving the quality of human capital which is very vital for the development of our nation. The confidence and behavior pattern of the neo-literates change tremendously when they are able to read & write.

As Freira observes literacy enables adults "read the world by reading the Word" Frank Lauback, who worked for the cause of literacy in more than one hundred countries has noted that "literacy begets new faith & new vision in the learner, it destroys his sense of inferiority and frustration, it stirs him to new self reliance, makes him feel that he belongs to the class of society that triumphs over difficulties, it gives him a new sense of mastery over his fate...It pulls him from the edges of society where he has lain stagnant mentally into the currents where he will be swept onwards as a part of the great moving course of human history. These observations were supported by several studies in different states.

Julius Nyerere rightly observed "a man develops himself through education which by broadening his mental horizon, widens his choices and capacity to take decisions since decision decides direction and direction decides destiny, literacy enables adults to take control of their destiny".

Poverty, literacy & development challenges for 21st century

The challenge set by the recent UNESCO commission report "Learning: The Treasure within" affirms its belief that education has a fundamental role to play in personal and social development and as one of the principal means available to faster, deeper and more harmonious form of human development and thereby to reduce poverty, exclusion ignorance, oppression and violence. It advocates with deep commitment and great moral passion. "LEARNING THROUGHOUT LIFE" as one of the keys of 21st Century. The Commission has put greater emphasis on LEARNING TO LIVE TOGETHER.: by developing an understanding of others and their history tradition and spiritual values and so on 'LEARNING THROUGH OUT LIFE' will require the development of infrastructure and institutional arrangements for providing educational services throughout the lives of adults.

Relevant issues relating to the Adult Education for the 21st Century were discussed in the international conference on Adult Learning at Hamburg 14-18 July'97 and the document entitled "Global Transformation and Education of Adults - An appeal for action states that "Adult learning....is indispensable in the quest to construct a better and fuller future for humanity. The challenges of 21st century cannot be met by Government, organisations or institutions alone, the energy and imaginations and genius of people and their full life, free and vigorous participation in every aspect of life are also needed.

In 21st century with the literacy programme utmost care should be taken to reduce poverty through different poverty alleviation schemes and focus on human development priorities - including basic health, basic education, safe drinking water and special attention for socially dis-advantaged groups should be given.

Rapid changes are accruing in all walks of life and people need update information and knowledge. With the changing science and technology the labour force should be more skilled to face the challenges in the next decade.

Women education needs to be strengthened to empower them, to play an active role as partner in the development process. In the 21st century sustainable development and education for sustainability is an important agenda before the nation. It is also very important to impart education to the adults on the complexity of the environment, population and development interrelationships.

Since India is facing population problem the policy should be formulated to impart population education along with literacy during 21st century. The literacy should be integrated with environment issues, economic programme, entrepreneurship development etc. for all-round development for human being. It is suggested to give more emphasis on the followings in the next century.

1. Establishment of continuing education centers for neo literates, school dropouts and senior citizens.
2. Establishment of study centers for equivalency programme.
3. Income generating & quality of life improvement programme.
4. Library & electronics media support to all village.
5. Involvement of voluntary agencies in the field of development.
6. Set up of vocational & technical institution in all block / village level.

In our country, most of the well thought out programmes/ schemes is implemented in isolation. But an integration and meaningful convergence of programmes and services can only achieve the desired goals of development in its real sense.

6

Impact of Education on Ethno-medicine and Health Care Practices Among the Tribal People of India

India is the home of several important traditional system of health care like Ayurveda. This system depends heavily on herbal products. Several millions of Indian households have been using through the ages nearly 8000 species of medicinal plants for their health care needs. Over one and half million traditional healers use a wide range of medicinal plants for treating ailments of both humans and livestock across the length and breadth of the country. Over 800 medicinal plant species are currently in use by the Indian herbal industry. The Indian sub-continent is inhabited by 88.2 million tribal populations belonging to over 577 tribal communities that come under 227 linguistic groups. They inhibit varied geographic and climatic Zones of the country. Their vocation ranges from hunting, gathering, cave dwelling nomadic to societies with settled culture living incomplete harmony with nature. Tribal thus mostly remained as stable societies and were unaffected by the social, cultural, material and economic evolutions that were taking place with the so called civilized societies. But this peaceful co-existence of the tribal has been disturbed in recent years by the interference in their habitats. Traditional communities living close to nature have, over the years acquired unique knowledge about the use of living biological resources. Modernisation, especially industrialization and urbanization has endangered the rich heritage of knowledge and expertise of age old wisdom of the traditional communities.

We must protect the forests for our children, grandchildren and children yet to be born. We must protect the forests for those who can't speak for themselves such as the birds, animals, fish and trees.

Anthropology as an integrated science of man deals with biological and cultural aspects of man. Presently anthropologists are more involved in applying their knowledge and techniques for human welfare. Ethno-medicine is a sub-field of medical anthropology and deals with the study of traditional medicines: not only those that have relevant written sources (e.g. Traditional Chinese Medicine, Ayurveda), but especially those, whose knowledge and practices have been orally transmitted over the centuries. In the scientific arena, ethno-medical studies are generally characterized by a strong anthropological approach, more than a bio-medical one. The focus of these studies is then the perception and context of use of traditional medicines, and not their bio-evaluation.

Tribes in India

The Indian sub-continent is inhabited by 88.2 million tribal populations belonging to over 577 tribal communities that come under 227 linguistic groups. They inhibit varied geographic and climatic Zones of the country. Their vocation ranges from hunting, gathering, cave dwelling nomadic to societies with settled culture living incomplete harmony with nature.

Forests have been their dear home and totally submitted themselves to forest settings. Their relationship with the forest was symbolic in nature. They have been utilizing the resources without disturbing the delicate balance of the eco-system. Tribal thus mostly remained as stable societies and were unaffected by the social, cultural, material and economic evolutions that were taking place with the so called civilized societies. But this peaceful co-existence of the tribal has been disturbed in recent years by the interference in their habitats. Traditional communities living close to nature have, over the years acquired unique knowledge about the use of living biological resources. Modernisation, especially industrialization and urbanization has endangered the rich heritage of knowledge and expertise of age old wisdom of the traditional communities.

A study on the utilization of local tribal revealed that they hold precious knowledge on the specific use of a large number of agents of wild plant and animal origins, the use of many are hitherto unknown to the outside world.

Herbal History and Tradition in Indian Context

The Rigveda, the oldest document of human knowledge mentions the use of medicinal plants in the treatment of man and animals. Ayurveda gives the account of actual beginning of the ancient medical science of India, which according to western scholars was written between 2500 to 600 B.C. Charaka and Susruta wrote around 1000 B.C. Charaka concentrates more on medicine while Susruta deals with surgery in details along with therapeutics.

Tribes and Ethno-Medicine

Ethno-medicine refers to "those beliefs and practices relating to disease which are the products of indigenous cultural development and are not explicitly derived from the conceptual frame work of modern medicine" (Hughes, 1968, cited from Misra et al, 2003). Various institutions are now concerned with the traditional health care system and means of traditional treatment.

The tribal people are the real custodians of the medicinal plants. Out of 45,000 species of wild plants, 7500 species are used for medicinal purposes. The World Health Organization (WHO) has been promoting a movement for 'Saving plants for saving lives'. This is because of the growing understanding of the pivotal role medicinal plants play in providing herbal remedies to health maladies.

India is the home of several important traditional system of health care like Ayurveda. This system depends heavily on herbal products. Several millions of Indian households have been using through the ages nearly 8000 species of medicinal plants for their health care needs. Over one and half million traditional healers use a wide range of medicinal plants for treating ailments of both humans and livestock across the length and breadth of the country. Over 800 medicinal plant species are currently in use by the Indian herbal industry.

In recent times with the increased knowledge of life and culture of the tribal communities, the social scientists are taking interest in ethno-medicinal studies. Many works have been reported especially from among the rural and tribal communities of India (Choudhury, 1986; Bhadra and Tirkey, 1997; Sharma Thakur, 1997).Ray and Sharma (2005) have given a description of ethno-medicinal beliefs and practices prevalent among the Savaras, a tribal community of Andhra Pradesh.

Kumari (2006) gave an account on the concept of illness and disease and the application of folk medicine among the Saureas of Jharkhand. However, ethno-medicinal studies are relatively less in Northeast India. Guha (1986) has reported from among the Boro-Kachari tribe of Assam. A glimpse of indigenous health practices among the plain tribes of Assam is given by Sharma Thakur (1999). The socio-economic condition of some of the tribes of Arunachal Pradesh and their problems of health and indigenous methods of treatment has been reported by Choudhury (2000), Duarah and Pathak (1997), Kohli (1999), Bhasin (1997, 1999,2002, 2003, 2005).

Ethno-Medicine and Health Care Practices among Sonowal Kacharis in Assam (India)

The Sonowal Kacharis is an endogamous group of Kachari tribe and a popular plain scheduled tribe population of Assam. Various types of locally available herbs and leaves of wild plants are used by them as medicine. Like many other communities of the region, there are few herbal specialists among the Sonowal Kachari. These specialists or medicine-men have considerable knowledge about the herbs and its medicinal use. Normally they learn about these medicinal plants and its uses from their ancestor. These medicine-men are referred by different term according to the cultural norms. Among the Sonowal Kachari's they are called as Bez (Barua and Phukan, 1958: 334). Of course in rural Assam, they are mainly known by this term.

It has been observed in the villages that use of herbal medicine for curing certain diseases are quite known to the people and besides medicine-men, many elderly persons known about the use of herbal medicines. Some of the diseases and their indigenous methods of treatment are given below:

(1) Fever: Lime (Citrus auran tifolia) juice mixed with sugar is applied on the forehead of the patient to get relief from fever.

(2) Diarrhoea: Dry goose berry (Emblica officinal is) powder and black salt mixed with cold water is taken. Bark of Long Pepper (Pipoli tree) mixed with Misiri water is also used to cure the disease.

(3) Dysentery: Lime (Citrus auran tifolia) juicewith hot water and little salt are used in dysentery. The juice of black Tulsi leaves (Ocimum sanctum) and Sirata (Swertiachirata) is also used for the purpose. The juice of tender leaves (three numbers) of mango (Mangifera indica), black berry (S.cuminii) and goose berry (Emblica officinal is) (equal proportions) together with honey are mixed with goat milk and is taken to cure blood dysentery. Honey together with the juice of Dubari grass (Family-Gramineae) can cure blood dysentery and need to be taken for three/ four days. They also use a kind of wild herb, locally called Manimuni (Centila asiatica).The juice of this herb mixed with sugar or honey should be taken continuously for a month to cure the disease. They also use limewater (Chun pani) mixed with juice of turmeric (Purcuma domestic) leave to get relief from blood dysentery and mucous.

(4) Blood Vomiting: A table spoon of carrot (Dancus carota) juice mixed with honey can cure blood vomiting.

(5) Liver Disease: Two to three raw or ripe Papayas (Carica papaya) daily can cure liver disease. A curry prepared from the bud of banana (Musa paradisiacal) and the meat of pigeon is also used as a medicine for the purpose.

(6) Jaundice: The medicine is prepared by pounding five or six number of Silikha (Myroballum) mixing with jaggery and it can cure jaundice. A glass of sugarcane (Saccharum officinarum) juice twice daily prescribed for the purpose. Boiled raw papaya (Carica papaya) is said to be good for curing the disease. Kardoi (Averrhoa carambola), Goose Berry (Emblica officinal is), Sugar cane (Saccharun officinarum), Neem leave (Azadirachta indica), a wild herb known as Duran ban (Lecas aspera), Brahmi sak (Herpestis monnieria), Purakol (Musa sapientum) are prescribed edibles for the patient.

(7) Nose Bleeding: Flower of Pomegranate (Punica granatum Linn) is crushed and 3-4 drops of juice is poured inside the nose to give immediate relief.

(8) Tonsilities: Juice is prepared by mixing one Amara seed (Sponolias mangifera), one Silikha seed (Mysoballum) and a piece of Turmeric (Purcuma domestic) and advice the patient gargles for a week regularly.

(9) Worms: Paste of five lemon seeds (Citrus aurantifolia) mixed with water and is prescribed to eat in empty stomach for a few days. The twigs of Chirata (Swertia chirata) are soaked in the water overnight and the water is prescribed to drink in empty stomach in the morning for one week regularly.

(10) Scabies: Lemon juice (Citrus aurantifolia) mixed with coconut oil is massaged for curing scabies. To remove scabies they take bath with hot water in which leaves of Neem (Azadirachta officinarum) were boiled. Twigs of Chirata (Swertia chirata) are crushed into paste with water to be used as an ointment and applied on the skin. Chirata water is prescribed to drink in the morning in empty stomach.

(11) Pain in the Ear: Juice of Tulsi (Ocimum sanctum) is boiled and put it in the ears to heal earache.

The patient is treated with available herbs, flora and minerals. Some of these are home remedies and some are specially prescribed by herbalist or folk medicine man available in the community. The practice of ethno-medicine is a complex multi-disciplinary system constituting the use of plants, spirituality and the natural environment and has been the source of healing for people for millennia. The spiritual aspects of health and sickness have been an integral component of the ethno-medicinal practice for centuries.

Diseases due to wrath of the supernatural

Disease	Supernatural agencies	Pujas (Rituals)
Dysentery, mental diseases, cancer	Deo	Propitiated by sacrificing two red cocks, one red hen, and one egg, besides other items of feast. Arrangement is made in the forest.
Asthama, Mental Disease, cancer	Lord of water	*Jalkhai puja*, worshipped by sacrificing one white duck and other items of feast, rice, salt vegetables, etc.
Accident, sudden illness	Burah-dangoria	No sacrifice. Only raw items, e.g. gram, rice, powdered rice, etc. are offered to propitiate Burah-dangoria.
Gastritis	Ancestral spirits	Ai puja, no sacrifice is made except offering of raw articles, powdered rice, gram with betel nut and leaves.
Epidemic and natural calamities	Mother goddess	Community level worship by arranging bhur-utuwa puja. One pair of betel nut and leaf is offered from each family. One red duck is offered on behalf of the villagers. All the offered articles are placed in a boat.
Epidemic and large scale death of men and animals	Mother goddes-sesof forest.	A white goat is a must for the Puja besides other offering.

Present Position of Tribes

The tribal health care practices and system of treating diseases are based on their deep observation and belief in nature. But with the development of education and their awareness towards importance of health and health care and also with the advent of modern health care facilities, Government health measures these people are becoming more interested in taking modern medicine instead of traditional herbal medicine.

Saving the Plant is Saving the Life

According to the text of Vishnu Samhita, causing any harm to the plants/animals is a sin. Even purloining of parts/ products of any of these living beings is a crime. The sinner/ criminals are liable to chastisement in this life and also after death. The punishments are of diverse nature:-pecuniary, corporal, expiatory and donation of specific articles to Brahmins.

Conclusions

The growing disinterest in the use of the ethno-medicinal plants and its significance among the younger generation of the tribes will lead to the disappearance of this practice. Educated younger generation of the tribes should be encouraged by the Government to protect and cultivate these valuable herbal plants before they get lost due to the impact of modernization and urbanization and also due to deforestation.

The role of Anthropology is also very important in the field of saving herbal plants. By educating tribal people we can preserve all these things for future generation. It is the Government duty to take necessary steps to preserve all these things.

References

1. Barua, I. and R. Phukan. 1990. "Socio-religious aspects of Health among Sonowal Kachari". The Eastern Anthropologist, 55: 4.
2. Bhasin, Veena. 1997. "Medical Pluralism and Health Services in Ladakh." J. Soc. Sci., 1: 43-69.

3. Bhasin, Veena. 1997. “The Human Settlements and Health Status of People of Sikkim”, (Pp. 153-187), in K.C. Mahanta (ed.), People of the Himalayas:Ecology, Culture, Development and Change. Delhi:Kamla-Raj Enterprises.
4. Bhasin, Veena. 1999. Tribals of Ladakh: Ecology, Human Settlements and Health. Delhi: Kamla-Raj Enterprises.
5. Bhasin, Veena. 2002. “Traditional Medicine among Tribals of Rajasthan.” J. Soc Sci., 6(3): 153-172.Bhasin, Veena. 2003.”Sickness and Therapy among Tribals of Rajasthan.” Stud. Tribes and Tribals, 1(1): 77 -83.
6. Choudhury, S. 2000. “Indigenous beliefs and Practices of herbal Medicine among the few Arunachalis”.Resarun, 26. 72-81, Govt. of Arunachal Pradesh, Department of Cultural Affairs.
7. Das, B. M. 2007. “Sonowal Kachari Nigostiya parichya”, (Pp. 1-3) in M. Sonowal (ed.), Sonowal Saurav Smarak Granth. Assam: Sonowal Kachari SanskriticMahotsava.

7

India Can Never be A Great Power Unless Illiteracy is Wiped Out

Francis Bacon had once declared that knowledge is power. It is today clear that if ever India wants to be a player of some consequence in the world, it can never do so unless all, repeat all, its citizens are literate and knowledgeable. Alas, the government seems ill prepared for the challenge. In India we today have an outdated and useless system of education that prepares quantity, not quality. And even the quantity is not enough because half of India remains illiterate. The money spent by the government is simply wasted in a system that is ill equipped to help India and Indians achieve a higher goal.

Schools are free, but there are too few schools in the villages to make a dent on illiteracy. The government constantly pleads its lack of resources to set up more schools in the villages. And municipal and government primary schools already set up are so pathetic that no middle class parents will ever want their children to attend them. So the choice is for private education at an affordable price. With the middle classes' strong voice not available, government schools only languish further — bad teachers, bad facilities, fewer and fewer students.

Then the students go to universities and colleges that are for the most part free (in the United States, students' lives are the opposite; they go to free schools and pay for college). In the 1980s, it was estimated that the Indian government spent Rs 200,000 per year per student enrolled in the IIT, the country's premier technology institutes. Yet, huge numbers of IIT students migrated out after completing their course, which effectively meant that precious money had been simply been lost. How many primary schools with decent facilities (such as blackboards, roofs, benches, toilets, and dedicated teachers) could have been set up with the money over the years is virtually incalculable.

This is not to condemn those who left (many of whom return later on). But why could the government not have charged the students at IIT? If a particular student could not pay, ensure that he or she is given a bank loan at a zero or low interest rate, to be repaid after his education is complete. Thus, the students could go abroad but certainly, few would mind sending home a few dollars to pay back an outstanding loan. IITs attract arguably India's finest brains, and securing a loan for them should never be a problem. In fact, the government can and should pass a law that no student, in any higher course, is to be denied a bank loan for higher studies.

There is another factor of our education policy and it is the emphasis on securing a degree. The real culprit for this is the government of India. Take for example, government recruitment. The government has four cadres, unimaginatively called A, B, C, and D. The last is for the menial workers (office boys, peons, cleaners, etc), who need to have cleared school (Class 10).

Cadre C is the clerical staff, cadre B the officer staff, and cadre A the top executive staff (for which the much sought after civil services exams have to be given). Now while it may be necessary to have graduates for Cadre B and A, why on earth is it necessary to be a graduate in any subject such as biology, zoology, geology, history, physics, chemistry, or you-name-it to join Cadre C where one just makes certain nothings and jottings on administrative files? Do we really need to force a needy person to acquire a degree for which he will have no further use ever again just to be clerk? This is a monstrous waste of time, money and talent.

It also explains why the government's initiative to push up vocational courses, diploma courses and other non-formal education has failed. Simply because the students who do such courses have very limited job opportunities available. Hence, only if one is guaranteed employment (usually a businessman's son) one will take up such a course, any other person (poor or middle class) will only seek a course which offers him or her maximum opportunity. This happens to be a degree, in any field, howsoever irrelevant to your final employment needs (how useful is it to know the inside of an earthworm as a clerk in the electricity billing department?).

To make matters worse, after doing a vocational course, further studies for those who are interested are not available, nor the pursuit of formal education. In today's fast-changing world, where persons may need to acquire further knowledge, such rigidity in Indian education rules is patently anachronistic.

Hence, the obsession with acquiring a formal degree. Tragically after graduation, thousands of students join the labour force with no specialised or marketable skill. They become drifters and wasters. To make matters worse, many go in for further studies such as a master's degree or law, only because they have nothing better to do! In fact, it was to curb this distressing tendency of uninterested students taking up law only to pass their time that the government introduced the five-year law course right after class 12 (intermediate). It hopes to cut down post-graduate law courses and on uninterested students.

What is worse is that in India, even master's degrees are subsidised. And the subsidy goes right up to the doctorate level. Today, many students do their masters and their doctorates only because it costs them nothing and gives them an excuse not to start working. Worse, students pursue courses to avail of hostel facilities, which, again are subsidised to ridiculous levels. These student spend the country's precious resources whiling away their time, playing politics, on a long free vacation with virtually no responsibilities save clearing the exams once a year. In India, there are no assignments, no project work, no research work involved even at the masters level.

In fact, students go right for the masters immediately after doing their bachelors without even knowing what jobs they are going to take up and whether the course has any relevance. Others take up masters but only prepare for their civil (why should they do masters for it is still questionable). Only a few do it genuinely as they want more knowledge. Is it any wonder that many of our worthies who finally boast a master's degree often know so little about their own subject. They can easily reproduce what is in the text-books but can rarely think for themselves about the subject.

It is time our planners gave serious thought to education. There is no need to subsidise higher education, because that only attracts the riff-raff rather than the serious students. The aim should be to make higher education available only to those who are genuinely interested. As mentioned above, let soft loans and grants are available to all students genuinely desirous of greater knowledge, loans that can be repaid. This will ensure that higher education is available to all regardless of wealth status, but also curb the uninterested. Anything free is unappreciated. Once the students pay for their education, they will treat it with greater respect than they do at present.

And the government would do well to spend the money thus saved on primary education. So that we may no longer have the dubious distinction of having the world's greatest number of illiterates! Thus, by diverting funds to primary education, we can wipe out illiteracy. And by charging for higher education, we will ensure that the students actually study their subjects and become an educated lot.

Let us remember that India can never aspire to great power status unless all its citizens can read and write, are aware of the times that we live in, and participate in the nation's destiny rather than be mere spectators.

8

Impact of Globalization on Teacher Education

A teacher who establishes rapport with the taught, becomes one with them, learns more from them than he teaches them. He who learns nothing from his disciples is, in my opinion, worthless. Whenever I talk with someone I learn from him. I take from him more than I give him. In this way, a true teacher regards himself as a student of his students. If you will teach your pupils with this attitude, you will benefit much from them - M.K. Gandhi.

Education has been around for as long as man has been, though its structure and perception has varied over centuries and civilizations. Now we are living in the highly scientific and technological world. Enormous changes are occurring in the day to day life of human beings because of globalization, privatization and liberalization. Education is seen as central to economic competitiveness, the reduction of poverty and inequality, and environmental sustainability. So, it is necessary to provide education for all; then only India will become developed country by 2020.

Globalization

Globalization is a term describing the increasing interdependence, integration and interaction among people, companies and corporations in disparate locations around the world. This umbrella term refers to a complex medley of economic, trade, social, technological, cultural and political relationships. The term has been used as early as 1944; however Theodore Levitt is usually credited with its first use in an economic context.

In defining and explaining globalization, Nsibambi (2001), incorporated five concepts. He defined globalization as "a process of advancement and increase in interaction among the worlds, countries and peoples facilitated by progressive technological changes in locomotion, communication, political and military power, knowledge and skills, as well as interfacing of cultural values, systems and practices". He noted that globalization is not a value-free, innocent, self-determining process. It is an international socio-politico-economic and cultural permeation process facilitated by policies of governments, private corporations, international agencies and civil society organizations. It essentially seeks to enhance and deploy economic, political, technological, ideological and military power and influence for competitive domination in the world.

Globalization is the worldwide process of homogenizing prices, products, wages, rates of interest and profits. Globalization relies on three forces for development: the role of human migration, international trade, and rapid movements of capital and integration of financial markets.

From the culture point of view, David (2002), states that globalization is the process of harmonizing different cultures and beliefs. Globalization is the process that eroding differences in culture and producing a seamless global system of culture and economic values (Castells, 1997). The harmonization, according to Awake (2002), is achieved due to advancement in communication and countries are increasingly being forced to participate. Therefore, globalization can be viewed as a process of shifting autonomous economies into a global market. In other words, it is the systematic integration of autonomous economies into a global system of production and distribution.

The world of separate nation-states is said to be ending enabling the process of globalization to run its logical course. The new technology, based on the computer and satellite communication have indeed revolutionized our traditional conception of the media, both print and electronic. Books, newspapers, radio, television and video programme are now being transposed into the multimedia world of the cyber space and available to all people of the world wherever they may live. Ajayi (2001) remarks that globalization is about competition and struggle for dominance which encourages more than anything else, the continuation and expansion of western imperialism in the new millennium.

Importance of Education

During the Vedic and Upanishadic period, India had some of the prominent institutions of higher education, which attracted scholars from distant places located in different parts of the world to come to India in pursuit of knowledge. The ancient universities of Takshashila and Nalanda, which survived till the end of the fifth and twelfth Century AD respectively, imparted knowledge in different areas according to the requirements of the contemporary society.

The importance of education is quite clear. Education is the knowledge of putting one's potentials to maximum use. One can safely say that a human being is not in the proper sense till he is educated.

This importance of education is basically for two reasons. The first is that the training of a human mind is not complete without education. Education makes man a right thinker. It tells man how to think and how to make decision.

The second reason for the importance of education is that only through the attainment of education, man is enabled to receive information from the external world; to acquaint him-self with past history and receive all necessary information regarding the present. Without education, man is as though in a closed room and with education he finds himself in a room with all its windows open towards outside world.

Education means the gradual process of acquiring knowledge. Education is a preparation for life. Swami Vivekananda, the great thinker and reformer of India had remarked: “We want that education by which character is formed, strength of mind is increased, intellect is expanded and by which one can stand on one’s own feet. Education is the manifestation of the perfection already in man.” The great Nobel Laureate and writer Rabindra Nath Tagore was one of the earliest educators to think in terms of the global education village, and his educational model has a unique sensitivity and aptness for education within multi-racial, multi-lingual and multi-cultural situations.

Development through Educational Institutions

Independent India has witnessed an upsurge in the growth of higher education. Yet from an international perspective, we are relatively slow, despite being steady in registering advancements in learning. Today India has the second largest education system in the world, next only to the USA. Yet, the total number of students represents hardly six percent of the relevant age group, i.e. 18-23 years, which is much below the average of developed countries which is about 47 percent. The gap is glaring. Hence the phenomenal challenge. The journey from being ‘Good’ to being ‘Great’ appears to be long and arduous.

India is a developing country. 70% of people are living in the villages. The rural area literacy percentage is very low when compared to urban area literacy rate. The main occupation of Indians is cultivation. The duty of higher educational institutions is to introduce courses which help to improve the rural people socio-economic status in the society. Through education it is possible to change the world. Because of globalization now world become a village. We get any type of information within the seconds. Educational institutions have prominent role in the development of rural people in the society.

The first citizen of India today, Dr.A P J Abdul Kalam, while envisioning India of 2020, recently observed - "Spirit of Inquiry, creativity, entrepreneurial and moral leadership are the capabilities central to nation building in a democracy. Educators should develop in our children these capacities and make them autonomous learners who are self-directed and self-controlled."

Earlier all over the world, education, especially higher education, was available only to a privileged few. In the context of a knowledge society and the goals of sustainable development, higher education/teacher education needs to percolate to the masses, not only just in terms of quantity, but also quality. In the last few years, this shift has been slowly taking place. Still, glaring deficiencies remain in the access to higher education, overall development of the student, sensitivity to human needs and equality in our society.

Also come into play, concerns in teacher education that come with globalization and rapidity of change like fast rate of obsolescence of knowledge, quality, competitiveness of education services, networking of institutions and innovations and new practices in delivery, combined with this are the concerns for sustainable development of the world.

Role of Teacher in Building Modern India

The role of the modern teacher is not confined to teaching alone. He/she is expected to participate in the development programmes of the community life. The question arises as to how this could be integrated with the teacher education programmes. Mudaliar Commission (1952-53) Report stated rightly, "we are convinced that the most important factor in the contemplated education reconstruction is the teacher-his personal qualities, his educational qualifications, his professional training and the place that he occupies in the school as well as in the community". On similar lines Kothari Commission (1964-66) stated that, "Nothing is more important than securing a sufficient supply of high quality recruits to the teaching profession, providing them with the best possible professional preparation and creating satisfactory conditions of work in which they can be fully effective".

The importance of the teachers in the Educational Programme of a country is too great. The greatness of a country does not depend on lofty buildings, gigantic projects and large armies, but on the quality of its citizens. If a nation has young men of sterling character and unimpeachable patriotism, she is found to make rapid progress in all fields. Young men are entrusted to the care of the teacher and it is therefore the sacred duty of the teacher to impart the right type of knowledge and make them good citizens. It is the teacher who impresses his children with his personality.

The teacher, a national integrator as he is, is the backbone of society, particularly so in the remote villages. He stands as an outstanding figure among the illiterate and semi-literate families. He is their friend, Philosopher and guide. The teacher actively shares the responsibility of reconstructing a social order, with all the cherished values and traditional beliefs, which are being eroded by the surge of new ideals and practices. He acts as a social reformer and counsellor to the community.

Impact of Globalization on Teacher Education

In the knowledge economy, the objectives of a society changes from fulfilling the basic needs of all round development to empowerment. The education system instead of going by text-book teaching will be promoted by reactive, interactive self learning, both formal and informal, with focus on values, merit and quality. The workers instead of being skilled or semi-skilled will be knowledgeable, self-empowered and flexibly skilled. Finally, the economy will be knowledge driven and not industry driven.

All fields of human activity, including education, have been influenced by the process of globalization clubbed with unexpected advancements in information and communication technology. Within the various sectors of education, teacher education has been affected the most. It is now increasingly realized that knowledge is universal and its creation and dissemination cannot be confined within national boundaries. The world is now like a global village, and continuous international interaction has become an essential component of human survival. The globalization of economy has led to internationalization of higher education including teacher education, not merely for economic benefits, but also for increased social interaction and promotion of international understanding.

Positive impact of Globalization on Teacher Education

1. A number of teacher educational institutions were increased.
2. Usage of technology increased in the educational institutions.
3. Information and communication technology were increased.
4. Teacher educational institutions were established in rural areas.
5. Government and private partnership in the field of teacher education.
6. Extension of internet facilities even to rural areas educational institutions.
7. Teachers are less worried for government jobs as MNC's and private or public sector are offering more lucrative jobs.
8. Free education for bright students.

Negative impact of Globalization on Teacher Education

1. Indian youths leaving education in mid-way and joining MNC's.
2. There has been an increase in the violence, particularly against women in the educational institutions.
3. Quality in education is decreasing (liberalization).
4. Degradation of values.
5. More availability of cheap and filthy material (CD's or DVD's of Hollywood movies, porn movies, sex toys, foreign channels like MTV) in the name of liberalization. It affects the psychology of teachers. Some teachers are miss-behaving with students.
6. Values of teacher are decreasing.

Conclusion

It is left to one's discretion to use a knife either to cut a fruit or to kill a person/animal. In the modernized and globalized world, it is necessary to be very cautious. Every single step should be taken with utmost care. It is the first duty of policy makers, politicians, officials and leaders to give priority for mother society and well being of their people. Globalization undoubtedly offers great opportunities for growth and development. However, no one can deny that its benefits are unevenly shared and its costs are unevenly spread among, across and within countries. This is particularly true with respect to developing and underdeveloped countries. Inspire of economic reforms the rates of unemployment and poverty in India is still high. Both in concept and practice, while globalization has positive, innovative, dynamic aspects, it also has negative, disruptive and marginalizing aspects (UNDP HDR 1999). Nsibambi (2001) suggested that globalization must be seen as a change process full of opportunities and challenges that must be carefully and skilfully harnessed and managed to ensure human development.

Teacher is a national builder. According to Indian philosophy teacher is a third god. It is very important to take care about teacher education. Through education only it is possible to preserve values and culture. Through education it is possible to solve any types of problems in the society.

It is apt to quote Mahatma Gandhi "I do not want my house to be walled in on all sides and my windows to be stuffed. I want the cultures of all the lands to be blown about my house as freely as possible. But, I refuse to be blown off my feet by any".

References

1. David F. (2002). Why National Pride Still Has a Home in the Global Village. Global Policy Forum. New York. The Scotsman May 18.
2. Gandhi, M. K. (1977), "*The Collected Works*, Ahmedabad: Navajivan.

3. Kumar, K. (1994), 'Mohandas Karamchand Gandhi' in Z. Morsy (ed.) *Thinkers on Education Volume 2*, Paris: UNESCO.
4. Nsibambi, A (2001). "The effects of globalization on the state in Africa: Harnessing the benefits and minimizing the costs. Paper presented at UN General Assembly, second committee: Panel discussion on globalization and the state, November 2, 2001.
5. Ruggie, John Gerard (1993), "Territoriality and Beyond: *Problematizing Modernity in International Relations*," International Organization 47; 139-74.
6. Scholte, Jan Aart (2000), "*Globalization: A Critical Introduction*" (New York: St. Martin's).

9

Globalization and Indian Education: Challenges and Career Development

Globalization A series of complex, independent yet under related process of stretching, intensifying and accelerating world-wide inter-connectedness in all aspects of human relations and transactions such that events, decisions and activities in one part of the world have immediate consequences for individuals, groups and states in other parts of the world. Globalization has transformed world trade, communications, economic relations, interest rate, air fare, petrol price and share rate world wide in the 21st century and is having a similarly profound effect on Education too. Now in Education, time and distance have been compressed to such an extent with new involving methodologies, that learning centers have now been converted into 'Global Market Place' of Higher Education. Globalization has transformed world trade, communications, economic relations, interest rate, air fare, petrol price and share rate world wide in the 21st century and is having a similarly profound effect on Education too. Now in Education, time and distance have been compressed to such an extent with new involving methodologies, that learning centers have now been converted into 'Global Market Place' of Higher Education.

In the History of Indian Education the following four types of trends are very clearly visible: Universalism, Nationalism, Internationalism and Indigenization.

General Agreement on Trade in Services (GATS) in Education Service

General Agreement on Trade in Services (GATS) in Education Service GATS rules promise that all the member countries of WTO have to give treatment of Most Favoured Nation (MFN) to all other member countries. There should be similar national treatment to all WTO countries and there will be no domestic discrimination.

WTO has identified four main modes of trade in Education that receive legal protection through GATS

WTO has identified four main modes of trade in Education that receive legal protection through GATS CROSS BORDER SUPPLY - through distance education or internet which can cross national boundaries. CONSUMPTION ABROAD - involves the education of foreign students and is the most common form of trade in educational services. COMMERCIAL PRESENCE - refers to the actual presence of foreign investors in a host country. This covers foreign universities setting up courses or entire institutions in another country. PRESENCE OF NATURAL PERSON - refers to the ability of people to move between countries to provide educational service.

AREA

AREA This education service covers all types of Education (Primary, Secondary, Higher, Adult, Others) including apprenticeship, training programme, foreign language instruction, training for career development, examination preparation, tutoring and educational support services, educational consultations, educational guidance, counseling, testing, student exchange programme etc.

Trade reforms may not help a country which:- spends all its exports revenues on weapons- lacks good governance - has crippling debt overhangs and - lacks domestic capacity or infrastructure to take advantage of new market access opportunities

Trade reforms may not help a country which:- spends all its exports revenues on weapons- lacks good governance - has crippling debt overhangs and - lacks domestic capacity or infrastructure to take advantage of new market access opportunities India faces a tough test on the bases of these conditions

CURRENT REALITIES: INDIA'S POSITION

CURRENT REALITIES: INDIA'S POSITION Globalization is based on interdependence where both the parties are dependent on each other on equal footing. But, in Education the reality is quite different. On the name of globalization, USA with 586000 foreign students is a leading exporter of Education service followed by UK (270000), Germany (227000) and Australia (174732) in the year 2002. The number of Indian student in USA in 1996-97 was 30641.This comprised the 6.70% of the total foreign students studying in USA, but in 2003-04, this number reached to 79736, which is the 13.9% of the total foreign students studying in USA.

NUMBER OF INDIAN STUDENTS STUDYING IN USA IN LAST EIGHT YEARS

India continues to remain the largest student sending country of origin, while the number of students from some countries (like China, Saudi Arabia, Pakistan, UAE, Egypt, Indonesia and Thailand) in USA experienced sharp decline in 2004. Indian students in US increased by 22.30% from the academic year 2001 to the next year. The number of Chinese students grew only 5.5% during this time which dropped China from number one spot. In Texas University itself the Indian students make up almost half (45.30%) of all international students studying there.

FOREIGN STUDENTS IN INDIA

FOREIGN STUDENTS IN INDIA The spirit of globalization should be reciprocal. A study by the Association of Indian Universities that covered 277 major Indian universities says that the number of foreign students in India shrunk from 12765 in 1992-93 to 7745 in 2003-04. If the country-wise position is analyzed the number of Malaysian students (806) is highest followed by Nepal (681), Iran (472) and Kenya (442). The significant numbers belonging to other countries are Bangladesh (319), UAE (232), Yemen (222) and Syria (25).

India has many advantages in the field of Higher Education

India has many advantages in the field of Higher Education The IITs of India have been ranked the third best technology university in the world for the year 2005 Management institutions (IIMs) have their own credentials here Quality Education is possible on low cost Comfortable with the International language English as medium of instruction

CHALLENGES AHEAD FOR INDIA

CHALLENGES AHEAD FOR INDIA cultural conflict equal share in educational business autonomy of institutions quality education to poorer classes local language and culture maintenance of native academic institutions lack of market oriented policies of the Government for the universities

Curriculum gives sufficient inputs about local culture, problems and needs but in the time of globalization, the prescribed curriculum will respond to the need of which country is difficult to say. The current realities of globalization reflect a highly skewed relationship between East and West. Between free trade and education there is a fundamental conflict because in new situations 'Invisible Hands' will regulate the Education of any country/ society rather than the Welfare Government. 'Right of Education' is an empowerment right, now this will be managed by 'Unforeseen Spirits'.

PATH AHEAD FOR INDIA

PATH AHEAD FOR INDIA Political Will Education should be the direct responsibility of the Central Government Industry and University collaboration Demand of multinational industries should be met by the universities Rethink and redesign the courses and curriculum Private universities Foreign collaboration of universities Open franchise overseas Bold and innovative leadership by academicians, administrators, political leaders and policy makers

10

A Study of Education in India and Asia-pacific

The development of any nation depends mainly on the standards of its educational institutions. Education is the most powerful and effective instrument for inducing radical changes in the behaviour of students. Education is a powerful instrument of national development-social, economic and cultural. Today's children are tomorrow's citizens. So, it is necessary to take care about children. Now we are living in the scientific, modern and technological world. The teacher occupies pivotal position in the system of education. Teaching has been one of the oldest and most respected professions in the world.

Education is the process of instruction aimed at the all round development of boys and girls. Education dispels ignorance. It is the only wealth that cannot be robbed. Learning includes the moral values and the improvement of character and the methods to increase the strength of mind. The history of education in India is very rich and interesting. One can trace the ancient India education to the 3rd century BC. Research shows that in the ancient days, sages and scholars imparted education orally, but after the development of letters, it took the form of writing. Palm leaves and barks of trees were used for education, and this in turn helped spread the written literature. Temples and community centers often took the role of schools. When Buddhism spread in India, education became available to everyone and this led to the establishment of some world famous educational institutions Nalanda, Vikramshila and Takshashila. These educational institutes in fact arose from the monasteries. History has taken special care to give Nalanda University, which flourished from the fifth to 13th century AD, full credit for its excellence. This university had around 10,000 resident students and teachers on its roll at one time. These students included Chinese, Sri Lankan, Korean and other international scholars.

It was in the 11th century that the Muslims established elementary and secondary schools. This led to the forming of few universities too at cities like Delhi, Lucknow and Allahabad. Medieval period saw excellent interaction between Indian and Islamic traditions in all fields of knowledge like theology, religion, philosophy, fine arts, painting, architecture, mathematics, medicine and astronomy.

Later, when the British arrived in India, English education came into being with the help of the European missionaries. Since then, Western education has made steady advances in the country. With hundreds of universities and thousands of colleges affiliated to them, in fact scores of colleges in every discipline, India has positioned itself comfortably as a country that provides quality higher education to its people in specific and to the world in general.

STAGES OF EDUCATION

India and China are big brothers in Asia-Pacific countries. 1/3 of total population of world is living in these two countries. Both are developing countries. Socio-economic, cultural and political impacts of these two countries are very much on other countries in these regions. It is very important to study about these two countries.

India: There are broadly four stages of school education in India, namely primary, upper primary, secondary and higher secondary (or high school). Overall, schooling lasts 12 years, following the "10+2 pattern". However, there are considerable differences between the various states in terms of the organizational patterns within these first 10 years of schooling. The government is committed to ensuring universal elementary education (primary and upper primary) education for all children aged 6-14 years of age. The general educational system in India was 10+2+3+2 for science and arts courses, 10+20+4 or 5 for engineering and medicine including school education.

China: The People's Republic of China has a nationwide system of public education, which includes primary schools, middle schools (lower and upper), and universities. Nine years of education is technically compulsory for all Chinese students. Education in China is the help of the Ministry of Education. The education system provides free primary education for six years (some provinces may have 5 years for primary school but 4 years

Country	Primary School		Middle School		High School		Colleges/ Universities	
	Age	Class	Age	Class	Age	Class	Age	Class
India	6-10	I-V	11-12	VI-VII	13-15	VIII-X	16-	XI-Ph.D
China	6/7-12	I-VI	13-15	VII-IX	16-18	X-XII	18-	....Ph.D

Total Literacy: Total literacy rates of India and China

Year	Literacy Rate by Sex in India and China					
	India			China		
	Literacy Rate (%)					
	Persons	**Males**	**Female**		**Males**	**Females**
1951	18.33	27.16	8.86		-	-
1961	28.30	40.40	15.35		-	-
1971	34.45	45.96	21.97		-	-
1981(1980)	43.57	56.38	29.76	62.35	78.6	52.7
1991(1981)	52.21	64:13	39.29	77.55	87.0	68.1
2001(2000)	64.84	75.26	53.67	84.8	92.3	77.3
2000/01-2010	67.30 (2005)	77.00 (2005)	57.00 (2005)	90.85	95.9 (2010)	85.8 (2010)

China and India: The adult literacy rates of China and India are given below.

Country	Adult Literacy Rate (%)	Youth Literacy Rate (%)
China	90.9	98.9
India	60.3	71.3

for middle school), starting at age seven or six, followed by six years of secondary education for ages 12 to 18. At this level, there are three years of middle school and three years of high school. The general school educational system in China was 6+3+3 or 5+4+3.

Adult literacy rate is for the age group 15 years and above. Youth literacy rate is for the age group 15-24 years. The youth literacy rate for India relates to 2001.

EDUCATIONAL INSTITUTIONS

India: Overall, according to the latest Government Survey undertaken by NUEPA (DISE, 2005-06), there are 1,124,033 schools. Overall, the % enrollment of pre-primary classes to total enrollment (primary) is 11.22% (DISE, 2005-06). In 1950-51, only 3.1 million students had enrolled for primary education. In 1997-98, this figure was 39.5 million. The number of primary and upper-primary schools was 0.223 million in 1950-51. This figure was 0.775 million in 1996-97. In 2006-7, an estimated 93% of children in the age group of 6-14 were enrolled in school. The Government of India aims to increase this to 100% by the end of the decade. To achieve this, the Government launched Sarva Shiksha Abhiyan.

Higher education in India has evolved in distinct and divergent streams with each stream monitored by an apex body, indirectly controlled by the Ministry of Human Resource Development and funded by the state governments. Most universities are administered by the States, however, there are 44 important universities called Central Universities, which are maintained by the Union Government. The increased funding of the central universities gives them an advantage over state competitors.

Indian higher education has been developing steadily. The Indian Institutes of Technology were placed 50th in the world and 2nd in the field of Engineering (next only to MIT) by Times Higher World University Rankings. There are several thousand colleges (affiliated to different universities) that provide undergraduate science, agriculture, commerce and humanities courses in India. Amongst these, the best also offer post graduate courses while some also offer facilities for research and PhD studies.

Technical Education has grown rapidly in recent years. With recent capacity additions, it now appears that the nation has the capability to graduate over 500,000 engineers (with 4-yr under-graduate degrees) annually, and there is also a corresponding increase in the graduation of computer scientists (roughly 50,000 with post-graduate degree). In addition, the nation graduates over 1.2 million scientists. Furthermore, each year, the nation is enrolling at least 350,000 in its engineering diploma programs (with plans to increase this by about 50,000). Thus, India's annual enrollment of scientists, engineers and technicians now exceeds 2 million.

China: The United Nations Development Programme reported that in 2003 China had 116,390 kindergartens with 613,000 teachers and 20 million students. At that time, there were 425,846 primary schools with 5.7 million teachers and 116.8 million students. General secondary education had 79,490 institutions, 4.5 million teachers, and 85.8 million students.

There also were 3,065 specialized secondary schools with 199,000 teachers and 5 million students. Among these specialized institutions were 6,843 agricultural and vocational schools with 289,000 teachers and 5.2 million students and 1,551 special schools with 30,000 teachers and 365,000 students.

In 2003 China supported 1,552 institutions of higher learning (colleges and universities) and their 725,000 professors and 11 million students (see List of universities in the People's Republic of China). While there has been intense competition for admission to China's colleges and universities among college entrants, Tsinghua and Beijing universities are amongst more than 100 other key universities that have been the most sought after. ***Tsinghua*** is a top university in Mainland China.

LITERACY FACTS AND FIGURES IN ASIA AND PACIFIC

The above figure shows that, in 2000-04; 52% of illiterates are in South and West Asia. 18% in Sub-Saharan Africa, 16% in East Asia and the Pacific, 7% in Arab States, 5% in Latin America and the Caribian and 2% of illiterates are in Other Regions. "More than two-thirds of the world's adult illiterates live in Asia and the Pacific Region." Political and cultural impacts are very much on literacy.

PUBLIC EDUCATION EXPENDITURE

	India		**China**	
	Year		Year	
Annual budget for nonformal education	1995	Rs, 2.3 billion (US$ 293 millions)	... .	... .
Public expenditure on education as percentage of GNP (%)	1995	3.5	1995	2.3
% share of nonformal education in total education budget	....	....	....	....

Indian Prime Minister Dr. Manmohan Singh declared that his government was allotted 4% of GND for Public Education Expenditure in the 11th Five Year Plan during the period 2007-2011.

THE MAIN POINTS RELATED TO EDUCATION IN THE PRESENT YEAR BUDGET OF INDIA

1. Education at the center of the social sector reforms
2. Rs. 34,400 crores to be allocated for education
3. Rs, 13,100 crores to be allocated for Sarva Shiksha Abhiyaan
4. Rs. 8,000 crores allocated for Mid-Day Meal Program
5. 6,000 model high schools to come up

6. 16 central universities to be established
7. 3 IITs to be set up in Bihar, Rajasthan and Andhra Pradesh
8. Rs. 85 crores allocated for the development of a knowledge society

EDUCATION AROUND THE WORLD

Studies reveal that United States of America is the only country investing the maximum in matters related to education. It has been ascertained that public education budget of United States of America, if taken into account equals the public education budget of the following nations, if combined together.

1. Central Asia
2. Caribbean and Latin America
3. Arab Regions
4. Eastern as well as Central Europe
5. Sub Saharan Africa
6. West and South Asia

SUGGESTIONS

The following suggestions are necessary to increase literacy rate and quality of education in the low literacy countries.

1. Frame very effective and strong educational policies.
2. Student-Teacher ratio should be 20:1.
3. Arrange good infrastructure for schools and colleges.
4. Student-Student; Teacher-Teacher; cultural exchange programme should be continued in every year.
5. Organization of regional seminars, conferences and workshops on the eve of education.
6. Minimize corruption in the field of education.
7. Give high-quality education for trainee teachers.
8. Use Science and Technology from the school stage.
9. Introduce computer education at primary level.
10. Adult and Continuing education should be strengthening.

11. Give autonomous status for monitoring bodies of education.
12. Raise the amount of public education expenditure.
13. Conduct regularly; in-service programmes for all teachers.
14. Continue mid-day meals programme for all schools up to X class.
15. Give free and compulsory education for all children up to X class and for girls up to Degree.
16. Minimize political influence in the field of education.
17. Take care in the framing of curriculum. i.e., it should be effective and easy to understand.
18. Establish some higher educational institutions both in rural and urban areas.
19. Give equal importance for science and arts subjects.
20. Conduct educational tours, field work in the systematic manner.
21. Give importance for student centered learning and activity based learning.
22. Introduce Yoga, Meditation and Value Education at school level.
23. Conduct sports and games regularly.
24. Give proper importance for cultural programmes in the curriculum.

CONCLUSIONS

Through education it is easy to motivate all type of people in the society. Now we are facing so many problems like terrorism, poverty, high-population and illiteracy. By inculcating values in the students; we can change the future generation. They will want peace & justice in a world that acknowledges the rule of law and in which no nation or individual need live in fear; Freedom and self reliance to be available to all; The dignity & work of every person to be recognized & safeguarded; All people to be given an opportunity to achieve their best in life; and They will seek equality before the law and the equality of opportunity for all."

REFERENCES

1. 2nd to 7th Educational Survey of India.
2. Carol Chapnick, Mukhopadhyay, Susan Seymour; 'Women, Education, Family Structure in India' (1994), published by West view Press.
3. Gopal Ji Malaviya in "Indian and Chinese Foreign Policies in Perspective", edited by Surjit Man Singh, 1998, Radiant Publishers, New Delhi.
4. Literacy mission of India, New Delhi.
5. National Council of Education Research and Training, New Delhi.
6. Times Higher Education Supplement- 2006, London.
7. UNDP report on education-2003.
8. www.accu.or.jp./litdbase/policy/index.htm

11

Preconception Health Plan
Preconception Diet & Nutrition

It is important that each individual following this plan, look within themselves at their motivations for their lifestyle habits. What pain are you covering? What beliefs do you hold about life that perpetuates fear and violence? Only through the flowering of self compassion and self love, can we fully accept our current life circumstances, and thus move beyond them.

I have struggled with my health for many years. I am finally seeing that health begins with a simple statement that is not just said, but felt and believed. That statement is some like, "I want to take care of myself." or "I want to honor myself." It takes effort and patience to really slow down enough in life to pay attention to our dietary habits. Yet to really regain your health, you need to carefully listen to the signals your body is telling you about how many foods to eat, and what types of foods to eat. I have done my best to condense the information into the shortest possible format; it still will take some amount of time to go through it all. Please be patient, as this information has real value. The information is also circular, so you can understand it better if you read everything, rather than skipping over certain parts.

At the bottom of the page is a disclaimer. As a reminder, I provide this information for informational use only, any efforts on your part to practice this information is done at your own responsibility. That being said, there is a great need for real preconception health care practitioners to exist in this country, and there are hardly any that can provide any meaningful health care service, hence the creation of this protocol.

Preparation health plan overview

1. Avoid modernized foods
2. Eat special foods, rich in fat-soluble vitamins
3. Choose at least one method to repair and restore the body
   - Raw Foods
   - Bowel Cleansing
   - Milk Cure
   - Herbal Cleansing (mentioned but not discussed)
4. Balance Blood Chemistry using raw or rare animal proteins/ fats and vegetables.
5. Eliminate Allergies with NAET, HK, and avoiding modernized foods.
6. Practice FAM to replace birth control pills or the IUD
7. Dynamic Movement and exercise for vibrancy and health.

Preconception health timetable

These guidelines have arisen out of the observations that some indigenous groups of people, have certain customs, that they know are essential to create healthy pregnancies and children. These customs call for the frequently consumption of special foods for men and women which are rarely consumed in our modern diet, prior to conception. An explanation for the modern problems of childbearing and conception can be found to some degree in the fact that a vast proportion of the United States population, no longer eats these special foods.

- Immediately begin the preconception health diet, no matter how close to conception you are.
- Replace IUD and Birth Control pills with Fertility Awareness Method (FAM).

All the foods on this list can be eaten at any time, and the list is inclusive. So keep adding these items to your diet and do not remove any foods that you are utilizing even if you shift to a different time period.

The foods listed for preconception health, during the 0-6 month period before conception, are high in fat-soluble vitamins, especially a vitamin and mineral known as Activator-X (naturally occurring vitamin K2 in animal foods). During the formation of the sperm and ova, which happens approximately during the three month time period before conception, it is essential that both the mother's and father's body be loaded with this ingredient of fertility. In addition to Activator-X, fat-soluble vitamins A and D are needed. The best sources of vitamins A and D are grassfed liver, and/or high vitamin or fermented cod liver oil. This will help create a superbly healthy child.

- Avoid modern processed foods
- Avoid smoking, alcohol and unnecessary drugs
- Eat two of the following three foods regularly (daily or almost daily)*
  1. Raw grassfed dairy foods
  2. Seafoods, including all edible organs
  3. Organs of land animals
- Animal proteins (wild fish, grassfed beef, lamb, chicken, oysters, clams, crab, lobster, eggs) should be usually eaten either raw, or fermented, or in stews, and usually eaten several times daily in small portions (1-3 ounces), or larger portions if you have a desire for more. (With plenty of fat)
- An abundance of vegetables
- Fermented foods, such as fermented beverages including fermented milk and fermented vegetables in abundance, they nourish, cleanse and heal the body

- Bone broths regularly as they restore, cleanse and nourish the body
- Special Preconception Foods (see the timeline: fish eggs, yellow butter, “mustard” and “tomalley”)

*As an alternative or as a supplement for one of the categories, fermented cod liver oil daily.

**Make adjustments do the diet based on your inner wisdom and how your body feels, this is not mean to be a rigid protocol, but a helpful map for good food selection. You’ll notice the diet is high in fat. Fat from healthy sources is good for us, it won’t make you fat, and high cholesterol is not a health hazard.

Fat-Soluble Vitamins

Fat-soluble vitamins are vitamins A, D, E, and K. They are severely lacking from our modern diet. The diet above pays special attention to the foods that will provide us rich sources of fat-soluble vitamins and other minerals necessary for optimal health. Those food sources are raw grassfed dairy foods, wild sea foods when the head or some of the organs are eaten, and organs of grassfed land animals.

Preconception for men

Preconception health is almost as important for men as it is for women. In the example on the birth defects page, I showed an example of a puppy that had a birth defect from the father’s seed.

Some coastal Indians of Peru, had father’s eat what is likely the testes of the angelote fish, which is similar to a skate, before conception. Eskimo people had the father’s eat the sperm sacs of salmon’s, the milt, before conception. Some fish merchants will provide the milt of a variety of fish; some sushi restaurants serve “soft roe” as a delicacy. Men and their children would benefit by obtaining this special food, and eating it occasionally or regularly, prior to conception. If milt is unobtainable, other special foods should suffice. (Fish eggs, yellow butter, “mustard” and “tomalley”)

Child spacing

Many Indigenous cultures had taboos and norms around the spacing of children. Other than the obvious fact that this will prevent the mother from going crazy taking care of two infants, spacing children allows for time for the Mother's body to recoup its nutrients in between conceptions. Ideally children should be spaced 2.5-5+ years apart. In my opinion, ideal child spacing is far enough apart to allow for the full, on cue, breastfeeding of the first child (4-7 years of spacing apart). Of course these guidelines must be adapted to the uniqueness of your circumstances.

Hazards of birth control pills and IUD

"Oral contraceptive pills usually contain two hormones (steroids), most often synthetic, estrogen and progestogen. The pill upsets the balance between copper and zinc levels, raising copper and lowering zinc... The pill also interferes with other mineral balances, especially magnesium, iron, iodine, and probably chromium and manganese." Buttram, H. For Tomorrow's Children

The levels of Vitamin A, Vitamin C, B1, B2, B3 and B6, magnesium, iron, iodine, chromium, manganese and perhaps other vitamins need to be restored over a period of time from oral conceptive use. Tese vitamins are depleted do the significant upset of body chemistry caused by the pill or IUD. Becoming pregnant in a depleted state and hormonally imbalanced state, as many mothers do coming immediately off the pill, is surely a significant contributing factor in a host of conception problems, like morning sickness, post-partum depression, and perhaps even minor or major defects in infants.

Liver, especially raw grassfed liver contains many of these vitamins. I suggest small portions of grassfed liver from any animal, preferably raw or rare cooked, once or several times per day to help recover from birth control pills. (High vitamin cod liver oil is a somewhat adequate replacement for fresh liver.) Spiraling as well as many other foods can also help restore various nutrient levels.

Fertility awareness method (FAM) can replace birth control pills and IUD

FAM is not the unreliable rhythm method of birth control. The failure rate of FAM when the method is strictly followed is between 0-2percent. This makes it as safe as or safer than condoms. Because of the harmful effects of birth control pills and the IUD, the FAM method, which relies primarily on two indicators, cervical fluid, and waking temperatures, is recommended.

This needs to be practiced ideally for several months or even several years before conception while the body has time to rebalance itself, and restore levels of important minerals lost from birth control pills or the IUD. For couples who are infertile, FAM is a way of increasing the likelihood of conception by timing exactly the fertile times, and also through charting, women can see if their ovulation cycles are normal. More information about FAM is at The Garden of Fertility, and Take Charge of Your Fertility.

Note: In case you are curious, many Indigenous groups used herbal methods of birth control to safety prevent pregnancy. This herbal knowledge can, and need to be reclaimed. Until then, we have FAM.

Modern foods cause physical degeneration

I use the term modern foods, or modernized foods, to describe whole foods that have been altered by commerce and industry to enhance profit. These alterations are not done with the consideration of the health effects on the final food product. Thus we have a society that consumes vast quantities of foods that even bugs and microorganisms will not eat. These foods make us sick, and cause diseases, like those mentioned on this website.

1. Sugar – White Sugar, Brown Sugar, Organic Sugar, Evaporated Cane Juice, Corn Syrup, Commercial Jams (Exceptions are, totally unheated honey, and stevia. Limit frequent consumption of excessively sweet fruit)
2. Flour & Grain Products – White Flour, Wheat Flour, Organic Flour, any unsoaked grain products. Examples: bread,

crackers, cookies, doughnuts, breakfast cereals, muffins, pastries, tortillas, bagels, and sandwiches (most store bought flour products even from the health food store need to be avoided). Only eat grains that are organic and both freshly ground and fermented. Many grains require the bran and germ to be removed.

3. Hydrogenated Oils - like Margarine and Low quality vegetable oils, Vegetable Oil, Soybean Oil, Crisco, Canola, and Safflower (replace with organic coconut oil, organic palm oil, organic olive oil or butter, suet, or tallow).
4. Any type of junk, convenience food, or modern fast foods
5. Coffee, Soft Drinks, Nutrasweet, and anything with artificial flavors, artificial colors, or artificial ingredients
6. Soymilk, Protein Powder, and Excess Tofu.
7. Pasteurized Milk, even if it is organic.
8. Non-grass-fed meat and eggs, and farm raised fish.
9. Alcohol, Cigarettes, and Drugs (including most prescription drugs & vaccines)

Preconception cleansing

During the time of pregnancy, the body does its best to create a clean, toxin free environment within the Mother, for the growing fetus. Because of our modern lifestyle, with food additives, environmental pollutants and chemicals, and pharmaceutical drugs and vaccinations, our bodies can be loaded with toxic accumulations. Rather than forcing your body to strain to eliminate toxins during pregnancy, you can eliminate a significant portion of toxins before pregnancy through special dietary modifications. The result, the possibility of a comfortable pregnancy.

Cleansing with Diet

"Raw liver was commonly used by the Plains Indians to rehabilitate exhausted and diseased people. Those in excellent health also regularly included raw liver in their diet. Even today raw fish is used by the Eskimos as well as by the South Sea

Islanders for the cure of disease." Bieler, H. Food is Your Best Medicine Aajonus Vonderplanitz describes in the book, The Recipe for Living without Disease., a program for healing and rejuvenating the body with raw foods. This raw food plan does not refer to eating lots of salads but rather...

The key sources of proteins are raw fish, raw beef, raw chicken, raw fertile eggs, raw milk, and raw cheese (all organic, or wild, and grassfed). The key sources of fats are raw grassfed butter, raw grassfed cream, organic avocados and cream made from coconuts. Fresh vegetable juice is also utilized, however, higher sugar vegetables like carrots and beets, are not used in large quantities for juice. A typical juice is homemade using the Greenstar Juicer and is about 80% celery and 20% parsley. Juices made that include cilantro can have the effect of binding to heavy metals and cleansing them for our bodies.

Eating raw grassfed eggs, with between 2-4+ cups of fresh vegetable juice per day, will help the body cleanse and renew itself. Usually the cleansing process if fairly uncomfortable lasts 2-10 days, and it involves a detoxifying sickness.

Even if you do not follow such a program, the lesson to be learned here is to utilize raw grassfed animal proteins and fats, and raw vegetable juices to aid in cleansing the body. Eating raw glands and organs, especially raw or rare cooked, grassfed liver (do not use conventional liver's or other conventionally raised organs as they are high in toxic substances) will help rejuvenate and heal your body.

Raw Milk Cure/Cleanse

"The therapy is simple. The patients are put at rest in bed and are given at half hour intervals small quantities of milk, totaling from five to ten quarts of milk a day. Most patients are started on three or four quarts of milk a day and this is usually increased by a pint a day. Diaphoresis [copious perspiration] is stimulated by hot baths and hot packs and heat in other forms. A daily enema is given."

In my preconception diet guidelines, I suggest utilizing special foods regularly along with animal foods. The late Melvin Page, DDS, found that degenerative diseases, like tooth decay are caused when our body chemistry becomes out of balance from our modern diet full of processed sugar, processed flour and other refined foods.

In this state of non-balance, couples can become infertile. Dr. Page developed the Page food plan for correcting this imbalance, primarily the focus is on regenerating the body through creating balanced blood sugar and balanced calcium/phosphorus ratios in the blood. In addition to elimination of all processed foods, and utilizing raw animal proteins, Dr. Page found good results by advising small to moderate portions of animal proteins throughout the day, and also strict elimination of sweets including sweet fruits (examples: bananas, pineapple, grapes, peaches, oranges). Dr. Page's health plan (PDF) is here. Dr. Page also used minute amounts of hormonal supplements and a system of special body measurements to create balanced body chemistry.

Emotion and preconception health

Our glandular system, the pituitary, thyroid, adrenal, ovaries, testes and so on, are directly influenced by our emotional health. When our body perceives a threat, our glands release toxic substances; this is a biological response to prepare us for fight, flight or freezing. While we need these defenses occasionally in life, our body misperceives threats almost daily, and thus we are engaged in a series of habitual biological responses, that create a hostile bio-chemical environment in our bodies. The solution, begin to notice your defensive postures, so as you can recognize and begin to deprogram these responses when they are used unnecessarily.

Stress and preconception health

Stress does result from our modern lifestyle, but the definition of stress I prefer, is a set of environmental circumstances that our body fails to meet. Working 16 hours a day is not stressful if you feel vibrant, alive and capable during those 16 hours.

Due to our modern habits of food, drink, drugs, and mismanagement of our hours of rising and sleeping, and a general not honoring of the life force, we experience stress in our daily lives because our bodies cannot cope with the work load we give them, due to our imbalanced lifestyle habits, such as eating deficient foods.

Stress does influence one's ability to conceive and have healthy children. I encourage you to explore, and ask about the root of what is causing you to choose these habits you have created so that the stress can be relieved.

Feeling all of feelings

There are benefits to taking some type of effort to acknowledge your feelings. Take a moment every day and ask yourself, how do I feel? Then just receive whatever response comes up, do not judge it or push it away. There is no such thing as a "wrong" or "bad" feeling. (Acting out negative feelings inappropriately can be wrong, but feeling and acknowledging them is okay.) Another practice is to sit in quiet, and align with the intention, "I want to feel all of my feelings." The way you feel prior to conception, as the seeds of life are being created, will be a part of a framework for how your pregnancy, birth, and parenting will be.

12

Entrepreneurial Leadership and New Venture Innovations

This study aims to contribute to the knowledge of leadership styles and entrepreneurial orientation at small and medium enterprises (SMEs) as well as their effects on business performance. Entrepreneurial leadership and continuous innovation are vital components of twenty-first-century communities and organizations. The concept of 'visionary leadership' has been changed to 'entrepreneurial leadership' in 21st century. Leadership is one of the most essential ingredients for entrepreneurial success yet it is conceptually elusive.

Most business leaders would agree that innovation is vital for delivering business results and maintaining competitive advantages. The climate demands that organizations must adopt a new model for improving profitability, increasing competitiveness, allowing for globalization and providing superior customer care. Entrepreneurial leaders must realize the importance of environmental, social, and global issues while creating an atmosphere of innovation designed to help followers become more entrepreneurial themselves. Research and

Development (R&D) culture is the engine for sustained product innovations and key driver of continual growth. R&D fuels sustainable economic expansion by creating high-wage jobs, world class exports and the growth of productivity. A model has also been developed to test the effectiveness of the leadership and innovations in Indian SMEs.

"Courage - not complacency - is our need today. Leadership not salesmanship. And the only valid test of leadership is the ability to lead. Our ends will not be won by rhetoric. We can have faith in the future only if we have faith in ourselves" - John F Kennedy.

Entrepreneur basically means 'Capitalist' and 'Industrialist' i.e., 'Producer', 'Maker', 'Manufacturer'. Here in the broader sense, the macro vision, entrepreneur does mean the producer of new things, new ideas, languages and all those innovations in the world. Thus an entrepreneur is the crown of all the present day academic, spiritual, cultural, scientific and technological innovations and developments in the world. Had not there been an entrepreneur we all would have been still in the primitive age moving in the jungles without proper food, clothing and shelter. It is by the zeal and perseverance of the entrepreneurs of the past that it has become possible for us to live in this modern age quite cozily with all the comforts in life. Unless one makes efforts and becomes a successful entrepreneur he will have to lead a stagnant and mundane life.

The entrepreneur must be able to recognize and seize external opportunities that relate to innovation in a specific industry. Specifically, it is important to apply innovation when sources of opportunity are presented through the entrepreneurial environment. There are three sources of innovative opportunities which are very much essential for smooth functioning of the business. They are incongruities, demographics, and perception change. An important aspect of these motivational models is the role of entrepreneurial goals in motivating business founders to sustain their pursuit of entrepreneurial activity.

What makes a good entrepreneur? What attributes do successful entrepreneurs possess? What are the qualities that make an entrepreneur effective? The answer to these questions must arise from an understanding of either what entrepreneurs actually do or what they are expected to do; it would require, in other words, an analysis of the entrepreneurial skills. Essential qualities of an entrepreneur are as follows:

Entrepreneurship is essential for international, social and economic well-being, as new ventures are the dominant source of job creation, market innovation, and economic growth in many societies. Entrepreneurship is a major contributing factor to the economic well-being of a country, both in terms of economic growth and job creation. Traditionally, entrepreneurial ability tended to be defined by the following four attributes:

- **Initiative** – the entrepreneur takes the initiative to bring together the economic resources of land, labour and capital to produce a commodity (whether a good or a service), with the hope that such production will create a profitable business venture.
- **Decision**-making – the entrepreneur makes the basic business policy decisions for the business, thereby setting the course of the enterprise.
- **Innovation** – the entrepreneur is an innovator who attempts to introduce new products and new ways of doing things.
- **Risk-taker** – the entrepreneur risks his or her time, effort, business reputation and invested funds in the entrepreneurial venture.

LITERATURE REVIEW

"Entrepreneurship, in its narrowest sense, involves capturing ideas, converting them into products and/or services and then building a venture to take the product to market" (Johnson, 2001, p. 138). Drucker (1994) made an important contribution to the theoretical construct of entrepreneurship in large organisations when he referred to "corporate entrepreneurship" or "intrapreneurship." Antoncic and Hisrich (2003) argued that intrapreneurship goes on within organisations, regardless of their size. Intrapreneurship research has studied the individual intrapreneur, the formation of new corporate ventures, and the characteristics of entrepreneurial organization (Antoncic & Hisrich, 2003). Innovation can be radical and incremental. Radical innovations refer to path breaking, discontinuous, revolutionary, original, pioneering, basic, or major innovations (Green, Gavin, & Aiman-Smith, 1995). Incremental innovations are small improvements made to enhance and extend the established processes, products, and services. However, this contradiction does not "necessarily correspond to the more fine-tuned reality" because "radicality is a continuum" (Katila, 2002 p. 307). The spirit of entrepreneurship includes imagination, inventiveness and openness to the new. This spirit of creative response aligns with the capacity to exercise moral imagination and to see ethical problems in a new light. To be sure, our most fundamental ethical values — values such as honesty, avoiding doing harm, keeping commitments — are grounded in timeless traditions and are not likely to be soon abandoned. But it is in the application of these ethical values to emerging, unique situations, where moral imagination and the entrepreneurial spirit can make a decisive difference.

ENTREPRENEURIAL LEADERSHIP: A NEW PARADIGM

Leadership is one of the essential ingredients for entrepreneurial success yet it is conceptually elusive. We recognize leadership when we see it but it is very hard to say what we are recognizing. The challenge is not just to understand leadership but also to provide recommendations on how leadership skills can be developed and used to enhance organizational performance. Entrepreneurial leadership can be classified into following eight categories. Thinking about leadership is developing rapidly. In some ways a new post-transformational integration which draws from the whole tradition on leadership thinking is emerging. By distilling this integration, entrepreneurial leadership can be thought of as having eight key elements.

1. **Personal Vision:** The entrepreneur's vision is the driving force behind leadership. It is the vision which transforms a disparate group of stakeholders into the people who will act to move the venture forward.
2. **Communication with stakeholders**: An entrepreneur must relate their vision to stakeholders through a variety of communication channels and forums. Such communications is not simply a passion of information; it is a call to action.
3. **Organisational culture**: It is the web of rules which define how it goes about its tasks. The relationship between leadership and culture is reciprocal. Leadership creates the organization's culture and in return, the organization's culture creates a space to be filled by a leader.
4. **Knowledge and expertise**: Entrepreneurs develops expertise in some specialist technology. For example, Bill Gate's knowledge of computing is an example of the above.
5. **Desire to lead**: The thing which ultimately underpins leadership is the desire to lead. No-one can be an effective leader unless he really wants to take on the role of leader.
6. **Credibility:** It is critical for leadership. If credibility can be built-up, then leadership becomes easier. If an entrepreneur loses credibility, then leadership is likely to be made more problematic if not lost altogether.
7. **Performance of the venture**: Credibility comes from the decisions which lead to successful outcomes. If credibility comes from being associated with success, it is not necessarily true that credibility is automatically lost as a result of the occasional failure.
8. **Leadership role:** The entrepreneur will usually be the most senior manager in the venture. They will be expected to take on a leadership role merely by virtue of being an entrepreneur.

RESEARCH DESIGN: INNOVATION AND ENTREPRENEURSHIP EQUATION

According to Frederic Sautet, "Entrepreneurship in Everything: Management Is

Doing Things Right; Leadership is doing the Right Thing." Innovation is a continual process of creative destruction where unproductive and irrelevant ideas, systems and mechanisms are replaced by new and more productive ones.

Innovation is generally a response to a change in the environment. However, innovations in financial products also have given rise to some new challenges for market participants and their supervisors in the areas of corporate governance and compliance. The process of innovation is not always painless as individually all innovations are not necessarily successful but collectively it is the process of innovations that leads us ahead in the path of progress. Recently we have seen this process of creative destruction at work more closely in the financial sector.

The business environment across the globe has been witnessing an unprecedented turmoil over the last couple of years. Financial innovations have become a conventional and popular phenomenon for the contemporary world of finance. These innovations have enabled them to win new customers by increasing demand for their products and have also increased their importance in the eyes of other businesses. The customers of today have become smarter and more knowledgeable. As a result, their demands and standards have also risen. In order to meet those demands, financial institutions have come up with their own set of innovations that they employ to achieve a high degree of customer satisfaction.

Leading innovation is a delicate and challenging process. You need to encourage expansive out-of-the-box thinking to generate new ideas, but also filter through these ideas to decide which to commercialize. Use a balanced "loose-tight" style of leadership for this purpose. "Loose-tight leadership alternates the creation of space for idea generation and free exploration with a deliberate tightening that selects and tests specific ideas for further investment and development."

Looseness usually dominates the early stages of the innovation process; in the later stages, tightening becomes more important to scrutinize the concepts and bring the selected ones to the market. A balanced approach is essential to loose-tight leadership. Those who remain loose too long generate plenty of ideas but have difficulty commercializing them. Those who lock into the tight mode choke off all but most obvious ideas, thus confining innovation to incremental line extensions of existing products that add little value.

The fast growth and business successes of eBay, Amazon.com, travel.com, priceline.com, and so forth, and the bankruptcy of numerous dot-com firms worldwide in 2000 have held potent management implications for IT innovation and entrepreneurial organizations worldwide. E-entrepreneurship and innovation are emerging disciplines for proactively responding to changes in the e-business world. The dot-com crash presented new challenges as well as new opportunities to e-business entrepreneurs and managers to rethink and reshape their business strategy. This author argues that a combination of entrepreneurship and innovation is a crucial factor to the long-term sustainability of ecommerce and e-businesses. In this frenetically changing competitive landscape, an integrative approach to e-entrepreneurship and innovation will enable organizations to gain competitive advantage and hold the key to e-business success.

Innovation = Idea + Leader + Team + Plan
Innovation = Invention X Entrepreneurship

Customer Value

Source: *Adapted from Govindarajan & Trimble (2010, L 439), Kim & Mauborgne (2005) and Pinchot & Pellman (1999)*

ENTREPRENEURIAL LEARNING: THE BATTLE OF THE DECADE

In order to compete in the environment, the right mix of

innovation and entrepreneurship is essential. To encourage each kind of innovation, entrepreneurial process needs to vet ideas effectively and move them forward systematically. With the recent focus on innovation, it can be easy for any organization to become wrapped around building a better axle. However, innovation alone does not breed success. There is a battle brewing between the time tested practice of entrepreneurship and the requirements of the emerging innovation economy. The question is whether innovation or entrepreneurship can exist in this new environment without the other, finding the right mix, and understanding the difference. In this article, we explore the critical differences between and the many types of innovation and entrepreneurship, as well as how to find the balance between the two and your optimal mix for competitive advantage.

Innovation is about new ideas. It may be new products, processes, services, business models and more. Entrepreneurship, however, is about realizing profit. The difference between innovation and entrepreneurship is key. You can build it, but they may not come. Delia Smith of Green Field Ventures gives a concise view of the difference when she notes that, "If innovation is the creation of new capacities for wealth creation, entrepreneurship is the exploitation of these capacities."

DIFFERENCES IN LEADERSHIP TYPES

Particulars	Transactional	Transformational	Entrepreneurial
Communications	As conditions demand	Symbolic	Intimate an dpersonal
Investment	Immediate payback	Committed investment	Staged investment
Strategy	Situational analysis	Long term	Medium term
Focus	Day-to-day activities	Organization Change	Opportunity Building
Approach	Development of tasks	Creative rearrangement	Creative destruction then rearrangement

In the accelerating business environment and evolving innovation economy, differentiators are key. Your business has to be unique in some advantageous way that draws your customers. The right mix of innovation and entrepreneurship is at the heart of creating advantage in this evolving economy. Steve Epner suggests, "an entrepreneur with an innovative idea is a rare and valuable find...everyone is capable of coming up with the idea. Put that together with someone who can execute a plan—and watch out."

LEADERSHIP AND INNOVATIONS: THE TWO FACES OF R & D

According to Jeff Timmons, "Entrepreneurship is the transformation of an idea into an opportunity." Entrepreneur provides a bridge between the small business manager and the chief executive of large firms. In growing the venture, the entrepreneur transforms the role of acquiring resources into that of creating intoning structures to management. Growth is a critical to entrepreneurial success. Organisational growth, however, means more than just an increase in size. It involves development and change within the organisation and changes in the way in which the organisation grows as coherent whole, organisational growth itself is best understood in a multi-faceted way. We have to steer it in the right direction with the abilities of a good entrepreneur.

According to Peter F. Drucker, The Father of Modern Management, "Innovation is the specific tool of entrepreneurs, the means by which they exploit change as an opportunity for a different business or a different service. It is capable of being presented as a discipline, capable of being learned, capable of being practiced. Entrepreneurs need to search purposefully for the sources of innovation, the changes and their symptoms that indicate opportunities for successful innovation. And they need to know and to apply the principles of successful innovation."

Investing in new and better products or services requires innovation "the successful exploitation of new ideas". No idea or innovation is successful, until its commercial manifestation is purchased in significant amounts. The evidence shows that innovative businesses deliver above average sales growth and profitability. New and better products or services may be created from new technology, a new application of old technology, by new design, through a new delivery model or just by better business processes. The stimulus for innovation can arise from either "technology push" or "market pulls" or sometimes a conjunction of the two. Often, novelty is created by the fusion of different technologies to meet a technical need in the market place. Involvement in R&D can provide technology, knowledge and expertise, but this can also be obtained from elsewhere. An important pre requisite, however, is to have the necessary skill to recognise, translate and apply the technology, wherever it comes from.

FINDINGS

Leadership is crucial for enhancing innovation practices and achieving strategic competitiveness in organizations. To sum up, the present research investigated the relationship of transformational leadership with technological innovation and the moderating effects of organizational culture and incentive compensation on these relationships. There are three levels of innovative practices i.e., Statesmanship, Entrepreneurship and Innovation. Statesmanship is the ability to work with and through other people, where as entrepreneurship is the ability to achieve results, regardless of obstacles. Innovation is the ability to generate new and usable ideas.

CONCLUSIONS

Entrepreneurs have an important effect on world economies and playing an important role in maintaining and developing to create new values. Organisational growth, however, means more than just an increase in size. It involves development and change within the organisation and changes in the way in which the organisation grows as coherent whole. Entrepreneurship education is a common course of study in educational settings. A question, which is always raised whether entrepreneurs born or are they taught?

Educational institutions seem to have an answer to this old question i.e., entrepreneurs can be taught. Universities, technical institutes, colleges, high schools, elementary schools, and out-of-school programs are teaching entrepreneurship. It involves development and change within the organisation and changes in the way in which the organisation grows as coherent and sets out a rationale for entrepreneurship in higher education. To be successful, an entrepreneur must not only identify an opportunity but also understand it in great depth through the acquiring of various skills.

REFERENCES

1. Johnson, D. (2001). What is innovation and entrepreneurship? Lessons for large organizations. Industrial and Commercial Training, 33(4), 135-140.
2. Antoncic, B., & Hisrich, R.D. (2003). Clarifying the intrapreneurship concept. Journal of Small Business and Enterprise Development, 10(1), 7-24.
3. Drucker, P.F. (1994). Innovation and entrepreneurship: Practice and principles. London: Heinemann.
4. Katila, R. (2002). Measuring innovation performance. In A. Neely (Ed.), Business performance measurement: Theory and practice (pp. 304-318). Cambridge: Cambridge University Press.
5. Green, S., Gavin, M., & Aiman-Smith, L. (1995). Assessing a multidimensional measure of radical technological innovation, IEEE Transactions on Engineering Management, 42(3), 203-214.

13

Women Entrepreneurs in India

Women have been confined to within four walls in our society in the past. Her involvement in economic activities was marked by low work participation rates and that too in low skill jobs in the unorganised sector of the economy. Ideologically as well as in prac-tice women are considered completely inferior to males. As a result they have been unrecognised and under-valued as well being placed as second sex in the society. But the transgression of values and the changing socio-economic conditions of women out of industrialisation and urbanisation altered the grim scenario drastically and opened new vista in social structural issues of women. The transformation of the social fabric of Indian society in terms of increased literacy among women and varied aspirations for better status, have witnessed a growing volume of unemployment. This problem necessitates a change in the life style of women in the country. Self-employment is recognised as panacea, which generates a category of entrepreneurs, who own economic enterprises at micro and macro levels. The development of micro enterprises in general and particularly for women opened the way for economic independence of women and shattered the glass ceilings anent women's image and status. This has made them to indulge in every line of business from pappad to power cables.

The challenges and opportunities provided to the women of digital era are growing rapidly that the job seekers are turning into job creators. They are flourishing as designers, interior decorators, exporters, publishers, garment manufacturers and still exploring new avenues of economic participation. In India, although women constitute the majority of the total population, the entrepreneurial world is still a male dominated one. Women in advanced nations are recognized and are more prominent in the business world. But the Indian women are still struggling to attain the position as in the advanced countries. However, there is a greater dynamism in the rate of growth of female employment.

In the 60 years' of independence, an emphasis on the socialistic pattern of the society and the role assigned to the Public sector, limited the scope for the growth of private entrepreneurship. The liberalization policy of the government has now thrown open a vast area of the economy for private entrepreneurship. As a consequence, many women have entered in to the world of business and become successful with all their hard work, diligence, competence and will power in their endeavor as entrepreneur.

WHO IS WOMEN ENTREPRENEUR

The word 'entrepreneur' appeared first in the French, in the early sixteenth century, men engaged in leading military expeditions were referred as entrepreneurs. Thus the term entrepreneurs were used at first to refer army leaders. In the 17th century, it was extended to cover the civil engineering activities such as construction of roads, bridges and harbours and fortification contractors. The same term was later applied to architects. In the early 18 the century, Cantillon R. Defined entrepreneur as "aperson or a dealer who buys factors services at a certain price and shells them certain prices in future. Peter .F. Trucker, William Diamond and others have refurbished the concept and now it is defined as follows.

Women entrepreneurs may be defined as the women or a group of women, who initiate, organize and operate a business enterprise. Women who innovate, imitate or adopt an economic activity can be called women entrepreneurs.

The Government of India has defined a women enterprise as "an enterprise owned and controlled by women having a minimum financial investment of 51 percent of the capital and giving at least 51 percent of the employment generated in the enterprise to women". On this basis government of India offer incentives and concessions to women entrepreneurs. However women entrepreneurs severely criticize this definition which sets out a condition of employing more than 50 percent women workers. They point out that any enterprise set-up by women should qualify for the concessions offered to women entrepreneurs

CHARACTERISTICS OF WOMEN ENTREPRENEURS IN INDIA

Most successful women entrepreneurs possess the following traits:

Women are ambitious

A successful woman entrepreneur is dreadfully strong-minded one, has an inner urge or drives to change contemplation into realism. Knowledge from her previous occupancy as an employee, relying on educational qualifications or lessons learnt from inborn business, she is ready to grab opportunities, sets goal, possess clear vision, steps confidently forward and is ambitious to be successful. Every successful woman entrepreneur is truly determined to achieve goals and make her business prosper. Thorough knowledge of the field is indispensable to success. She comes with new innovative solutions to old problems to tide over issues.

Women are confident

A successful woman entrepreneur is confident in her ability. She is ready to learn from others, search for help from experts if it means adding value to her goals. She is positive in nature and is keener to take risks. A winning woman entrepreneur uses common intelligence to make sound judgments when encountering everyday situations. This is gleaned from past experience and information acquired over the years. It is essential not to get aggravated and give up when you face obstacles and trials. The aptitude to explore uncharted territories and take bold decisions is the hallmark of a successful woman entrepreneur. A successful woman usually loves what she does. She is extremely fervent about her tasks and activities. Her high energy levels motivate her to contribute immensely towards building, establishing and maintaining a prosperous business.

Women is open and willing to learn

A successful woman entrepreneur keeps side by side of changes, as she is fully conscious of the importance of evolving changes. She is ahead of her competitors and thrives on changes. She adapts her business to changes in technology or service prospect of her patrons. She is inquisitive, concerned to learn and accommodative to innovations.

Women are cost conscious

A successful woman entrepreneur prepares pragmatic budget estimates. She provides cost effective quality services to her clients. With minimized cost of operations, she is able to force her team to capitalize on profits and gather its benefits.

Women values cooperation and allegiance

A woman has the ability to work with all levels of populace. She is keen on maintaining Associations and communicates evidently and efficiently. This helps her to negotiate even responsive issues without difficulty. She is sympathetic to people around her and have good networking skills that help her to get better contacts and utilize opportunities.

Women can balance home and work

A successful woman entrepreneur is good at balancing varied aspects of life. Her multitasking aptitude combined with support from spouse and relatives enables her to bring together business priorities with domestic responsibilities competently and efficiently.

Women are aware of her legal responsibility to the social order

A successful woman entrepreneur is eager to share her achievement with the society. She is dedicated to assist others and enjoys her liability.

Women focus on their Plans

Women Entrepreneur's plan their work and work with plan. Set long-term and short-term goals and take consistent action in moving toward them.

Women are Resourceful

Women entrepreneurs take advantage effectively coordinating the available factors and resources such as mentoring, training and coaching and build a strong base of education, training and experience which can help lead to success.

An effectual Women Entrepreneur requires certain additional essential **qualities,** which can be listed as follows. Innovative thinking and farsightedness, Often relatively comfortable with ambiguity, uncertainty and risk, Quick and effective choice making skill,Strongly influence events (or self-efficacy),Strong determination, Have high levels of work motivation, Preparedness to take risks, Characterized by high levels of social competence and social intelligence, Accepting changes in right time, Has an ability to build relationships and to connect with others on a social and interpersonal level, Access and alertness to latest scientific and technological information, Single-minded and devoted to their unique passions, Efficient execution of decisions imposed on them, May judge ambiguous business conditions in more positive, enthusiastic, and optimistic terms,Clear vision and ambition on the improvement of family and children, Takes advantage of resources such as mentoring, counseling and other small business development assistance, Patience and bearing the sufferings on behalf of others,Has some blend of critical analytical thinking, creativity, and practical implementation of ideas and Ability to work physically more at any age.

Many women have these traits but they never got a platform to showcase their talents and for this reason they don't know their real abilities. Matching the basic qualities required for entrepreneurs and the basic characters of Indian women reveal that, much potential is available among the Indian women on their entrepreneurial ability. This potential is to be documented, brought out and exposed for utilization in productive and service sectors for the progress of the nation

TYPE OF WOMEN ENTREPRENEURS

Entrepreneurs can be of different types. Some may prefer to go it alone or share the risk in groups with others. They are found in every economic system and every form of economic activity as well as in other social and cultural activities. They are seen from amongst farmers, labourers, fishermen, tribals, artisans, artists, importers, exporters, bankers, professionals, politicians, bureaucrats and so many others. Basing on the above features entrepreneurs classified into five types. These are discussed below.

Business Entrepreneur

Business entrepreneurs are those entrepreneurs who develop an idea for a new product or service and then establish an enterprise to materialise their idea into reality. Most of the entrepreneurs belong to this category because majority of entrepreneurs are found in the field of small trading and manufacturing concerns.

Trading Entrepreneur

An entrepreneur who undertakes trading activities whether domestic or overseas is known as a trading entrepreneur. He has to identify the potential market for his product in order to stimulate the demand for the same. He pushes many ideas ahead of others in the form demonstration to promote his business.

Industrial Entrepreneur

Industrial entrepreneurs are essentially manufacturers who manufacture products and services which have an effective demand in the marketing they have the ability to convert the economic resources and technology into a profitable venture.

Corporate Entrepreneur

Corporate entrepreneur is one who through his innovative ideas and skill able to organise, manage and control a corporate undertaking very effectively and efficiently. Usually, he is a promoter of the undertaking/corporation engaged himself either in business, trade or industry.

Agricultural Entrepreneur

Agricultural entrepreneur is one who undertakes agricultural as well as allied activities in the field of agriculture. He engages himself in raising and marketing of crops, fertilisers and other inputs of agriculture through employment of modern techniques, machines and irrigation.

FUNCTIONS OF WOMEN ENTREPRENEURS

A Woman entrepreneur has also to perform all the functions involved in establishing an Enterprise,

- Functions for establishment of an enterprise
- Idea generation and screening
- Determination of objectives
- Undertaking a risk and handling of economic uncertainties involved in business.
- project preparation
- Product analysis
- Introduction of innovations, imitations of innovations.
- Form of business
- Co ordination, administration and control.
- Raising funds
- Supervision and leadership.

- Procuring men, machine and materials and operations of business.

In nutshell, women entrepreneur are those women who think of a business enterprise, initiate it, organize and combine the factors of production, operate the enterprise, undertake risk and handle economic uncertainties involved in running a business enterprise.

CONSTRAINTS TO WOMEN ENTREPRENEURS

Women owned businesses are highly increasing in the economies of almost all countries. The hidden entrepreneurial potentials of women have gradually been changing with the growing sensitivity to the role and economic status in the society. Skill, knowledge and adaptability in business are the main reasons for women to emerge into business ventures. 'Women Entrepreneur' is a person who accepts challenging role to meet her personal needs and become economically independent. A strong desire to do something positive is an inbuilt quality of entrepreneurial women, who is capable of contributing values in both family and social life. With the advent of media, women are aware of their own traits, rights and also the work situations. The glass ceilings are shattered and women are found indulged in every line of business from pappad to power cables. The challenges and opportunities provided to the women of digital era are growing rapidly that the job seekers are turning into job creators. They are flourishing as designers, interior decorators, exporters, publishers, garment manufacturers and still exploring new avenues of economic participation. In India, although women constitute the majority of the total population, the entrepreneurial world is still a male dominated one. Women in advanced nations are recognized and are more prominent in the business world. But the Indian women entrepreneurs are facing some major constraints like

a) Lack of confidence – In general, women lack confidence in their strength and competence. The family members and the society are reluctant to stand beside their entrepreneurial growth.

To a certain extent, this situation is changing among Indian women and yet to face a tremendous change to increase the rate of growth in entrepreneurship.

b) Socio-cultural barriers – Women's family and personal obligations are sometimes a great barrier for succeeding in business career. Only few women are able to manage both home and business efficiently, devoting enough time to perform all their responsibilities in priority.

c) Market-oriented risks – Stiff competition in the market and lack of mobility of women make the dependence of women entrepreneurs on middleman indispensable. Many business women find it difficult to capture the market and make their products popular. They are not fully aware of the changing market conditions and hence can effectively utilize the services of media and internet.

d) Motivational factors – Self motivation can be realized through a mind set for a successful business, attitude to take up risk and behavior towards the business society by shouldering the social responsibilities. Other factors are family support, Government policies, financial assistance from public and private institutions and also the environment suitable for women to establish business units.

e) Knowledge in Business Administration – Women must be educated and trained constantly to acquire the skills and knowledge in all the functional areas of business management. This can facilitate women to excel in decision making process and develop a good business network.

f) Awareness about the financial assistance – Various institutions in the financial sector extend their maximum support in the form of incentives, loans, schemes etc. Even then every woman entrepreneur may not be aware of all the assistance provided by the institutions. So the sincere efforts taken towards women entrepreneurs may not reach the entrepreneurs in rural and backward areas.

g) Exposed to the training programs - Training programs and workshops for every type of entrepreneur is available through the social and welfare associations, based on duration, skill and the purpose of the training program. Such programs are really useful to new, rural and young entrepreneurs who want to set up a small and medium scale unit on their own.

h) Identifying the available resources – Women are hesitant to find out the access to cater their needs in the financial and marketing areas. In spite of the mushrooming growth of associations, institutions, and the schemes from the government side, women are not enterprising and dynamic to optimize the resources in the form of reserves, assets mankind or business volunteers.

Highly educated, technically sound and professionally qualified women should be encouraged for managing their own business, rather than dependent on wage employment outlets. The unexplored talents of young women can be identified, trained and used for various types of industries to increase the productivity in the industrial sector. A desirable environment is necessary for every woman to inculcate entrepreneurial values and involve greatly in business dealings. The additional business opportunities that are recently approaching for women entrepreneurs are eco-friendly technology, Bio-technology; IT enabled enterprises, Event Management, Tourism industry, Telecommunication, Plastic materials, Vermiculture, Mineral water, Sericulture, Floriculture, Herbal & health care, Food, fruits & vegetable processing.

Empowering women entrepreneurs is essential for achieving the goals of sustainable development and the bottlenecks hindering their growth must be eradicated to entitle full participation in the business. Apart from training programs, Newsletters, mentoring, trade fairs and exhibitions also can be a source for entrepreneurial development. As a result, the desired outcomes of the business are quickly achieved and more of remunerative business opportunities are found. Henceforth, promoting entrepreneurship among women is certainly a short-cut to rapid economic growth and development. Let us try to eliminate all forms of gender discrimination and thus allow 'women' to be an entrepreneur at par with men.

WOMEN ENTREPRENEURS IN INDIA

Entrepreneurship has gained currency across the sphere and female- entrepreneurship has become an important module. India is one of the fastest emerging economies and the importance of entrepreneurship is realized across the gamut.

Women entrepreneurs may be defined as the women or a group of women, who initiate, organize and operate a business enterprise. Women who innovate, imitate or adopt an economic activity can be called women entrepreneurs.

The Government of India has defined a women enterprise as "an enterprise owned and controlled by women having a minimum financial investment of 51 percent of the capital and giving at least 51 percent of the employment generated in the enterprise to women". On this basis government offers incentives and concessions to women entrepreneurs. However women entrepreneurs severely criticize this definition which sets out a condition of employing more than 50 percent women workers. They point out that any enterprise set-up by women should qualify for the concessions offered to women entrepreneurs

Generally women will have a second thought to become an entrepreneur. However, many will start entrepreneurship to earn quick money. Women have a deep-seated need for a sense of independence along with a desire to do something meaningful with their time and to have their own identity instead of remaining behind the shadow of their husband. Women also find entrepreneurship as a tool of meeting their career needs and childcare role. However, there are drastic differences in the way the men and women-owned enterprise views their activities. It is also found that compared to men, women are less concerned with making money and often choose business proprietorship as a result of career dissatisfaction.

Most women business owners in Indian organization are either housewives or fresh graduates with no previous experience of running a business. These women business owners are in traditionally women - oriented business like garments, beauty care, and fashion designing, which either do not require any formalised training or developed from a hobby or an interest into a business.

Women, who have started out their own business without any mentor or legacy have created their own plateau and also earned many feats. Women on the other hand, who inherited a small business from the family, had taken their small business to a greater extent and turned it out into a large organization. There are also some women who have inherited from the large organization, taken the organization to a much higher plateau. What motivates these women to venture out in the no man's land? The primary motives for engaging in some economically gainful activity are: (1) Making money/making more money (2) and a desire for gainful time structuring.

The first motive is found at the lower end of the socio-economic scale. However, the factors that initiate a woman to take the plunge are usually environmental, for example, failure of husband business, sudden death of a father in a women only household or husband' inability or unwillingness to shoulder the responsibility of the family, and many other similar reasons.

What have been the processes of change for women in the context of the tapestry being woven globally and nationally? Let us look at some of the key changes for women over the last five decades.

Women entrepreneurs of the fifties

Women Entrepreneurs of the fifties fall into two categories. The first category refers to those women who create and manage an entrepreneurial activity where there was no income generating male in the family. The second category was the one who lived by social roles and took charge of the enterprise of the husband had left. Thus, Compulsive factors led to the creation of women entrepreneurs in fifties.

Women Entrepreneurs of the Sixties

Sixties were the decade when many women got education in schools and colleges and began to have aspirations. These were largely unarticulated. Women accepted the social coding of the socio-cultural traditions and married. But soon they took small steps to start small and one-woman enterprises at home and from home. These were still activities for self-occupation and engagement but behind these were the seeds of aspirations to discover a meaning for the self and economic choices. This was still not for economic autonomy or economic self-sufficiency. Thus in sixties women began to aspire but also accepted the social cultural traditions

Women Entrepreneurs of the Seventies

In this decade, a critical mass of women completed their education and entered in the work force as professionals. The women in this decade opened up new frontiers. These women were unlike their mothers not only had aspirations to become an entrepreneur but also had ambitions. They opted for self-employment - be the enterprise, a one woman enterprise or who employed several others. This was an active step in the life of women folk. This choice was not out of compulsions or helplessness. It was an active choice to take charge of one's' life. For many, this choice began in their parental family and continued in their own personal homes. Thus, women were educated in highly sophisticated, technological and professional education and became equally contributing partners in seventies.

Women Entrepreneurs of the Eighties

The women entrepreneurs of 50's and 60's, and 70's had accepted both their social and occupational roles. They played the two roles and tried to balance both. But in eighties, the women had highly sophisticated technological and professional education. Many had medical, engineering and diplomas as well similar other degrees. Many entered their fathers or husbands industry as equally contributing partners and others opened up their own clinics and nursing homes and small boutiques, small enterprises of manufacturing and entered garment exports. This was the decade of breakthrough for women in many fields and many frontiers. Women made personal choices, stood up for their convictions and had the courage to make new beginnings. However, all these choices and beginnings were a not smooth sailing. For many, the society was hostile, the family was opposing and non-supportive and the women carried the guilt of not playing the traditional and appropriate social roles viz. that of being a good mother and so on.

Women Entrepreneurs of the Nineties

The women entrepreneurs of the nineties were qualitatively a different breed of women. These women already had a role model in the two earlier generations of women and become capable, competent, confident and assertive. They were clear of the type of choices to make and what they wanted to do. They went ahead with all clarity and did it. The nineties had thrown up many names of women who initiated an enterprise, fostered it and nurtured it to grow. There were many others who entered the big enterprises of their fathers and husbands and contributed to it with their competencies and capabilities. Sometimes they outshone the names of their fathers and husbands.

This was the first time the concept of 'the best' rather than a 'male heir' began to be talked about. The fathers thought of 'inheritance' or a 'legacy' to a 'daughter' rather than just a son who may have been incapable and incompetent. Women in the nineties had often questioned their traditional coding of their roles and had become conscious of the voice of their own identity. With economic independence, women have acquired a high self-esteem and have also discovered that they are able to deal with situations single-handedly. In situations of mis-match in marriages, physical violence, demands for dowry, pushing the women into socially confirming roles and other forms of social psychological harassment women do stand up to make their statements and make difficult choices. Today's women are fearless and have learnt to live alone, travel alone, and rear children alone when failures in marriage and life partnerships occur. Some women have preferred to remain single, are leading happy and contended lives and are successful in their work. Many couples today, opt for leading a life without children, and prefer to focus on work, relationships, and the joy of experiencing freedom. Many and more and more women in nineties have made up their minds to have a single child in order to meet the demands of home and work and have very well been able to integrate their multiple roles in multiple systems.

The Women Entrepreneurs of the 21st Century

The status of women in India has been changing as a result to mounting industrialization and urbanization and social legislation in the 21st century. Over the years, more and more women are going in for higher education, technical and professional education and their proportion in the workforce has also been increased. With the spread of education and awareness, women have shifted from the kitchen, handicrafts and traditional cottage industries to non-traditional higher levels of activities. The Government has also laid special weight age on the requirement for conducting special entrepreneurial training programs for women to enable them to start their own ventures. Financial institutions and banks have also set up particular cells to help women entrepreneurs. This has rebound the women entrepreneurs on the economic scene in the recent years although many women's entrepreneurship enterprises are still remained a much neglected field. Though, for women there are quite a lot of handicaps to enter into and manage business ownership due to the intensely entrenched conventional state of mind and strict principles of the Indian society

CONCLUSION

Empowering women entrepreneurs is essential for achieving the goals of sustainable development and the bottlenecks hindering their growth must be eradicated to entitle full participation in the business. Apart from training programs, Newsletters, mentoring, trade fairs and exhibitions also can be a source for entrepreneurial development. As a result, the desired outcomes of the business are quickly achieved and more of remunerative business opportunities are found. Henceforth, promoting entrepreneurship among women is certainly a short-cut to rapid economic growth and development. Let us try to eliminate all forms of gender discrimination and thus allow 'women' to be an entrepreneur at par with men.

References

1. Anwar, S. Farhat, Management of rural women entrepreneurs: the case study of Banglades, Journal of Business Admzinistration, vol. 18, No. 3 and 4, 1992.
2. Acharya, Meena, The Statistical Profile on Nepalese Women: An Update in the Policy Context, Kathmandu, Institute for Integrated Development Studies, 1994.
3. Armendariz, B., and J. Morduch (2007): The Economics of Microfinance. MIT Press,Cambridge, MA.
4. Banerjee, A. V., and E. Duflo (2005): Growth Theory through the Lens of Development Economics," in Handbook of Growth Economics, Vol. 1A, ed. by P. Aghion, and S. Durlauf, pp. 473{552. Elsevier, Amsterdam.
5. Banerjee, A. V., E. Duflo, R. Glennerster, and C. Kinnan (2009): The Miracle of Microfinance? Evidence from a Randomized Evalutation," mimeo, MIT.
6. Bertrand, M., D. Karlin, S. Mullainathan, E. Shafir, and J. Zinman (forthcoming): \What's Psychology Worth? A Field Experiment in the Consumer Credit Market,"Quarterly Journal of Economics.
7. Charumathi, B., Women entrepreneur's challenges and prospects, in C. Swara Lakshmi ed.,Development of Women Entrepreneurship in India: Problems and Prospects, New Delhi, Discovery Publishing House, 1998.
8. De Mel, S., D. McKenzie, and C. Woodruff (2008):\Returns to Capital in Microenterprises: Evidence from a Field Experiment," Quarterly Journal of Economics, 123(4),1329{1372.
9. Genicot, G., and D. Ray (2009): \Aspirations, Inequality, Investment and Mobility, "mimeo, Georgetown and New York University.

10.Karlan, D. S., and M. Valdivia (2008): \Teaching Entrepreneurship: Impact Of Business Training On Micro_nance Clients and Institutions,," mimeo, Yale University.

11.Macours, K., and R. Vakis (2008): \Changing Households' Investments and Aspirations through Social Interactions: Evidence from a Randomized Transfer Program in a Low-income Country," World Bank Research Paper.

12.Matiur-Rahman, S.K., M.K. Bhattacharjee and R.K. Lahiri, Entrepreneurship development and the women entrepreneurial pilgrims of Bangladesh, in C. Swarajya Lakshmi, ed., Development of Women Entrepreneurship in India: Problems and Prospects New Delhi, Discovery Publishing House, 1998.

13.Ray, D. (2006): \Aspirations, Poverty and Economic Change," in Understanding Poverty, ed. by A. V. Banerjee, R. Benabou, and D. Mookherjee. Oxford University Press, Oxford,UK.

14

Indigenous' Peoples Rights for Inclusion

Indigenous populations are communities or ethnic groups that live within, or are attached to, geographically distinct traditional habitats or ancestral territories, and who identify themselves as being part of a distinct cultural group, descended from groups present in the area before modern states were created and current borders defined. They generally maintain cultural and social identities, and social, economic, cultural and political institutions, separate from the mainstream or dominant society or culture. This term became a political term in the late twentieth century to refer to ethnic groups have historical ties to groups that existed in a territory prior to colonization or formation of a nation state, and which normally preserve a degree of cultural and political separation from the mainstream culture and political system of the nation state within the border of which the indigenous group is located.

The political sense of the term indigenous people, defines these groups as particularly vulnerable to exploitation and oppression by nation states, and as a result a special set of political rights in accordance with international law have been set forth by

International Organizations such as the United Nations, the International Labour Organisation and the World Bank. The United Nations have issued a Declaration on the Rights of Indigenous people, the purpose of which it is to protect the collective rights of indigenous peoples to their culture, identity, language, employment, health, education and natural resources.

Different states designate the groups within their boundaries that are recognized as indigenous peoples according to international legislation by different terms, for example "Native Americans" "Pacific Islander" (USA), "Inuit", Metis "First Nations " (Canada), Aborigines (Australia), Hill tribes (South East Asia), indigenous ethnic minorities, Scheduled tribes or Adivasi (India), tribal groups, or autochthonous groups.

CONDITIONS OF THE INDIGENOUS PEOPLE

Worldwide around 370 million Indigenous People, embody and nurture 80% of the world's cultural and biological diversity, and occupy 20% of the world's land surface. The Indigenous Peoples of the world are very diverse. They live in nearly all the countries on all the continents of the world and form a spectrum of humanity, ranging from traditional hunter-gatherers and subsistence farmers to legal scholars. In some countries, Indigenous peoples form the majority of the population; others comprise small minorities. Indigenous Peoples are concerned with preserving land, protecting language and promoting culture. Some Indigenous Peoples strive to preserve traditional ways of life, while others seek greater participation in the current state structures. Like all cultures and civilizations, Indigenous peoples are always adjusting and adapting to changes in the world. Indigenous peoples recognize their common plight and work for their Self-determination; based on their respect for the earth.

Despite such extensive diversity in Indigenous communities throughout the world, all Indigenous Peoples have one thing in common - they all share a history of injustice. Indigenous Peoples have been killed, tortured and enslaved. In many cases, they have been the victims of genocide. They have been denied the right to participate in governing processes of the current state systems. Conquest and colonization have attempted to steal their dignity and identity as indigenous peoples, as well as the fundamental right of self -determination. As a result of inexplicable suppression and oppression of the indigenous people, the United Nations Human Rights Council adopted the U.N. Draft Declaration on the Rights of Indigenous Peoples on June 29, 2006.

DRAFT DECLARATION ON THE RIGHTS OF INDIGENOUS PEOPLES

This is the most comprehensive statement of the rights of indigenous peoples to date; establishing collective rights to a greater extent than any other document in International Human rights Law. It emphasizes the right of indigenous peoples to maintain and strengthen their own institutions, cultures and traditions and to pursue their development in accordance with their aspirations and needs. On the other hand this adoption of the declaration also will help the indigenous people in their effort against discrimination, racism, oppression, marginalization and exploitation. The draft declaration divided into nine parts. They are Fundamental Rights, Life and security, Culture, Religion, and Language Law, Education Media and Employment, Participation and Development, Land and Resources, Self Government& Indigenous, Implementation and Minimum Standard.

It was originally drafted in 1985 by the working group on Indigenous people, the world's largest human rights forum, the draft declaration was adopted by the United Nations sub-commission on the promotion and protection of Human Rights in 1994. This draft was submitted to the commission on Human Rights, which established the working group on draft declaration on the rights of indigenous peoples. The working group consists of more than 200 indigenous people's organisation which meets and participates once a year. Its goal was to facilitate the general Assembly's adoption of the declaration by the final year (2004)of the international Decode for the world's indigenous peoples.

The universal declaration of human rights (1948) is the first international document that states that all human beings are "equal in dignity and rights". Everybody is entitled to the rights in the declaration of any kind, such as race, colour, sex, language, religion, political or other opinion, national or social origin, property, birth or other statutes.

After taking more than 20 years to draft and to accept the draft, on June 29, 2006, the United Nations Human rights Council adopted the UN Draft Declaration on the rights of Indigenous people. The declaration emphasizes the rights to maintain and strengthen their own institutions, cultures and traditions and pursue their development in accordance with their aspirations and needs.

SUBSTANTIVE RIGHTS OF INDIGENOUS PEOPLE

Indigenous Peoples' rights overlap with many other human rights. Many important Indigenous Peoples' rights are not framed in specific Indigenous Peoples' rights treaties, but are part of more general treaties, like the Universal Declaration of Human rights or the Convention on the Prevention and punishment of the Crime of Genocide, International covenant on civil and political rights, and International Covenant on Economic, Social and Cultural Rights. The Rights endorsed to the indigenous people from many International instruments other than meant for Indigenous people is termed as substantive Rights. The following are the Substantive Rights of the Indigenous people.

1. *Right to life*
2. *Freedom from Torture*
3. *Freedom from Slavery*
4. *Right to Fair Trail*
5. *Freedom to Speech*
6. *Freedom of thought and Conscience and Religion*
7. *Rights Debates*
8. *Future Generation*
9. *Sexual Orientation and Gender Identity*
10. *Right to Trade*

11. Right to water

12. Reproductive Rights

13. Right to Information and Information Technologies

SPECIFIC RIGHTS OF INDIGENOUS PEOPLE

1. Right against Racial Discrimination

Right against Racial Discrimination is the first specific right of the indigenous people. Racial discrimination is often used to describe discrimination on an ethnic or cultural basis, independent of their somatic (i.e"racial") differences. Albeit the racial discrimination is common phenomena, it is virulent in its form anent the indigenous people are concerned. Especially indigenous people are been inflicted to various harmful activities such as extremism, hatred, xenophobia, exploitation, separatism, racial supremacy, mass murder and vigilantism upon being an indigenous. Therefore, so as to protect the interested of the indigenous people, they are bestowed with the right against the pernicious practices of racial discrimination.

2. Self-Determination

Self-determination refers to the right to choose their sovereignty and the political status without external interference. The United Nations International Covenant on Civil and Political Rights and the International Covenant on Economic, Social and Cultural Rights state that all peoples have the right of self –determination by virtue of which they "freely determine their political status and freely pursue their economic, social and cultural development." So, the Indigenous peoples are also not an exception for the right to self-determination. By virtue of this right indigenous people can freely determine their political status and freely pursue their economic, social and cultural development

3. Forced Assimilation

Forced assimilation is a process of forced cultural assimilation of religious or ethnic minority groups, into an established and generally larger community. This presumes a loss of many characteristics which make the minority different. The indigenous people who are known for minority by status and culture are given right to be an independent cultural group. Forcing them to assimilate with the larger cultural groups is a total violation of the human rights meant for them. Forcing in any form may cause a danger to the existence of the indigenous people's culture and their identity. So States shall provide effective mechanisms for prevention, and redress such forced assimilation of the indigenous people

4. Forced Relocation

Indigenous People should not be forced to move away from their lands or territories either upon the state policy or international authority or on the basis of ethnicity or religion. Banishment or exile of Indigenous People also can be attributed to the similar process. In other words Indigenous peoples and individuals have the right to belong to an indigenous community or nation, in accordance with the traditions and customs of the community or nation concerned. No discrimination of any kind may arise from the exercise of such a right. Forceful transfer or relocation of Indigenous People may not suit to their way of life and cause the substantial harm to them. In addition they will lose all their moveable and immovable property. Hence the indigenous people should not be forced to relocate to any areas that are unfamiliar to them without the free, prior and informed consent of the indigenous peoples concerned and after agreement on just and fair compensation and, where possible, with the option of return.

5. Cultural Heritage

Cultural heritage is often unique and irreplaceable, which places the responsibility of preservation of it on the current generation. Indigenous peoples have the right to practice and revitalize their cultural traditions and customs. This includes the right to maintain, protect and develop the past, present and future manifestations of their cultures, such as tangible culture (such as buildings, monuments, landscapes, books, works of art, and artefacts), intangible culture (such as folklore, traditions, language, and knowledge), and natural heritage (including culturally-significant landscapes, and biodiversity). States shall take effective measures to ensure that this right is protected and also to ensure that indigenous peoples can understand and be understood in political, legal and administrative proceedings, where necessary through the provision of interpretation or by other appropriate means.

6. Freedom of Religion

The religion of indigenous people is a mixer of Animisam and Theism. Just because the indigenous people's religion is out of the ordinary by its nature, there should not any movement to prevent them by not practicing their religious practices. Indigenous people have the right to manifest, practice, develop and teach their religious and spiritual traditions, customs and ceremonies; the right to maintain, protect, and have access in privacy to their religious and cultural sites; the right to the use and control of their ceremonial objects; and the right to the repatriation of their human remains As the freedom of religion is considered by many people and nations as a fundamental human right, the believers in other faiths should not be persecuted.

7. Cultural Diversity

Cultural diversity of the indigenous people is to be respected by others. The many separate societies that emerged around the globe differed markedly from each other, and many of these differences persist even to this day. The more obvious cultural differences that exist between people are language, dress and traditions. There are also significant variations in the way societies organize themselves, in their shared conception of morality, and in the ways they interact with their environment. So, the indigenous people also given right to the dignity and diversity of their cultures, traditions, histories and aspirations which shall be appropriately reflected in education and public information. The States shall take effective measures, in consultation and cooperation with the indigenous peoples concerned, to combat prejudice and eliminate discrimination and to promote tolerance, understanding and good relations among indigenous peoples and all other segments of society

8. Indigenous Land Rights

Indigenous people have the right over the land that they are cultivating or for using inhabitation either owned by them individually or collectively. Land and resource-related rights are of fundamental importance to indigenous peoples for a range of reasons, including: the religious significance of the land, self-determination, identity, and economic factors.

The claim by the Indigenous people over the land has been addressed, with varying degrees of success on the national and international level. Such claims may be based upon the principles of international law, treaties, common law or domestic constitution or legislation. The foundational documents for indigenous land rights in international law include indigenous and Tribal people's convention, 1989 and the declaration on the rights of the Indigenous people and the International covenant on civil and political Rights.

9. Traditional knowledge and indigenous knowledge

The traditional knowledge typically distinguishes one community from another. Traditional Environmental Knowledge and Local Knowledge generally refer to the long-standing traditions and practices of certain regional, indigenous, or local communities. Traditional knowledge also encompasses the wisdom, knowledge, and teachings of these communities. In many cases, traditional knowledge has been orally passed for generations from person to person. Some forms of traditional knowledge are expressed through stories, legends, folklores, rituals, songs, and even laws. Other forms of traditional knowledge are expressed through different means. Some communities depend on their traditional knowledge even for survival. So, the indigenous people should be allowed to preserve and practice the traditional knowledge and indigenous knowledge they have possessed with themselves.

10. Intellectual Property Rights

Indigenous people initially have shown concern over the territorial rights and traditional resource rights of their communities. Then they showed concern for the misappropriation and misuse of their "intangible" knowledge and cultural heritage. Indigenous peoples and local communities have resisted, among other things: the use of traditional symbols and designs as mascots, derivative arts and crafts; the use or modification of traditional songs; the patenting of traditional uses of medicinal plants; and the copyrighting and distribution of traditional stories. Thus, the Indigenous peoples and local communities have sought to prevent the patenting of their traditional knowledge and resources where they have not given express consent.

11. An Indigenous Language

The indigenous people have the right to protect and develop their language as it is from a linguistically distinct community that has been settled in the area for many generations. An indigenous language or autochthonous language is a language that is native to a region and spoken by indigenous people but has been reduced to the status of a minority language or may have fallen out of use caused by colonisation, where the original language is replaced by that of the colonists. So instead of forcing the indigenous people to speak some other language which is alien to them, they should be allowed to use their own language.

RIGHTS AT STAKE

In spite of international recognition and acceptance of the Universal Declaration of Human Rights, which guarantees the fundamental rights of all human beings, in practical terms, Indigenous Peoples' human rights remain without specifically designated safeguards. Indigenous Peoples continue to face serious threats to their basic existence due to systematic government policies and there on sought recognition of their identities. In many countries, Indigenous Peoples are in the most disadvantageous and vulnerable conditions and continue to face sheer discrimination in every walks of their life schools and are exploited in the workplace. In many countries, they are not even allowed to study their own languages in schools. Sacred lands and objects are plundered from them through unjust treaties. National governments continue to deny Indigenous Peoples the right to live in and manage their traditional lands; often implementing policies to exploit the lands that have sustained them for centuries. In some cases, governments have even enforced policies of forced assimilation in efforts to eradicate Indigenous Peoples, cultures, and traditions. Over and over, governments around the world have displayed an utter lack of respect for Indigenous values, tradition and human rights and failed to protect the group rights of the indigenous people

CONCLUSION

Indigenous Peoples are a significant and important portion of humanity. Their heritage, their ways of life, their stewardship of this planet, and their cosmological insights are an invaluable treasure house for us. They are like any other human being living in the civilized world. But they are put into untold sufferings .Dispossession from the land or restriction of access to natural resources, therefore, brings not only economic impoverishment but also the loss of identity and threatens their cultural survival. So it is realized that an equal platform can be provided to indigenous people, if proper implementation is given to these rights. The government also should help them to overwhelm their grievous and atrocious situation by giving proper education to them .

REFERENCES

1. Bijoy, C.R. and Raman, K.R., 2003, "The Real Story: Adivasi Movements to Recover Land" in EPW, Vol. 38, No. 20 (May 17-23).
2. Dietrich, G., 2000, "Dams and People: Adivasi Land Rights" in EPW, Vol. 35 No. 38 (September 16-22).
3. Ekka, A., 2000-01, "Jharkhand Tribal's: Are They Really a Minority?" in EPW, Vol. 35. No. 52/53 (December 30, 2000-January 5, 2001).

4. Griggs, R.R.A., 1993, Role of World Nations; Washington: Centre for World Indigenous Peoples.
5. Hardiman, D., 1987, The Coming of the Devi: Adivasi Assertion in Western India; Delhi: OUP.
6. Kosambi, D.D., 1956, An Introduction to the Study of Indian History, Bombay: Popular Prakashan.
7. Kumar, S., 2001, "Adivsias of South Orissa: Enduring Poverty" in EPW, Vol. 36, No. 43 (October 27-November 2).
8. Massey, J., 1994, "Indigenous People: Dalits: Dalit Issues in Today's Theological Debate".
9. Pati, B., 2001, "Identity, Hegemony, Resistance: Conversions in Orissa" in EPW, Vol. 36, No. 44 (November 3-9).
10. Prasad, A., 2003, Against Ecological Romanticism: Verier Elwin and the Making of an Anti-Modern Tribal Identity, New Delhi: Three Essays Collective.
11. Rahul, 1998, "Bhil Women of Nimad: Growing Assertion" in EPW, Vol. 33, No. 9 (February 28-March 6).
12. Raman, K.R., 2002, "Breaking New Ground: Adivasi Land Struggle in Kerala" in EPW, Vol. 37, No. 10 (March 9-15).
13. Viswanath, C.K., 1997, "Adivasis: Protesting Land Alienation" in EPW, Vol. 32, No. 32 (August 9-15).

15

Women Employment in India

India's economy has undergone a substantial transformation since the country's independence in 1947. Agriculture now accounts for only one-third of the gross domestic product (GDP), down from 59 percent in 1950, and a wide range of modern industries and support services now exist. In spite of these changes, agriculture continues to dominate employment, employing two-thirds of all workers. India faced economic problems in the late 1980s and early 1990s that were exacerbated by the Persian Gulf Crisis. Starting in 1992, India began to implement trade liberalization measures. The economy has grown-the GDP growth rate ranged between 5 and 7 percent annually over the period and considerable progress has been made in loosening government regulations, particularly restrictions on private businesses. Different sectors of economy have different experiences about the impact of the reforms. In a country like India, productive employment is central to poverty reduction strategy and to bring about economic equality in the society. But the results of unfettered operation of market forces are not always equitable, especially in India, where some groups are likely to be subjected to disadvantage as a result of globalization. Women constitute one such vulnerable group.

Since the times immemorial, worth of the work done or services rendered by women has not been recognized. India is a multifaceted society where no generalization could apply to the entire nation's various regional, religious, social, and economic groups. Nevertheless, certain broad circumstances in which Indian women live affect the ways they participate in the economy. Indian society is extremely hierarchical with virtually everyone ranked relative to others according to their caste (or caste-like group), class, wealth, and power. This ranking even exists in areas where it is not openly acknowledged, such as certain business settings. Though specific customs vary from region to region within the country, there are different standards of behavior for men and women that carry over into the work environment. Women are expected to be chaste and especially modest in all actions that may constrain their ability to perform in the workplace on an equal basis with men. Another related aspect of life in India is that women are generally confined to home thus restricting their mobility and face seclusion. The women face constraints beyond those already placed on them by other hierarchical practices. These cultural rules place some Indian women, particularly those of lower caste, in a paradoxical situation: when a family suffers economically, people often think that a woman should go out and work, yet at the same time the woman's participation in employment outside the home is viewed as "slightly inappropriate, subtly wrong, and definitely dangerous to their chastity and womanly virtue". When a family recovers from an economic crisis or attempts to improve its status, women may be kept at home as a demonstration of the family's morality and as a symbol of its financial security. As in many other countries, working women of all segments of Indian society faces various forms of discrimination including sexual harassment. Even professional women find discrimination to be prevalent: two-thirds of the women in one study felt that they had to work harder to receive the same benefits as comparably employed men.

A section of Indian women—the elite and the upper middle class—have gained by the exposure to the global network. More women are engaged in business enterprises, in international platforms like the Inter-Parliamentary Union, and have greater career opportunities as a result of international network. Freer movement of goods and capital is helpful to this section. But most women continue to remain marginalized as they are generally employed in a chain of work and seldom allowed independent charge of her job. Sharing of responsibility at work place or taking independent decisions is still a remote possibility for them. Economic independence of women is important as it enhances their ability to take decisions and exercise freedom of choice, action. Many of the workingwomen, who control their own income, do contribute towards the economic needs of family as and when required. They often participate in discussions at their work place and their views are given due weightage before any final decision. Workingwomen do use and spend their income at their own sweet will but sometimes permission of the husband becomes necessary for the purpose. However when it comes to making investments, they often leave it to their husband or other male member of the family to invest on their behalf. Many of them do not take decision even in case of important investments, like, life insurance, national saving schemes or other tax saving investments. Workingwomen do feel concerned about the economic needs of the family but when not consulted in such matters, they regret being ignored especially when they contribute monetarily towards economic well being of the family. After globalization women are able to get more jobs but the work they get is more casual in nature or is the one that men do not prefer to do or is left by them to move to higher or better jobs. Globalization has indeed raised hopes of women for a better and elevated status arising out of increased chances to work but, at the same time, it has put them in a highly contradictory situation where they have the label of economically independent paid workers but are not able to enjoy their economic liberty in real sense of the term. India is the first among countries to give women equal franchise and has a highly credible record with regard to the enactment of laws to protect and promote the interests of women, but women continue to be denied economic, social and legal rights and privileges. Though they are considered to be equal partners in progress, yet they remain subjected to repression, marginalization and exploitation. It has been advocated by many researchers (Amartya Sen, 1990) that independent earning opportunities reduce the economic dependence of woman on men and increase her bargaining power in the family. This bargaining power depends on the nature of work she is employed in. But the income earning activities increase the workload of a woman unless the man accepts an increased share in domestic work. Since globalization is introducing technological inputs, women are being marginalized in economic activities, men traditionally being offered new scopes of learning and training. Consequently, female workers are joining the informal sector or casual labor force more than ever before. For instance, while new rice technology has given rise to higher use of female labor, the increased work-load for women is in operations that are unrecorded, and often unpaid, since these fall within the category of home production activities. The weaker sections, especially the women, are denied the physical care they deserve. There is, thus, hardly any ability for the majority of Indian women to do valuable functioning; the "capability" to choose from alternatives is conspicuous by absence.

Although most women in India work and contribute to the economy in one form or another, much of their work is not documented or accounted for in official statistics. Women plow fields and harvest crops while working on farms, women weave and make handicrafts while working in household industries, women sell food and gather wood while working in the informal sector. Additionally, women are traditionally responsible for the daily household chores (e.g., cooking, fetching water, and looking after children). Although the cultural restrictions women face are changing, women are still not as free as men to participate in the formal economy. In the past, cultural restrictions were the primary impediments to female employment now however; the shortage of jobs throughout the country contributes to low female employment as well. The Indian census divides workers into two categories:

"main" and "marginal" workers. Main workers include people who worked for 6 months or more during the year, while marginal workers include those who worked for a shorter period. Many of these workers are agricultural laborers. Unpaid farm and family enterprise workers are supposed to be included in either the main worker or marginal worker category, as appropriate. Women account for a small proportion of the formal Indian labor force, even though the number of female main workers has grown faster in recent years than that of their male counterparts.

Since Indian culture hinders women's access to jobs in stores, factories, and the public sector, the informal sector is particularly important for women. More women may be involved in undocumented or "disguised" wage work than in the formal labor force. There are estimates that over 90 percent of workingwomen are involved in the informal sector and not included in, official statistics. The informal sector includes jobs such as domestic servant, small trader, artisan, or field laborer on a family farm. Most of these jobs are unskilled and low paying and do not provide benefits to the worker. Although such jobs are supposed to be recorded in the census, undercounting is likely because the boundaries between these activities and other forms of household work done by women are often clouded thus, the actual labor force participation rate for women is likely to be higher than that which can be calculated from available data. Women working in the informal sector of India's economy are also susceptible to critical financial risks. Particularly vulnerable are the poorest of the poor. Should they become ill, lose their job, or be unable to continue working, they and their families may fall into debt and find themselves in the depths of poverty. At risk are millions of poor who depend on the income generated by one or more women in their household. These women do not have regular salaried employment with welfare benefits like workers in the organized sector of the labor market. Female workers tend to be younger than males. According to the 2001 census, the average age of all female workers was 33.6 compared with the male average of 36.5.These data are reported by local employment offices that register the number of people looking for work. The accuracy of, these data is questionable because many unemployed people may not register at these offices if there are no perceived benefits to registering. In addition, the offices operate more extensively in urban areas, thus likely undercounting unemployment in rural areas. One would expect that as cultural impediments to work decrease, younger women would be the ones entering the workforce; older women who have never worked in the formal sector are not likely to start working later in life. Throughout the economy, women tend to hold lower-level positions than men even when they have sufficient skills to perform higher-level jobs. Researchers have estimated that female agricultural laborers were usually paid 40 to 60 percent of the male wage. Even when women occupy similar positions and have similar educational levels, they earn just 80 percent of what men do, though this is better than in most developing countries. The public sector hires a greater share of women than does the private sector, but wages in the public sector are less egalitarian despite laws requiring equal pay for equal work. There is evidence that suggests that technological progress sometimes has a negative impact on women's employment opportunities. When a new technology is introduced to automate specific manual labor, women may lose their jobs because they are often responsible for the manual duties. For instance, one village irrigated its fields through a bucket system in which women were very active. When the village replaced the manual irrigation system with a tube well irrigation system, women lost their jobs. Many other examples exist where manual tasks such as wheat grinding and weeding are replaced by wheat grinding machines, herbicides, and other modern technologies. These examples are not meant to suggest that women would be better off with the menial jobs rather they illustrate how women have been pushed out of traditional occupations. Women may not benefit from jobs created by the introduction of new technology. New jobs (e.g., wheat grinding machine operator) usually go to men, and it is even rare for women to be employed in the factories producing such equipment. National Sample Survey data exemplify this trend. Since the 1970s, total female self-employment and regular employment have been decreasing as a proportion of total employment in rural areas, while casual labor has been increasing (NSSO, 1994). Other data reinforce the conclusion that employment options for female agricultural workers have declined, and that many women seek casual work in other sectors characterized by low wages and low productivity. Other agricultural work includes workers involved with livestock, forestry, fishing and hunting, plantations, orchards, and related activities.

Even if a woman is employed, she may not have control over the money she earns, though this money often plays an important role in the maintenance of the household. In Indian culture women are expected to devote virtually all of their time, energy, and earnings to their family. Men, on the other hand, are expected to spend time and at least some of their earnings on activities outside the household. Research has shown that women contribute a higher share of their earnings to the family and are less likely to spend it on themselves. Research has suggested that as the share of the family income contributed by woman increases, so does the likelihood that she will manage this income. However, the extent to which women retain control over their own income varies from household to household and region to region. Many women still sought their husbands' permission when they wanted to purchase something for themselves. In northern India, where more stringent cultural restrictions are in place, it is likely that few women control family finances. Conditions of working women in India have improved considerably in the recent years. Ironically, despite the improvement in their status, they still find themselves dependent on men. It is because of the fact that man in patriarchal society has always wielded economic independence and power to take decision. Since the working woman earns an independent income in the same patriarchal set-up, where the basic infrastructure of society has hardly changed, though her own role within the same structure is passing through a transitional phase, it is but natural that she would remain vulnerable to exploitation even in her economically independent state. Society perhaps yet needs to accord due recognition to women to take the lead role and women, at the same time; need to be oriented vigorously towards assuming this role in the society.

16

Educational Problems of Women in India

In spite of certain outstanding examples of individual achievement of Indian woman and a definite improvement in their general condition over the last one hundred years, it remains true that our woman still constitute a large body of under - privileged citizens. Women of course do not form a homogenous group in class or caste terms. Nevertheless, they face distinctive problems that call for special attention. The Backward Classes Commission set up by the Government of India in 1953 classified women of India as a backward group requiring special attention.

The ministry of Education clubs girls with Scheduled Castes and Tribes as the three most backward groups in education. Ram Manohar Lohia considered the lot of women to be similar to that of Harijans. Realizing the enormity of the problems of Indian women the Government of India has appointed a separate committee on the Status of Women in India, The social backwardness of Indian women points to the great hiatus between their legal status which is more or less equal to that of men, and their actual position in society, which is still far from the ideal which exists on paper. The educational, economic, political and social backwardness of women makes them the largest group hindering the process of rapid social change.

It is inevitable that when this 'backward' group has the major responsibility of bringing up future generations the advancement of society cannot be rapid or take any significant form of development. In the report of the committee appointed by the National Council for Women's Education it was emphatically stated that what was needed to convert the equality of women from de jure to be facto status was widespread education for girls and women and a re-education of men and women to accept new and scientific attitudes towards each other and to themselves. A changing society and a developing economy cannot make any headway if education, which is one of the important agents affecting the norms of morality and culture, remains in the hand of traditionalists who subscribe to a fragmented view of the country's and the world's heritage. The differences between the positions of men and women in society will not lessen; leave aside disappear, as long as there are differences between the education of men and women. Inadequate education or no education is the most important factor contributing to the backwardness of our masses, especially our womenfolk. It is the low literacy among women which brings national literacy figure so low.

This gap which exists between the literacy rates of the two sexes also exists between the enrolment of girls and boys at all levels of education. Right from the primary school to the university, we find that the number of girl students is considerable lower than the number of boy students. According to Article 45 of the Constitution, universal compulsory and free education until the age of 14 was to be achieved by the year 1960. Looking at the present condition of primary education in villages, it seems doubtful that 100 per cent enrolment of girls can be achieved by the end of this century. There is no doubt that we have made great headway in the education of women in the last century. It is unfortunately true of our society that children are sent to school not according to their intelligence or aptitude but according to their sex. Such attitudes need to be changed without further delay if we want to achieve 100 per cent enrolment of the primary school-going children. Although the disparity between the enrolment of girls and boys has been lessening in the urban areas, the gap between their enrolments is still very wide specially in rural areas. The reasons for this are both economic and social.

The economic structure of rural areas is such that children, especially girls, are required to help in household work and perform their chores. Young girls have to look after their younger brothers and sisters, have to get water from the well, have to carry food to the father in the field, etc. Since there is so much to be done at home, they cannot be spared for the luxury of attending a school. The resources of the poor farmer are so limited that he does not have anything to spare for the education of his children. If there are resources available it the boy who is sent to school first. Parents also do not see the value of educating their children specially daughters who would get married after all and be only housewives. Since they cannot see any direct relationship between education and economic betterment, they have very little motivation to send their children to school.

It is still not being realized that there is definite connection between education, good motherhood and efficient house management. The management of millions of household and the upbringing of millions of children in thus is the hands of illiterate women. It is here that a change is required if our democratic and socialistic intensions are not to remain a mere pretence. People can be motivated to have their children educated only if educational system is directly linked with economic and social development. As long as our education remains oblivious of the felt needs of people to solve their immediate problems and on the contrary, actually alienates them from their natural, social and cultural surroundings, they will rightly resist sending their children to school. It is the area of primary education, especially in rural areas, which should be given maximum attention. Primary education for both girls and boys is what we should be concerned about while planning our policies and allocation funds. It is this sector of our education structure that gets neglected in favor of all sorts of institutes of 'higher learning' and 'research' of a kind that are neither relevant nor pertinent to our pressing problems. The role of women outside home is becoming an important and even essential feature of our present day reality.

17

Chronic Hunger and the Status of Women in India

You can tell the condition of a nation by looking at the status of its women.

—Jawaharlal Nehru

However much a mother may love her children, it is all but impossible for her to provide high-quality child care if she herself is poor and oppressed, illiterate and uninformed, anemic and unhealthy, has five or six other children, lives in a slum or shanty, has neither clean water nor safe sanitation, and if she is without the necessary support either from health services, or from her society, or from the father of her children.

—Vulimiri Ramalingaswami,
"The Asian Enigma"

The women who participate in and lead ecology movements in countries like India are not speaking merely as victims. Their voices are the voices of liberation and transformation....The women's and ecology movements are therefore one, and are primarily counter-trends to a patriarchal maldevelopment.

—Vandana Shiva

Amartya Sen - The Unheeded Conscience: *We will lionise him, but will we ever listen to what he's saying?*

> *Sen points out that when he took up issues of women's welfare, he was accused in India of voicing "foreign concerns." "I was told Indian women don't think like that about equality. But I would like to argue that if they don't think like that they should be given a real opportunity to think like that."*
>
> —Parmita Shastri, Outlook India, 1998

Executive Summary

The persistence of hunger and abject poverty in India and other parts of the world is due in large measure to the subjugation, marginalization and disempowerment of women. Women suffer from hunger and poverty in greater numbers and to a great degree than men. At the same time, it is women who bear the primary responsibility for actions needed to end hunger: education, nutrition, health and family income. Looking through the lens of hunger and poverty, there are seven major areas of discrimination against women in India:

Malnutrition: India has exceptionally high rates of child malnutrition, because tradition in India requires that women eat last and least throughout their lives, even when pregnant and lactating. Malnourished women give birth to malnourished children, perpetuating the cycle.

Poor Health: Females receive less health care than males. Many women die in childbirth of easily prevented complications. Working conditions and environmental pollution further impairs women's health.

Lack of education: Families are far less likely to educate girls than boys, and far more likely to pull them out of school, either to help out at home or from fear of violence.

Overwork: Women work longer hours and their work is more arduous than men's, yet their work is unrecognized. Men report that "women, like children, eat and do nothing." Technological progress in agriculture has had a negative impact on women.

Unskilled: In women's primary employment sector - agriculture - extension services overlook women.

Mistreatment: In recent years, there has been an alarming rise in atrocities against women in India, in terms of rapes, assaults and dowry-related murders. Fear of violence suppresses the aspirations of all women. Female infanticide and sex-selective abortions are additional forms of violence that reflect the devaluing of females in Indian society.

Powerlessness: While women are guaranteed equality under the constitution, legal protection has little effect in the face of prevailing patriarchal traditions. Women lack power to decide who they will marry, and are often married off as children. Legal loopholes are used to deny women inheritance rights.

India has a long history of activism for women's welfare and rights, which has increasingly focused on women's economic rights. A range of government programs have been launched to increase economic opportunity for women, although there appear to be no existing programs to address the cultural and traditional discrimination against women that leads to her abject conditions.

The Inextricable Link

The greatest tragedy facing humanity today is the persistence of chronic hunger - an intolerable phenomenon that takes the lives of 24,000 of us every day. For fully one-fifth of humanity, life is a daily struggle to survive in conditions of relentless poverty. Day after day, the lives of one billion individuals are cut short or terribly diminished by chronic, persistent hunger. Day after day, one billion people are denied the opportunities they need to lead healthy and productive lives. People living with chronic hunger exist in conditions of severe poverty. What they lack is the chance to change their situation, to develop their own self-sufficiency. The most potent confirmation of this fact can be seen in the lives of women. They, along with their children, are the main victims of hunger, and they are also most lacking in opportunities to end their own and their families' hunger.

The Hunger Project has come to the recognition that the persistence of hunger in India - and elsewhere in the world where hunger is still an overriding social issue - is, to a large degree, due to the subjugation, marginalization and disempowerment of women. Furthermore, women's suppression is rooted in the very fabric of Indian society - in traditions, in religious doctrine and practices, within the educational and legal systems, and within families. Ironically, much of the essential work of ending hunger rests in women's hands. Traditionally, women bear primary responsibility for the well-being of their families. Yet they are systematically denied access to the resources they need to fulfill their responsibility, which includes education, health care services, job training, and access and freedom to use family planning services.

In order to gain a shared understanding of the condition of the status of women in India and its impact on the persistence of hunger, this document surveys papers done by leading scholars in Indian development issues. It is organized in a framework of seven issues that characterize the plight of resource-poor women, with a focus on rural women, in India: malnutrition, poor health, lack of education, overwork, lack of skills, mistreatment and powerlessness. The link between these issues and the persistence of hunger in India was underscored in a 1996 study: The Asian Enigma, by Vulimiri Ramalingaswami: In short, the poor care that is afforded to girls and women by their husbands and by elders is the first major reason for levels of child malnutrition that are markedly higher in South Asia than anywhere else in the world.

India: An Overview

India, with a population of 989 million, is the world's second most populous country. Of that number, 120 million are women who live in poverty. India has 16 percent of the world's population, but only 2.4 percent of its land, resulting in great pressures on its natural resources. Over 70 percent of India's population currently derives their livelihood from land resources, which includes 84 percent of the economically-active women.

India is one of the few countries where males significantly outnumber females, and this imbalance has increased over time. India's maternal mortality rates in rural areas are among the world's highest. From a global perspective, Indian accounts for 19 percent of all lives births and 27 percent of all maternal deaths. "There seems to be a consensus that higher female mortality between ages one and five and high maternal mortality rates result in a deficit of females in the population. Chatterjee (1990) estimates that deaths of young girls in India exceed those of young boys by over 300,000 each year, and every sixth infant death is specifically due to gender discrimination." Of the 15 million baby girls born in India each year, nearly 25 percent will not live to see their 15th birthday. "Although India was the first country to announce an official family planning program in 1952, its population grew from 361 million in 1951 to 844 million in 1991. India's total fertility rate of 3.8 births per woman can be considered moderate by world standards, but the sheer magnitude of population increase has resulted in such a feeling of urgency that containment of population growth is listed as one of the six most important objectives in the Eighth Five-Year Plan."

Since 1970, the use of modern contraceptive methods has risen from 10 percent to 40 percent, with great variance between northern and southern India. The most striking aspect of contraceptive use in India is the predominance of sterilization, which accounts for more than 85 percent of total modern contraception use, with female sterilization accounting for 90 percent of all sterilizations.

The Indian constitution grants women equal rights with men, but strong patriarchal traditions persist, with women's lives shaped by customs that are centuries old. In most Indian families, a daughter is viewed as a liability, and she is conditioned to believe that she is inferior and subordinate to men. Sons are idolized and celebrated. May you be the mother of a hundred sons is a common Hindu wedding blessing. The origin of the Indian idea of appropriate female behavior can be traced to the rules laid down by Manu in 200 B.C.: "by a young girl, by a young woman, or even by an aged one, nothing must be done independently, even in her own house". "In childhood a female must be subject to her father, in youth to her husband, when her lord is dead to her sons; a woman must never be independent."

A study of women in the Swayam Shikshan Prayog (SSP), based in 20 villages in four districts in Maharashtra state was introduced in this way: The primary issue all women in the SSP were struggling with was that of everyday survival. Insufficient incomes and the lack of employment were reported to be their most pressing concerns. Survival is a constant preoccupation and at its most basic, survival means food (Chambers 1983). The most common problems were the lack of basic amenities such as food, water, fuel, fodder and health facilities. In addition, the deterioration of the natural environment and the fact that many of their traditional occupations were no longer viable were conditions that were making it increasingly hard for women to continue sustaining their families, as they had done in the past. SSP is a loose, informal network of women's collectives, voluntary organizations, action groups and unions.

Women Are Malnourished

The exceptionally high rates of malnutrition in South Asia are rooted deeply in the soil of inequality between men and women. "...the poor care that is afforded to girls and women by their husbands and by elders is the first major reason for levels of child malnutrition that are markedly higher in South Asia than anywhere else in the world." This point is made in the article, The Asian Enigma, published by UNICEF in the 1996 Progress of Nations, in which the rates of childhood malnutrition in South Asia are compared with those in Africa. We learn that malnutrition is far worse in South Asia, directly due to the fact that women in South Asia have less voice and freedom of movement than in Africa. "Judgement and self-expression and independence largely denied, millions of women in South Asia have neither the knowledge nor the means nor the freedom to act in their own and their children's best interests."

"Gender disparities in nutrition are evident from infancy to adulthood. In fact, gender has been the most statistically significant determinant of malnutrition among young children and malnutrition is a frequent direct or underlying cause of death among girls below age 5. Girls are breast-fed less frequently and for shorter durations in infancy; in childhood and adulthood, males are fed first and better. Adult women consume approximately 1,000 fewer calories per day than men according to one estimate from Punjab. Comparison of household dietary intake studies in different parts of the country shows that nutritional equity between males and females is lower in northern than in southern states." Nutritional deprivation has two major consequences for women: they never reach their full growth potential and anaemia. Both are risk factors in pregnancy, with anaemia ranging from 40-50 percent in urban areas to 50-70 percent in rural areas. This condition complicates childbearing and result in maternal and infant deaths, and low birth weight infants.

One study found anaemia in over 95 percent of girls ages 6-14 in Calcutta, around 67 percent in the Hyderabad area, 73 percent in the New Delhi area, and about 18 percent in the Madras area. This study states, "The prevalence of anaemia among women ages 15-24 and 25-44 years follows similar patterns and levels. Besides posing risks during pregnancy, anaemia increases women's susceptibility to diseases such as tuberculosis and reduces the energy women have available for daily activities such as household chores, child care, and agricultural labor. Any severely anaemic individual is taxed by most physical activities, including walking at an ordinary pace.

Women Are in Poor Health

Surviving through a normal life cycle is a resource-poor woman's greatest challenge. "The practice of breast-feeding female children for shorter periods of time reflects the strong desire for sons. If women are particularly anxious to have a male child, they may deliberately try to become pregnant again as soon as possible after a female is born. Conversely, women may consciously seek to avoid another pregnancy after the birth of a male child in order to give maximum attention to the new son." A primary way that parents discriminate against their girl children is through neglect during illness. When sick, little girls are not taken to the doctor as frequently as are their brothers. A study in Punjab shows that medical expenditures for boys are 2.3 times higher than for girls.

As adults, women get less health care than men. They tend to be less likely to admit that they are sick and they'll wait until their sickness has progressed before they seek help or help is sought for them. Studies on attendance at rural primary health centers reveal that more males than females are treated in almost all parts of the country, with differences greater in northern hospitals than southern ones, pointing to regional differences in the value placed on women. Women's socialization to tolerate suffering and their reluctance to be examined by male personnel are additional constraints in their getting adequate health care.

Maternal Mortality

India's maternal mortality rates in rural areas are among the highest in the world. A factor that contributes to India's high maternal mortality rate is the reluctance to seek medical care for pregnancy - it is viewed as a temporary condition that will disappear. The estimates nationwide are that only 40-50 percent of women receive any antenatal care. Evidence from the states of Bihar, Rajasthan, Orissa, Uttar Pradesh, Maharashtra and Gujarat find registration for maternal and child health services to be as low as 5-22 percent in rural areas and 21-51 percent in urban areas.

Even a woman who has had difficulties with previous pregnancies is usually treated with home remedies only for three reasons: the decision that a pregnant woman seeks helps rests with the mother-in-law and husband; financial considerations; and fear that the treatment may be more harmful than the malady. It is estimated that pregnancy-related deaths account for one-quarter of all fatalities among women aged 15 to 29, with well over two-thirds of them considered preventable. For every maternal death in India, an estimated 20 more women suffer from impaired health. One village-level study of rural women in Maharashtra determined on the basis of physical examinations that some 92 percent suffered from one or more gynecological disorder.

Contraception Use

Women's health is harmed by lack of access to and the poor quality of reproductive services. "About 24.6 million couples, representing roughly 18 percent of all married women, want no more children but are not using contraception. (Operations Research Group, 1990). The causes of this unmet need remain poorly understood, but a qualitative study in Tamil Nadu suggests that women's lack of decision-making power in the family, opportunity costs involved in seeking contraception, fear of child death, and poor quality of contraceptive service all play an important role." (Ravindran 1993).

Some estimates suggest that some 5 million abortions are performed annually in India, with the large majority being illegal. As a result, abortion-related mortality is high. Although abortion has been legal since 1972 in India, "studies suggest that although official policy seeks to make pregnancy-termination services widely available, in practice guidelines on abortion limit access to services, particularly in rural areas. In 1981, of the 6,200 physicians trained to perform abortions, only 1,600 were working in rural areas."

Job Impact on Maternal Health

Working conditions result in premature and stillbirths.

The tasks performed by women are usually those that require them to be in one position for long periods of time, which can adversely affect their reproductive health. A study in a rice-growing belt of coastal Maharashtra found that 40 percent of all infant deaths occurred in the months of July to October. The study also found that a majority of births were either premature or stillbirths. The study attributed this to the squatting position that had to be assumed during July and August, the rice transplanting months.

Impact of Pollution on Women

Women's health is further harmed by air and water pollution and lack of sanitation. The impact of pollution and industrial wastes on health is considerable. In Environment, Development and the Gender Gap, Sandhya Venkateswaran asserts that "the high incidence of malnutrition present amongst women and their low metabolism and other health problems affect their capacity to deal with chemical stress. The smoke from household biomass (made up of wood, dung and crop residues) stoves within a three-hour period is equivalent to smoking 20 packs of cigarettes. For women who spend at least three hours per day cooking, often in a poorly ventilated area, the impact includes eye problems, respiratory problems, chronic bronchitis and lung cancer. One study quoted by WHO in 1991 found that pregnant women cooking over open biomass stoves had almost a 50 percent higher chance of stillbirth.

Anaemia makes a person more susceptible to carbon monoxide toxicity, which is one of the main pollutants in the biomass smoke. Given the number of Indian women who are anaemic - 25 to 30 percent in the reproductive age group and almost 50 percent in the third trimester - this adds to their vulnerability to carbon monoxide toxicity. Additionally, with an increasing population, diseases caused by waste disposal, such as hookworm, are rampant. People who work barefooted are particularly susceptible, and it has been found that hookworm is directly responsible for the high percentage of anaemia among rural women.

Women Are Uneducated

Women and girls receive far less education than men, due both to social norms and fears of violence. India has the largest population of non-school-going working girls. India's constitution guarantees free primary school education for both boys and girls up to age 14. This goal has been repeatedly reconfirmed, but primary education in India is not universal. Overall, the literacy rate for women is 39 percent versus 64 percent for men. The rate for women in the four large northern states - Bihar, Uttar Pradesh,

Rajasthan and Madhya Pradesh - is lower than the national average: it was 25 percent in 1991. Attendance rates from the 1981 census suggest that no more than 1/3 of all girls (and a lower proportion of rural girls) aged 5-14 are attending school.

Although substantial progress has been achieved since India won its independence in 1947, when less than 8 percent of females were literate, the gains have not been rapid enough to keep pace with population growth: there were 16 million more illiterate females in 1991 than in 1981.

Sonalde Desai in Gender Inequalities and Demographic Behavior asserts that "parents' reluctance to educate daughters has its roots in the situation of women. Parents have several incentives for not educating their daughters. Foremost is the view that education of girls brings no returns to parents and that their future roles, being mainly reproductive and perhaps including agricultural labor, require no formal education. As more and more boys are engaged in education, there is a growing reliance on the labor of girls. Girls are increasingly replacing their brothers on the farm while carrying on their usual responsibilities in housework. A large proportion of the roughly 40 million "nonworking" girls who are not in school are kept at home because of responsibilities in housework."

The role of parents is to deliver a chaste daughter to her husband's family. Sonalde Desai goes on to point out that "another disincentive for sending daughters to school is a concern for the protection of their virginity. When schools are located at a distance, when teachers are male, and when girls are expected to study along with boys, parents are often unwilling to expose their daughters to the potential assault on their virginity."

There is little response to counter these obstacles: school hours remain inflexible to the labor demands of girls; many villages do not have a school; and less than 1/3 of India's primary and middle-school teachers are women. According to Mapping Progress, "educational funds were cut by 801.3 million rupees in the 1991-92 budgets. Funds for the mass literacy movement, in which women participate enthusiastically, have been reduced by 5 percent from the previous year. Budgetary provisions for non-formal education have been cut by 17 percent, leading to closure of many night schools and adult education programs in which working-class women participate. Reduction in government expenditures on higher education and encouragement to private colleges will reduce women's opportunities for higher education since privatization in education promotes only male-dominated professional and technical courses, as they are lucrative."

Hours worked

Women work roughly twice as many as many hours as men. Women's contribution to agriculture - whether it be subsistence farming or commercial agriculture - when measured in terms of the number of tasks performed and time spent, is greater than men. "The extent of women's contribution is aptly highlighted by a micro study conducted in the Indian Himalayas which found that on a one-hectare farm, a pair of bullock's works 1,064 hours, a man 1,212 hours and a woman 3,485 hours in a year."

In Andhra Pradesh, (Mies 1986) found that the work day of an woman agricultural labourer during the agricultural season lasts for 15 hours, from 4 am to 8 pm, with an hour's rest in between. Her male counterpart works for seven to eight hours, from 5 am to 10 am or 11 am and from 3 pm to 5 pm. Another study on time and energy spent by men and women on agricultural work (Batliwala 1982) found that 53 percent of the total human hours per household are contributed by women as compared to 31 percent by men. The remaining contribution comes from children. The linking of agricultural activities to male dominance is described by Roy Burman (in Menon 1991): The anxiety of man to monopolize his skill in plough culture is reflected in the taboo that is observed almost all over India, against the women's handling the plough. In many societies, she is not even allowed to touch it.

Mies further observed that "whereas operations performed by men were those that entailed the use of machinery and draught animals, thereby using animal, hydraulic, mechanical or electrical energy, women almost always relied on manual labour, using only their own energy." Rice transplantations, the most arduous and labour intensive task in rice cultivation, is carried out entirely by women without the help of any tools. "Girls learn to assist their mothers in almost all tasks, and from the age of 10 years participate fully in the agricultural work done by women. Mies cites the case of Laxmi, a three-year-old infant who, along with her mother, pulled seedlings for transplanting. Boys on the other hand were seldom seen transplanting or weeding though they did help out in ploughing or watering the fields." "Not only do women perform more tasks, their work is also more arduous than that undertaken by men. Both transplantation and weeding require women to spend the whole day and work in muddy soil with their hands. Moreover, they work the entire day under the intensely hot sun while men's work, such as ploughing and watering the fields, is invariably carried out early in the morning before the sun gets too hot. Mies argues that because women's work, unlike men's, does not involve implements and is based largely on human energy, it is considered unskilled and hence less productive. On this basis, women are invariably paid lower wages, despite the fact that they work harder and for longer hours than do men." In contrast, a study in Uttar Pradesh reports that men "only reluctantly conceded that their womenfolk really work. The researchers in this area were repeatedly told that women, like children, simply eat food and do nothing."

The invisibility of women's work

Women's work is rarely recognized. Many maintain that women's economic dependence on men impacts their power within the family. With increased participation in income-earning activities, not only will there be more income for the family, but gender inequality should be reduced. This issue is particularly salient in India because studies show a very low level of female participation in the labor force. This under-reporting is attributed to the frequently held view that women's work is not economically productive. In a report of the National Commission on Self-Employed Women and Women in the Informal Sector, the director of social welfare in one state said, "There are no women in any unorganized sector in our state." When the Commission probed and asked, "Are there any women who go to the forest to collect firewood? Do any of the women in rural areas have cattle?" the director responded with, "Of course, there are many women doing that type of work." Working women are invisible to most of the population.

If all activities - including maintenance of kitchen gardens and poultry, grinding food grains, collecting water and firewood, etc. - are taken into account, then 88 percent of rural housewives and 66 percent of urban housewives can be considered as economically productive. Women's employment in family farms or businesses is rarely recognized as economically productive, either by men or women. And, any income generated from this work is generally controlled by the men. Such work is unlikely to increase women's participation in allocating family finances. In a 1992 study of family-based textile workers, male children who helped in a home-based handloom mill were given pocket money, but the adult women and girls were not.

The impact of technology on women

The shift from subsistence to a market economy has a dramatic negative impact on women. According to Sandhya Venkateswaran, citing Shiva, the Green Revolution, which focused on increasing yields of rice and wheat, entailed a shift in inputs from human to technical. Women's participation, knowledge and inputs were marginalized, and their role shift from being "primary producers to subsidiary workers." Where technology has been introduced in areas where women worked, women labourers have often been displaced by men. Threshing of grain was almost exclusively a female task, and with the introduction of automatic grain threshers - which are only operated by men - women have lost an important source of income.

Combine harvesters leave virtually no residue. This means that this source of fodder is no longer available to women, which has a dramatic impact on women's workload. So too, as cattle dung is being used as fertilizer, there is less available for fuel for cooking. "Commercialization and the consequent focus on cash crops have led to a situation where food is lifted straight from the farm to the market. The income accrued is controlled by men. Earlier, most of the produce was brought home and stored, and the women exchanged it for other commodities. Such a system vested more control with the women."

Women Are Unskilled

Women have unequal access to resources. Extension services tend to reach only men, which perpetuates the existing division of labour in the agricultural sector, with women continuing to perform unskilled tasks. A World Bank study in 1991 reveals that the assumption made by extension workers is that information within a family will be transmitted to the women by the men, which in actual practice seldom happens. "The male dominated extension system tends to overlook women's role in agriculture and proves ineffective in providing technical information to women farmers." Mapping Progress, states, "in the farm sector, the process of mechanization of agricultural activities has brought in tendencies for gender discrimination by replacing men for a number of activities performed by women and also by displacing the labor of women from subsistence and marginal households. Women are employed only when there is absolute shortage of labor and for specific operations like cotton-picking. "To supply food-processing industries being set up with foreign collaboration, there has already been a major shift from subsistence farming method of rice, millet, corn and wheat to cash-crop production of fruit, mushrooms, flowers and vegetables. This shift has led to women being the first to lose jobs."

A number of factors perpetuate women's limited job skills: if training women for economic activities requires them to leave their village, this is usually a problem for them. Unequal access to education restricts women's abilities to learn skills that require even functional levels of literacy. In terms of skill development, women are impeded by their lack of mobility, low literacy levels and prejudiced attitudes toward women. When women negotiate with banks and government officials, they are often ostracized by other men and women in their community for being ‘too forward.’ Government and bank officials have preconceived ideas of what women are capable of, and stereotypes of what is considered women’s work.

Women Are Mistreated.

Violence against women and girls is the most pervasive human rights violation in the world today. Opening the door on the subject of violence against the world’s females is like standing at the threshold of an immense dark chamber vibrating with collective anguish, but with the sounds of protest throttled back to a murmur. Where there should be outrage aimed at an intolerable status quo there is instead denial, and the largely passive acceptance of ‘the way things are.’ Male violence against women is a worldwide phenomenon. Although not every woman has experienced it, and many expect not to, fear of violence is an important factor in the lives of most women. It determines what they do, when they do it, where they do it, and with whom. Fear of violence is a cause of women’s lack of participation in activities beyond the home, as well as inside it. Within the home, women and girls may be subjected to physical and sexual abuse as punishment or as culturally justified assaults. These acts shape their attitude to life, and their expectations of themselves.

The insecurity outside the household is today the greatest obstacle in the path of women. Conscious that, compared to the atrocities outside the house, atrocities within the house are endurable, women not only continued to accept their inferiority in the house and society, but even called it sweet. In recent years, there has been an alarming rise in atrocities against women in India. Every 26 minutes a woman is molested. Every 34 minutes a rape takes place. Every 42 minutes a sexual harassment incident occurs. Every 43 minutes a woman is kidnapped. And every 93 minutes a woman is burnt to death over dowry. One-quarter of the reported rapes involve girls under the age of 16 but the vast majority are never reported. Although the penalty is severe, convictions are rare.

Selective Abortions

The most extreme expression of the preference for sons is female infanticide and sex-selective abortion. A study of amniocentesis in a Bombay hospital found that 96 percent of female fetuses were aborted, compared with only a small percentage of male fetuses. "Government officials event suspect that the disproportionate abortion of female fetuses may be a major underlying cause of the recent decline in the nation's sex ratio. In 1971 there were 930 females for every 1,000 males. A decade later this figure had increased to 934, but by 1991, instead of continuing to rise, the ratio dropped to 927, lower than the 1971 figure. This sex ratio is one of the lowest in the world."

Sonalda Desai reports that there are posters in Bombay advertising sex-determination tests that read, "It is better to pay 500 Rs. now than 50,000 Rs. (in dowry) later." Government has passed legislation to curb the misuse of amniocentesis for sex selection and abortion of female fetuses. Women activists have been critical of this act because of its provision that calls for punishing the women who seek the procedure. These women may be under pressure to bear a male child.

Marriage

Women are subordinate in most marriages. Exposure to and interactions with the outside world are instrumental in determining the possibilities available to women in their daily lives. The situation of women is affected by the degree of their autonomy or capacity to make decisions both inside and outside their own household. "The position of women in northern India is notably poor. Traditional Hindu society in northern rural areas is hierarchical and dominated by men, as evidenced by marriage customs. North Indian Hindus are expected to marry within prescribed boundaries: the bride and groom must not be related, they have no say in the matter, and the man must live outside the woman's natal village. "Wife givers" are socially and ritually inferior to "wife takers", thus necessitating the provision of a dowry. After marriage, the bride moves in with her husband's family. Such a bride is "a stranger in a strange place." They are controlled by the older females in the household, and their behavior reflects on the honor of their husbands. Because emotional ties between spouses are considered a potential threat to the solidarity of the patrilineal group, the northern system tends to segregate the sexes and limit communication between spouses - a circumstance that has direct consequences for family planning and similar "modern" behaviors that affect health. A young Indian bride is brought up to believe that her own wishes and interests are subordinate to those of her husband and his family. The primary duty of a newly married young woman, and virtually her only means of improving her position in the hierarchy of her husband's household, is to bear sons."

Sonalde Desai points out that the perception that sons are the major source of economic security in old age is so strong in the north that "many parents, while visiting their married daughters, do not accept food or other hospitality from them. However, given women's low independent incomes and lack of control over their earnings, few can provide economic support to their parents even if parents were willing to accept it."

In the south, in contrast, a daughter traditionally marries her mother's brother or her mother's brother's son (her first cousin). Such an arrangement has a dramatic impact on women. "In southern India, men are likely to marry women to whom they are related, so that the strict distinction found in the north between patrilineal and marital relatives is absent. Women are likely to be married into family households near their natal homes, and are more likely to retain close relationships with their natal kin." "Over the past several decades, however, marriage patterns have changed markedly. Social, economic, and demographic developments have made marriages between close relatives less common, and the bride price has given way to a dowry system akin to that in the north. Nevertheless, as long as the underlying ethic of marriage in the south remains the reinforcement of existing kinship ties, the relatively favorable situation of southern Indian women is unlikely to be threatened."

Child Marriages

Child marriages keep women subjugated. A 1976 amendment to the Child Marriage Restraint Act raised the minimum legal age for marriage from 15 to 18 for young women and from 18 to 21 for young men. However, in many rural communities, illegal child marriages are still common. In some rural areas, nearly half the girls between 10 and 14 are married. Because there is pressure on women to prove their fertility by conceiving as soon as possible after marriage, adolescent marriage is synonymous with adolescent childbearing: roughly 10-15 percent of all births take place to women in their teens.

A May 1998 article in the New York Times states

Child marriages contribute to virtually every social malaise that keeps India behind in women's rights. The problems include soaring birth rates, grinding poverty and malnutrition, high illiteracy and infant mortality and low life expectancy, especially among rural women.

The article cites a 1993 survey of more than 5,000 women in Rajasthan, which showed that 56 percent of them had married before they were 15. Barely 18 percent of them were literate and only 3 percent used any form of birth control other than sterilization. Sixty-three percent of the children under age 4 of these women were severely undernourished. "Each year, formal warnings are posted outside state government offices stating that child marriages are illegal, but they have little impact."

One man interviewed for the article has seven daughters. He borrowed some 60,000 rupees to pay for the dowries for six of his daughters, ranging in age from 4-14. He reported that "the weddings mean that he can now look forward to growing old without being trapped in the penury by the need to support his daughters." (NYT)

Dowries

Women are kept subordinate, and are even murdered, by the practice of dowry. In India, 6,000 dowry murders are committed each year. This reality exists even though the Dowry Prohibition Act has been in existence for 33 years, and there are virtually no arrests under the Act. Since those giving as well as those accepting dowry are punishable under the existing law, no one is willing to complain. It is only after a "dowry death" that the complaints become public. It is estimated that the average dowry today is equivalent to five times the family's annual income and that the high cost of weddings and dowries is a major cause of indebtedness among India's poor.

A December 1997 article in India Today, entitled, Victims of Sudden Affluence states, "A woman on fire has made dowry deaths the most vicious of social crimes; it is an evil endemic to the subcontinent but despite every attempt at justice the numbers have continued to climb. With get-rich-quick becoming the new mantra, dowry became the perfect instrument for upward material mobility." A study done by a policy think-tank, the Institute of Development and Communication, states, "the quantum of dowry exchange may still be greater among the upper classes, but 80 percent of dowry deaths and 80 percent of dowry harassment occurs in the middle and lower stratas."

The article goes on to state, "So complete is the discrimination among women that the gender bias is extended even toward the guilty. In a bizarre trend, the onus of murder is often put on the women to protect the men. Sometimes it is by consent. Often, old mothers-in-law embrace all the blame to bail out their sons and husbands." Despite every stigma, dowry continues to be the signature of marriage. Says Rainuka Dagar, "It is taken as a normative custom and dowry harassment as a part of family life."

Divorce

Divorce is not a viable option. Divorce is rare - it is a considered a shameful admission of a woman's failure as a wife and daughter-in-law. In 1990, divorced women made up a miniscule 0.08 percent of the total female population.

Maintenance rights of women in the case of divorce are weak. Although both Hindu and Muslim law recognize the rights of women and children to maintenance, in practice, maintenance is rarely set at a sufficient amount and is frequently violated. Both Hindu and Muslim personal laws fail to recognize matrimonial property. Upon divorce, women have no rights to their home or to other property accumulated during marriage; in effect, their contributions to the maintenance of the family and accumulation of family assets go unrecognized and unrewarded.

Inheritance

Women's rights to inheritance are limited and frequently violated. In the mid-1950s the Hindu personal laws, which apply to all Hindus, Buddhists, Sikhs and Jains, were overhauled, banning polygamy and giving women rights to inheritance, adoption and divorce. The Muslim personal laws differ considerably from that of the Hindus, and permit polygamy. Despite various laws protecting women's rights, traditional patriarchal attitudes still prevail and are strengthened and perpetuated in the home.

Under Hindu law, sons have an independent share in the ancestral property. However, daughters' shares are based on the share received by their father. Hence, a father can effectively disinherit a daughter by renouncing his share of the ancestral property, but the son will continue to have a share in his own right. Additionally, married daughters, even those facing marital harassment, have no residential rights in the ancestral home. Even the weak laws protecting women have not been adequately enforced. As a result, in practice, women continue to have little access to land and property, a major source of income and long-term economic security. Under the pretext of preventing fragmentation of agricultural holdings, several states have successfully excluded widows and daughters from inheriting agricultural land.

Women in Public Office (Revised May, 1999)

Panchayat Raj Institutions

> *The highest national priority must be the unleashing of woman power in governance. That is the single most important source of societal energy that we have kept corked for half a century.*
>
> —Mani Shankar Aiyar, journalist, India Today

Through the experience of the Indian Panchayat Raj Institutions (PRI) 1 million women have actively entered political life in India. The 73rd and 74th Constitutional Amendment Acts, which guarantee that all local elected bodies reserve one-third of their seats for women, have spearheaded an unprecedented social experiment which is playing itself out in more than 500,000 villages that are home to more than 600 million people. Since the creation of the quota system, local women-the vast majority of them illiterate and poor-have come to occupy as much as 43% of the seats, spur the election of increasing numbers of women at the district, provincial and national levels. Since the onset of PRI, the percentages of women in various levels of political activity have risen from 4-5% to 25-40%.

According to Indian writer and activist Devaki Jain, "the positive discrimination of PRI has initiated a momentum of change. Women's entry into local government in such large numbers, often more than the required 33.3 %, and their success in campaigning, including the defeat of male candidates, has shattered the myth that women are not interested in politics, and have no time to go to meetings or to undertake all the other work that is required in political party processes...PRI reminds us of a central truth: power is not something people give away. It has to be negotiated, and sometimes wrested from the powerful."

Contrary to fears that the elected women would be rubber stamp leaders, the success stories that have arisen from PRI are impressive. A government-financed study, based on field work in 180 villages in the states of Uttar Pradesh, Rajasthan and Madhya Pradesh, and coordinated by the Center for Women's Development Studies in New Delhi, has found that a full two-thirds of elected women leaders are actively engaged in learning the ropes and exercising power. Says Noeleen Heyzer, executive director of UNIFEM, "This is one of the best innovations in grass-roots democracy in the world."

Women leaders in the Panchayati Raj are transforming local governance by sensitizing the State to issues of poverty, inequality and gender injustice. Through the PRI, they are tackling issues that had previously gone virtually unacknowledged, including water, alcohol abuse, education, health and domestic violence. According to Sudha Murali, UNICEF Communications Officer in Andhra Pradesh, women are seeing this power as a chance for a real change for them and for their children and are using it to demand basic facilities like primary schools and health care centers.

The PRI has also brought about significant transformations in the lives of women themselves, who have become empowered, and have gained self-confidence, political awareness and affirmation of their own identity. The panchayat villages have become political training grounds to women, many of them illiterate, who are now leaders in the village panchayats. Says Sudha Pillai, joint secretary in India's Ministry for Rural Development, "It has given something to people who were absolute nobodies and had no way of making it on their own. Power has become the source of their growth."

By asserting control over resources and officials and by challenging men, women are discovering a personal and collective power that was previously unimaginable. This includes women who are not themselves panchayat leaders, but who have been inspired by the work of their sisters; "We will not bear it," says one woman. Once we acquire some position and power, we will fight it out...The fact that the Panchayats will have a minimum number of women [will be used] for mobilizing women at large." It is this critical mass of unified and empowered women which will push forward policies that enforce gender equity into the future. An observation by Deepak Tiwari in This Week, India's No.1 Weekly News Magazine, displays the promising future made possible by the PRI. He notes, "'Learning politics' is the latest fad for young village girls, who dream of joining the growing band of women panchayat representatives, 164,060 at last count, in the state."

Conclusion

As UN Secretary General Kofi Annan has stated, "Gender equality is more than a goal in itself. It is a precondition for meeting the challenge of reducing poverty, promoting sustainable development and building good governance." This recognition is currently missing in India. Transforming the prevailing social discrimination against women must become the top priority, and must happen concurrently with increased direct action to rapidly improve the social and economic status of women. In this way, a synergy of progress can be achieved.

As women receive greater education and training, they will earn more money. As women earn more money - as has been repeatedly shown - they spend it in the further education and health of their children, as opposed to men, who often spend it on drink, tobacco or other women. As women rise in economic status, they will gain greater social standing in the household and the village, and will have greater voice. As women gain influence and consciousness, they will make stronger claims to their entitlements - gaining further training, better access to credit and higher incomes - and command attention of police and courts when attacked.

As women's economic power grows, it will be easier to overcome the tradition of "son preference" and thus put an end to the evil of dowry. As son preference declines and acceptance of violence declines, families will be more likely to educate their daughters, and age of marriage will rise. For every year beyond 4th grade that girls go to school, family size shrinks 20%, child deaths drop 10% and wages rise 20%. As women are better nourished and marry later, they will be healthier, more productive, and will give birth to healthier babies. Only through action to remedy discrimination against women can the vision of India's independence - an India where all people have the chance to live health and productive lives - be realized.

Bibliography

1. Abzug, Bella., and Davis, Susan. 1998. "India." Mapping Progress: Assessing Implementation of the Beijing Platform.
2. Bunch, Charlotte. "The Intolerable Status Quo: Violence Against Women and Girls." The Progress of Nations 1997 New York: UNICEF

3. Burns, John F. "Though Illegal, Child Marriage is Popular in Part of India." The New York Times. May 11, 1998.
4. Carr, Marilyn., and Chen, Martha., and Jhabvala, Renana. 1996. Speaking Out: Women's Economic Empowerment in South Asia. Southampton Row, London: Intermediate Technology Publications LTD.
5. Desai, Sonalde. 1994. Gender Inequalities and Demographic Behavior: India. New York: The Population Council, Inc.
6. Neft, Naomi., and Levine, Ann D. 1997. Where Women Stand: An International Report on the Status of Women in 140 Countries. New York: Random House.
7. Omvedt, Gail. 1990. "Violence Against Women: New Movements and New Theories in India." Kali Primaries.
8. Purushothaman, Sangeetha. 1998. The Empowerment of Women in India: Grassroots Women's Networks and the State. New Delhi: Sage Publications.
9. Rajan. "Will India's Ban on Prenatal Sex Determination Slow Abortion of Girls?" Internet.
10. Ramalingaswami, Vulimiri., and Jonsson, Urban., and Rohde, Jon. "The Asian Enigma." The Progress of Nations. 1996 New York: UNICEF
11. Reardon, Geraldine. 1995. Power and Process. Oxford: Oxfam
12. Times of India. "Protest Against Atrocities in Women." Internet. p.3
13. Tinker, Anne. 1996. Improving Women's Health in India. Development in Practice Series. The World Bank
14. Venkateswaran, Sandhya. 1995. Environment, Development and the Gender Gap. New Delhi: Sage Publications.

18

Women and the Economy in India

The economy has grown—the GDP growth rate ranged between 5 and 7 percent annually over the period 1993-97 (The World Bank, 1998)—and considerable progress has been made in loosening government regulations, particularly restrictions on private businesses. Nevertheless, India remains one of the world's most tightly regulated major economies (Heitzman and Worden, 1996).

India is a multifaceted society where no generalization could apply to the entire nation's various regional, religious, social, and economic groups. Nevertheless, certain broad circumstances in which Indian women live affect the ways they participate in the economy. Indian society is extremely hierarchical with virtually everyone ranked relative to others according to their caste (or caste-like group), class, wealth, and power. This ranking even exists in areas where it is not openly acknowledged, such as certain business settings.

Indian women, particularly those of lower caste, in a paradoxical situation: when a family suffers economically, people often think that a woman should go out and work, yet at the same time the woman's participation in employment outside the home is viewed as "slightly inappropriate, subtly wrong, and definitely dangerous to their chastity and womanly virtue" (Dube and Palriwala, 1990, p. 131). When a family recovers from an economic crisis or attempts to improve its status, women may be kept at home as a demonstration of the family's morality and as a symbol of its financial security. As in many other countries, working women of all segments of Indian society face various forms of discrimination including sexual harassment. Even professional women find discrimination to be prevalent: two-thirds of the women in one study felt that they had to work harder to receive the same benefits as comparably employed men. It is notable that most of the women in this study who did not perceive discrimination worked in fields (e.g., gynecology) where few, if any, men competed against them (Liddle and Joshi, 1986).

Much of Women's Economic Activity Not Reflected in Statistics

Although most women in India work and contribute to the economy in one form or another, much of their work is not documented or accounted for in official statistics. Women plow fields and harvest crops while working on farms; women weave and make handicrafts while working in household industries; women sell food and gather wood while working in the informal sector. Additionally, women are traditionally responsible for the daily household chores (e.g., cooking, fetching water, and looking after children). Although the cultural restrictions women face are changing, women are still not as free as men to participate in the formal economy. In the past, cultural restrictions were the primary impediments to female employment; now, however, the shortage of jobs throughout the country contributes to low female employment as well.

The 1991 Indian census divides workers into two categories: "main" and "marginal" workers. Main workers include people who worked for 6 months or more during the year, while marginal workers include those who worked for a shorter period. Detailed data on marginal workers have not been tabulated from the 1991 census, but many of these workers are agricultural laborers. Unpaid farm and family enterprise workers are supposed to be included in either the main worker or marginal worker category, as appropriate (Registrar General and Census Commissioner (RGCC), 1993).

Women account for a small proportion of the formal Indian labor force, even though the number of female main workers has grown faster in recent years than that of their male counterparts. The 1991 census shows that the number of male main workers increased 23 percent since the 1981 census while the number of female main workers increased 40 percent. However, women still accounted for only 23 percent (64.3 million) of the total. The reported labor force participation of women is very low. Fewer than one-quarter (22 percent) of women of all ages were engaged in work either as a main or a marginal worker in 1991, compared with just over half of men. Rural women were more likely than urban women to be counted in the census as working, 27 percent versus 9 percent, respectively (RGCC, 1993).

Informal Sector Important Source of Work for Women

Since Indian culture hinders women's access to jobs in stores, factories, and the public sector, the informal sector is particularly important for women. More women may be involved in undocumented or "disguised" wage work than in the formal labor force. There are estimates that over 90 percent of working women are involved in the informal sector and not included in official statistics (The World Bank, 1991). The informal sector includes jobs such as domestic servant, small trader, artisan, or field laborer on a family farm. Most of these jobs are unskilled and low paying and do not provide benefits to the worker. Although such jobs are supposed to be recorded in the census, undercounting is likely because the boundaries between these activities and other forms of household work done by women are often clouded (Dube and Palriwala, 1990). Thus, the actual labor force participation rate for women is likely to be higher than that which can be calculated from available data.

Women's Unemployment Rates Similar to Men's

Unemployment is difficult to estimate in India and most unemployment statistics are likely to underestimate the true level of unemployment, particularly for women. This is due, in part, to the fact that many potential workers do not bother looking for work because they feel jobs are too scarce. Such people are rarely included in unemployment statistics. Also, there is not a strong motivation to register at employment offices because of the perceived minimal benefits of doing so. Different sources provide disparate pictures of the nature of unemployment in the country. According to employment-office statistics for 1996, there were 37.4 million unemployed people, of whom 22 percent were female (International Labour Office (ILO), 1997).2 The most useful unemployment data, however, come from the Indian

National Sample Survey Organization that conducts periodic surveys to estimate employment and unemployment rates. The most recent available survey (1990-91) showed that female unemployment rates were virtually the same as male rates; just over 2 percent for each gender in rural areas, and just over 5 percent in urban areas. Data show substantial drops in unemployment rates since 1977- 78, particularly for women. At that time, the female unemployment rate was 4.1 percent in rural areas and 10.9 percent in urban areas, while the male rates were 3.6 percent and 7.1 percent, respectively (National Sample Survey Organization (NSSO), 1994).

The above trend in unemployment rates does mask other less-positive developments, however. Although female unemployment rates were falling, there was not a corresponding increase in employment rates. For example, in 1977-78, 23.2 percent of all rural females were employed, but by 1990-91, these are of rural females employed remained essentially unchanged. For males, on the other hand, drops in their unemployment rate translated almost directly into comparable increases in their employment rate (NSSO, 1994).

Female Workers Relatively Young

Female workers tend to be younger than males.3 According to the 1991 census; the average age of all female workers was 33.6 compared with the male average of 36.5. Among the youngest workers (ages 5 to 14), girls worked at nearly the same rate as boys—about 5 percent of children worked as main or marginal workers. As age increases, the ratio of female to male workers decreases. In the 25 to 29 age group, there were only 406 female workers for every 1,000 male workers, and for the age group 50 to 59, the ratio declined further to 340. Little has changed since 1981, though the number and the proportion of children under the age of 15 who were working has declined.

Vast Majority of Indians Work in Agriculture

Most female and male main workers are employed in agriculture. Agricultural employment is divided into three categories in the census: cultivators, agricultural laborers, and other agricultural work.4 Cultivators usually have some right to the land—they or their family own the land or lease it from the government, an institution, or another individual. In addition, cultivators may supervise or direct others. In contrast, agricultural laborers work on another person's land for monetary wages or in-kind compensation. These workers have no right to the land on which they work. More than half (55 percent) of female agricultural workers are considered laborers, compared with just one-third of male agricultural workers. This suggests that most female workers are employed in lower-skilled, lower-paid positions, and are not the supervisors or owners of capital. Most female cultivators are members of a family that owns the land, rather than being the owners themselves (Kishwar and Vanita, 1985). The share of total female agricultural workers who were cultivators increased slightly between 1981 and 1991, from 41 to 43 percent.

The only other sector of the economy that employs more than 5 percent of working women is the service sector (Figure 2). This sector, which includes occupations such as social work, government, teaching, religious activities, and entertainment, accounts for about 8 percent of all female main worker labor. Household and no household industries5 each employ about 4 percent of female main workers.

Technology Does Not Always Improve Women's Employment

There is evidence that suggests that technological progress sometimes has a negative impact on women's employment opportunities. When a new technology is introduced to automate specific manual labor, women may lose their jobs because they are often responsible for the manual duties. For instance, one village irrigated its fields through a bucket system in which women were very active. When the village replaced the manual irrigation system with a tube well irrigation system, women lost their jobs (Kishwar and Vanita, 1985). Many other examples exist where manual tasks such as wheat grinding and weeding are replaced by wheat grinding machines, herbicides, and other modern technologies.

These examples are not meant to suggest that women would be better off with the menial jobs; rather, they illustrate how women have been pushed out of traditional occupations. Women may not benefit from jobs created by the introduction of new technology. New jobs (e.g., wheat grinding machine operator) usually go to men, and it is even rarer for women to be employed in the factories producing such equipment. Recent National Sample Survey data exemplify this trend. Since the 1970s, total female self-employment and regular employment have been decreasing as a proportion of total employment in rural areas, while casual labor has been increasing (NSSO, 1994). Other data reinforce the conclusion that employment options for female agricultural workers have declined, and that many women seek casual work in other sectors characterized by low wages and low productivity (National Commission for Women in India, 1993).

Female Employment Does Not Insure Economic Independence

Even if a woman is employed, she may not have control over the money she earns, though this money often plays an important role in the maintenance of the household. In Indian culture, as in many other countries, women are expected to devote virtually all of their time, energy, and earnings to their family. Men, on the other hand, are expected to spend time and at least some of their earnings on activities outside the household. Research has shown that women contribute a higher share of their earnings to the family and are less likely to spend it on themselves (Dwyer and Bruce, 1988). Research has suggested that as the share of the family income contributed by woman increases, so does the likelihood that she will manage this income (The World Bank, 1991). However, the extent to which women retain control over their own income varies from household to household and region to region. One study found that fewer than half of women gave their earnings to their husbands (Dwyer and Bruce, 1988).6 the study also showed, however, that many women still sought their husbands' permission when they wanted to purchase something for themselves. In northern India, where more stringent cultural restrictions are in place, it is likely that few women control family finances.

Relationship between Women's Education and Work Is Not Straightforward

The level of education is low in India; in 1991, only 39 percent of women and 64 percent of men were literate. The majority of those who are literate have only a primary education or less (RGCC, 1993). For men, as the level of education rises, the share that is main workers generally increases. Just over one-third of literate men who have no formal education work as main workers, while three quarters of those with post-high school educations are similarly employed.

Surprisingly, women with university degrees do not have relatively high employment rates; only 28 percent of these women are employed as main workers. The confounding of the usual relationship between education and employment may be related to the likelihood that poorer and lower educated families require female members to work. Often, girls and young women work instead of receiving an education. Well-off and better-educated families may send their daughters to school, but are able to afford to follow the cultural practice of keeping women at home after schooling is complete. Not until women receive specialized post-secondary education do they see significant improvements in their employment rates.

Women Have Distinct Work Experiences in Different Areas of the Country

Employment rates for women vary substantially across India's diverse states and territories. States with proportionately larger rural populations typically have higher employment rates because most people throughout India are engaged in agriculture. For instance, the territory of Dadra and Nagar Haveli, a small area in western India, had the highest female employment rate (49 percent) in the country according to the 1991 census. In this area, 90 percent of all female employment was in agriculture. Delhi, on the other hand, with an urban population of nearly 90 percent, had a female employment rate of just 7.4 percent. Exceptions to the relationship between proportionately large rural populations and above-average female employment exist. Regions in northern India have lower employment rates than southern regions (Figure 3). Though the share of the population involved in agriculture in these states was near the national average, the female employment rate was very low—10.8 percent in Haryana and just 4.4 percent in Punjab. According to survey data, rural female unemployment is also very low in these areas—1.4 percent in Punjab and virtually nil in Haryana. Around half of all rural women in these areas are engaged in domestic duties compared to the national average of 37.8 percent (NSSO, 1994). Identifying the exact reasons for the disparity between the northern and southern regions is difficult.

The northern states, particularly Punjab, are agriculturally fertile and the population is comparatively well off. Thus, it is not as important for the women of families in these regions to work. More importantly, however, cultural practices vary from region to region. Though it is a broad generalization, northern India tends to be more patriarchal and feudal than southern India.

Women in northern India have more restrictions placed on their behavior, thereby restricting their access to work. Southern India tends to be more egalitarian, women have relatively more freedom, and women have a more prominent presence in society.

References

1. Dube, Leela and Rajni Palriwala, eds., 1990, Structures and Strategies: Women, Work, and Family, New Delhi.
2. Dwyer, Daisy and Judith Bruce, eds., 1988, A Home Divided: Women and Income in the Third World, Stanford, CA.
3. Heitzman, James and Robert L. Worden, eds., 1996, Area Handbook Series, India–A Country Study, Washington, DC. International Labour Office, 1997, Yearbook of Labour Statistics 1997, Geneva.
4. Kishwar, Madhu and Ruth Vanita, eds., 1985, In Search of Answers: Indian Women's Voices From Manushi, London.
5. Liddle, Joanna and Rama Joshi, 1986, Daughters of Independence: Gender, Caste and Class in India, New Brunswick,
6. NJ. Madheswaran, S. and T. Lakshmanasamy, 1996, "Occupational Segregation and Earnings
7. Differentials by Sex: Evidence from India," Artha Vijnana, Vol. 38, No. 4, pp. 372-386.
8. National Commission for Women India, 1993, Proceedings of the National Workshop on "Employment, Equality and Impact of Economic Reform on Women," New Delhi.7
9. National Sample Survey Organization, 1994, Sarvekshana, Vol. 17, No. 3, January-March.
10. Registrar General and Census Commissioner, 1993, Census of India 1991, Final Population Totals: Brief Analysis of Primary Census Abstract, Series 1, New Delhi.

19

Perspectives on Women in Management in India

Today, India is a force in the global economy, with a high demand for talent. A key source of talent is educated Indian women. While Corporate India has not yet fully recognized or utilized this talent pool, the growing gender diversity in Indian managerial ranks offers a pathway for change for Indian women. Cultural and societal change means a shift from traditional views and stereotypes.

This article provides a glimpse into the status of women in management in India. Based on in-depth interviews by the Society for Human Resource Management (SHRM) with Indian professional men and women and findings from Indian research studies, this article aims to present perspectives that offer an increased awareness of the challenges and opportunities for women in management in India.

Cultural context

Historically, India has been a male-dominated society. Yet, in the past two decades or so, social change has opened the possibility for women to attain managerial roles in corporate India. Amartya Sen, Indian author and winner of the Nobel Prize in Economics, discusses gender inequality in his book The Argumentative Indian: Writings on Indian History, Culture and Identity. He points out that, "In the course of the evolution of women's movement [...] women are not passive recipients of welfare-enhancing help brought about by society, but are active promoters and facilitators of social transformations. Such transformations influence the lives and well-being of women, but also those of men and children—boys as well as girls. This is a momentous enrichment of the reach of women's movement."1 The growing gender diversity in Indian managerial ranks now offers a pathway for change for Indian women.

Today, the number of women students in business schools has grown significantly. These changes are in large part due to a significant cultural shift in parental perspective that allows for the possibility of women working outside the home, contributing economically to the family and even pursuing a career. The percentage of women in management in India is roughly 3% to 6%, 2 with approximately 2% of Indian women managers in Indian corporations.5 However, almost 96% of women workers are in the unorganized sector3.

As a brief comparison, in the United States women are projected to account for 49% of the increase in total labor force growth between 2006 and 2010. In 2008, the largest percentage of employed women (39%) worked in management, professional and related occupations and women accounted for 51% of all workers in the high-paying management, professional and related occupations. Globally, the number of women senior managers in large corporations is low. The March 2009 report, Women CEOs of the Fortune 1000, published by Catalyst (the U.S. firm working to expand opportunities for women and business), identifies the women CEOs of the Fortune 500 and 1000 companies. Of the Fortune 500 companies, 15 CEOs are women, including one Indian woman, Indra K. Nooyi, PepsiCo, Inc. (#59). Of the Fortune 501-1000, there are nine women CEOs5. The statistics at the CEO level of these large companies clearly show that there is much progress to be made for women worldwide at this level of management.

Movement for Change

As social values change, Indian women have been entering the workforce in the past couple decades. Globalization has brought an influx of multinational corporations to India, with Western HR practices and concepts such as gender diversity in leadership roles. As opportunities for women in management in India slowly increase, women are entering professions previously seen as the domain of men in the corporate world: advertising, banking, civil services, engineering, financial services, manufacturing, police and armed forces, and emerging fields such as IT and communications. At a recent speech to the Ladies' Circle International, Her Excellency, the President of India, Shrimati Pratibha Devisingh Patil, pointed out that to bring about gender equality, it is necessary to focus on educating and empowering women. Ms. Patil emphasized the need to strengthen processes that will promote economic and social development of women and urged this organization to increasingly concentrate its energies in this area.

Dr. Sudhir Varma, a specialist in the field of gender and development in India, and an ex IAS, has noted, "In spite of cultural and social taboos, more and more educated women are able to reach very high levels in the government, and the number of women in the corporate sector is gradually growing. There is no doubt that they have to constantly prove their efficiency to go up each step of the ladder. Corporate Indian women, earlier docketed into the routine repetitive work sectors like information technology, now head several national and Indian offices of international banks. They are also heading business and manufacturing houses." Dr. Varma, currently the Director of the Social Policy Research Institute (SPRI) in Jaipur, India, points out that "it is true that women face a certain amount of opposition from their male colleagues, but they now have full government support to grow along with men in their respective spheres. More and more women are now enrolling in MBA and other highly professional courses, and there is no bias against them during their placements." Professor Pawan S. Budhwar, Head of Group, Aston Business School at Aston University in the United Kingdom, has written extensively on human resource management issues in India. In the 2005 study Women in Management in the New Economic Environment, he and his research team point out that "developments in information technology and related services sectors are helping women in India to move out of their traditional household roles and develop a career in organizations." At the same time, they emphasize that merely having programs for women in the workplace will not be sufficient. Rather, there must be a true commitment on the part of senior management to hire women managers, including a policy for advancement linked to the business strategy.

Key Strengths of Indian Women as Managers

- Ability to network with colleagues
- Ability to perceive and understand situations
- Strong sense of dedication, loyalty and commitment to their organizations
- Ability to multitask
- Collaborative work style—solicit input from others, with respect for ideas
- Crisis management skills
- Willingness to share information (interactive leadership style)
- Sensitivity in relationships (e.g., compassionate, empathetic, understanding)
- Behaving in a gender-neutral manner

Source: *Adapted from Budhwar, P. S., Saini, D. S., & Bhatnagar, J. (2005, June). Women in management in the new economic environment: The case of India. Asia Pacific Business Review, 11(2), 179-193.*

Significant change in the workplace takes time. Professor Sujoya Basu, a member of the Faculty of Behavioral Sciences at the Indian Institute of Management Calcutta, argues that transformation in the Indian context for women in management can happen through policy and regulations that promote gender diversity and quality contact. She emphasizes that change can occur through the collective will to change the mindset of people to overcome gender differences at the educational and organizational levels.

Research Studies

The Indian literature on Indian women managers highlights challenges and opportunities for women and for organizations. A number of studies, spanning the years 2002 to 2008, document positive progress for women in the Indian management space as well as barriers to their progress. Research shows that the economic development of India has been positively influenced by entrepreneurial enterprises. Further, entrepreneurship has provided women in India the opportunity to enter social and political circles previously closed to them. Family background and support play an important role to achieve independence and move above the confines of a male-dominated traditional society. For most women entrepreneurs, financial stability in the household and family support is critical for their success. "A supportive family, both before and after marriage, is a key factor for Indian professional women to succeed."

However, women in management face challenges due to stereotyping. A 2002 study Gender Stereotypes at Work: Implications for Organizations notes that stereotypes and perceptions of Indian women in the workplace appear to have had a significant negative impact on the position of women managers. This study suggests Indian women are viewed as working in PR, HR and administrative positions at low to junior levels, and in fields such as fashion and beauty. Women in Indian organizations felt that such stereotypes result from not being given challenging assignments. Yet, male managers saw women as being treated more leniently than men when making mistakes11. 2008 study Gender Stereotypes in Corporate India: A Glimpse explored existing gender stereotypes in corporate India. According to this research, Indian men managers held similar managerial gender stereotypes as found in earlier Western studies. That is, they associate managerial success with men more than with women ("think manager—think male"). In contrast, Indian women managers did not project gender stereotypes on managerial positions.

A 2005 study of senior women in public and private sector firms, titled Women in Management in the New Economic Environment: The Case of India, found that women look for work from economic necessity and for personal goals. Women in lower to middle socioeconomic status seek income opportunities, and those in the upper middle class pursue a career for professional ambitions. Women with higher education have more interest in independence, are career-oriented and interested in quickly moving up the organizational ladder. The key challenge for women managers is managing both their traditional role as housewives and their career. Women experience great pressure to work hard to prove themselves in the workplace, and one of the greatest obstacles is how women managers are treated by men.

They often receive differential treatment, reinforcing the stereotypical view of being inferior and less important than men, resulting in not being offered challenging jobs and not being part of important organizational issues. Yet, despite social and attitudinal barriers, Indian women have gained some equality. Indian organizations are beginning to realize that women can do the same work as men, although in some cases, they have different needs. Finally, a 2006 study Women Managers in India explored key issues for women managers in corporate India in service and manufacturing. The study found that when it comes to hiring practices, most men and women managers see employment as based on merit, not gender (90% men and 79% women), but only about one-third think that organizations look for ways to increase the number of women in senior management roles.

In terms of organizational perceptions of importance of gender issues, overall, Indian organizations lack sensitivity about these issues and under appreciate women's capabilities and talents.

The study also examined management skills and leadership style and found that generally, men tend to want women to act like men, and most men are not comfortable working for a woman manager. Overall, women prefer an interactive style, and men prefer a command and control style.

To be successful in business, women develop management styles that make it more comfortable for men to work with and/or report to a female manager. Lastly, the study concluded that major barriers to women's advancement to corporate leadership include lack of mentoring of women, lack of awareness by women of company politics and an inhospitable corporate culture.

Perspectives of Indian Women Professionals

To learn more about Indian women managers, SHRM conducted interviews with four Indian women professionals:

- Archana Bhaskar, HR Director, Shell Companies in India
- Hema Hattangady, Vice Chairman and CEO, Schneider Electric Conzerv India
- Dr. Juhi Kumar, Assistant Professor, Weill Cornell Medical College
- Navodita Varma, SPHR, President, Maanasvi LLC

Each of them offers a broad range of experience from her respective career—physician, business owner, HR director and CEO. All emphasize the importance of family support, higher education, mentors, belief in one's capabilities and a strong focus on personal and professional goals. While biases still exist in Indian society, each of these Indian women professionals sees expanding opportunities for women in India. As one of the interviewees points out, "we have indeed come a long way, from a nation condoning practices like female infanticide, dowry deaths and sati to one that endorses and encourages education, economic remuneration for the family, and economic and social reforms that have resulted in macro-level changes in the country and within organizations."

Recommended HR Management Practices to Create a "Women-Friendly" Organization

- Senior management commitment to gender issues
- Career development programs for women
- Exposure of women to top management
- Leadership development programs for women
- Job rotation for women
- Recruitment of women at senior-level positions
- Regular survey of women to assess job satisfaction
- Mentoring programs for women
- Child care facilities at work

Source: *Adapted from Saini, D. S. (2006). Labour law in India. In H. J. Davis, S. R. Chatterjee & M. Heur (Eds.), Management in India: Trends and Transition (pp. 60-94). New Delhi: Response Books.*

Socioeconomics

Dr. Juhi Kumar, Assistant Professor in Pediatric Nephrology at the Weill Cornell Medical College, New York City, remarks on the changes that she has seen. "In the past 10 years that I have been away from my country, things have changed tremendously. Ten years ago, there were limited numbers of women in the workforce, in traditional professions like teaching and clerical-level positions in banks. Now, when I go back to India, I see women in increasing numbers in managerial positions." As a result of economic changes, the earning potential of women has increased in importance. As Archana Bhaskar, HR Director for Shell Companies in India, observes, "there is certainly positive change for women in India in the workplace.

Today, women are thought of as great managers, often pursued strongly by search firms. In fact, several firms have targets to achieve on women numbers." She goes on to explain that the real change, though, has happened with the advent of the IT and business process outsourcing (BPO) industries, which has employed significant numbers of women and brought in best practices to enable women staff. In her experience, "Shell is absolutely a fantastic place for women to work. The diversity and inclusion practices and thinking are very advanced and well engrained. The core values of respect and inclusion for people and work/life balance, as well as flexible work practices, are seriously pursued, resulting in an environment where women thrive."

Hema Hattangady, Vice Chairman and CEO of Schneider Electric Conzerv India (formerly Conzerv Systems), notes that the presence of Indian women managers ranges between a high of 6% and a low of 3%. Women can be seen mainly in HR, IT, administration and other support functions. She emphasizes that there is still a lot to achieve with regard to women in management positions in India. "Although ever-evolving HR practices, diversity practices and factors like education have led to an increase in the number of women working in India, there is still a lot left to be done to develop, encourage and empower women for management positions."

Family and Education

The stories of the four women interviewed for this article point to the criticality of family support and education for career success. As principal of her own HR consulting firm, Navodita Varma, SPHR, points out that coming from a family that valued education was very important. "I come from a well-educated family. After my MBA in human resources, I was fortunate to get good jobs. My husband pushed me to achieve as much as I could." "Today, most urban Indian men want educated and well-informed life partners."

Hema Hattangady, who heads up India's largest energy management company, said," My education has played a key role in my professional success in terms of helping me get some leverage in the business world where credentials can play an important part with regard to 'getting a foot in the door.' The fact that I was armed with an MBA from IIM, one of the premier management institutes in India, helped convince my people that

I could definitely be of some use in our then small family-run enterprise." Born into a family of teachers, Dr. Juhi Kumar received constant encouragement from her family on her professional journey. Her mother highly qualified. "It is these major influences that continue to guide me and help me live my life by a certain set of values and principles," says Dr. Kumar. She points out that her husband provided tremendous support. It was through his encouragement that she could do her master's degree in the United States and her residency in pediatrics and fellowship in pediatric nephrology. She has now has a teaching position at a prestigious medical university.

Education and family support strongly contributed to the career aspirations of Archana Bhaskar, who now has a high-level position in human resources in a multinational corporation. She came from a typical middle class background in a tier 2 city. "My parents laid great emphasis on excellence in education and were willing to go to great lengths to support me in getting the right academic opportunities. My mother is very well, but she did not work after marriage. She was fierce about my being able to be financially independent and what that means to a woman's life."

Social Expectations

In India, the roles expected of a man, as the bread-winner, and a woman, as the home maker, have been refined. Ms. Varma notes, "The expectations from the husband's family after marriage—which include the woman giving up her career after marriage, childbirth and then expectations that if she works outside of the home, she still needs to look after the in-laws, the house, the children and the husband—can prove to be too much for many women to handle, and they end up giving up their careers midway." Ms. Bhaskar's experience illustrates some of the difficulties in the workplace for women. "When I started working after my post-graduation in business management, there was not much support for women managers. You had to be like one of the men to succeed. Work/life balance was almost thrown out of the window. The one or two women that were in my organization were busy trying to compete with each other rather than help! Male colleagues and managers consistently refused to take me seriously, saying I was in the job for entertainment rather than to make a professional success."

Success Factors

A number of factors contribute to success for the modern Indian women in the workplace. Ms. Varma emphasizes that "a good education, effective communication skills (both written and oral), as well as a very professional attitude toward your work and co-workers, are the key to attain managerial roles. Mentors are also important, and I was lucky to get good bosses early in my career who gave me full freedom to work and to take decisions and who were mentors for me." Hema Hattangady's says "Once you have a mentor who backs you, you have the confidence to move forward." "Mentoring is one of the principle reasons that I was successfully able to turn a fledgling family-owned concern into a world-class energy management organization." Being a lifelong learner is also essential for success. According to Ms. Hattangady, "tacking a new education line onto your resume proves to your employer that you're committed to improving your skills and that you care about being good at your job. Besides simply raising your, a master's in business administration can also help decrease the gender gap.

Finally, as Archana Bhaskar shares from her experience, success is a mix of tradeoffs, perseverance and focus. "I succeeded largely due to my professional excellence and intellectual abilities and, of course, unstinting support from my husband. However, there were times when I had to often make choices and limit my sphere of impact (that is, perform below my capacity) in order to optimize my life and career. Somewhat later into my career, sponsorship and mentoring played a key role in getting the right breaks. Being able to define clear personal/professional choices was important."

Recommendations for Indian Organizations

As cultural mores change and Indian society more broadly supports Indian women in managerial positions, organizations need to be more open and make appropriate changes in their workplace. From the Indian research study Women in Management in the New Economic Environment: The Case of India, the following are recommendations for Indian organizations to promote a supportive workplace for women.

- Develop policies that create a women-friendly workplace environment.
- Establish training programs for women, such as mentorship, career guidance and leadership development.
- Promote awareness initiatives that highlight the value of women managers.
- Elicit input from women employees regarding policies, promotion and performance review processes.
- Make accommodations for women in areas such as need-based postings. That is, as done in civil services, have a policy to post both spouses to the same district or state.
- Have a true commitment to hire and promote women and include women in the annual business strategy.

In Closing

In today's global economy, Corporate India needs talent in order to be competitive. Generally, women as managers are underutilized in corporate India. To advance women in managerial roles, support by top management is essential. Promoting diverse management practices and opening doors to women in management—through proactive human resource policies and programs—is one way for Indian organizations to expand their talent pool and, ultimately, their leadership pipeline. As highlighted by the Indian women professionals interviewed for this article, specific success factors—a good education, mentoring, family support, strong communication skills and life-long learning—are essential for Indian women managers today. While traditional Indian cultural viewpoints are slow to change (and not all women want a career in management), positive change for women in the business world in India is moving forward.

References

1. Sen, A. (2005). The argumentative Indian: Writings on Indian history, culture and identity. New York: Farrar, Straus and Giroux.
2. Budhwar, P. S., Saini, D. S., & Bhatnagar, J. (2005, June). Women in management in the new economic environment: The case of India. Asia Pacific Business Review, 11(2), 179-193.
3. Women workers in India in the 21st century—Unemployment and underemployment. (2004, February). Retrieved April 30, 2009, from www.cpiml.org/liberation/year_2004/febraury/WomenWorkers.htm
4. United States Department of Labor/Women's Bureau. (2008). Quick stats on women workers, 2008. Retrieved August 25, 2009, from www.dol.gov/wb/stats/main.htm
5. Catalyst. (2009, March). Women CEOs of the Fortune 1000. Retrieved April 2, 2009, from http://www.catalyst.org/
6. Budhwar, P. S., Saini, D. S., & Bhatnagar, J. (2005, June). Women in management in the new economic environment: The case of India. Asia Pacific Business Review, 11(2), 179-193.
7. President of India. (2009, August 21). Speech by Her Excellency, the President of India, Shrimati Pratibha Devisingh Patil, at the meeting with the Ladies' Circle International. Retrieved August 24, 2009, from http://presidentofindia.nic.in/sp210809.html
8. Budhwar, P. S., Saini, D. S., & Bhatnagar, J. (2005, June). Women in management in the new economic environment: The case of India. Asia Pacific Business Review, 11(2), 179-193.
9. Basu, S. (2008). Gender stereotypes in Corporate India: A glimpse. New Delhi: Response Books.
10. Handy, F., Ranade, B., & Kasam, M. (2007, Summer). To profit or not to profit: Women entrepreneurs in India. Nonprofit Management & Leadership, 17(4), 383-401.

11. Khandelwal, P. (2002, April-June). Gender stereotypes at work: Implications for organizations. Indian Journal of Training and Development. XXXII(2), 72-83.

12. Basu, S. (2008). Gender stereotypes in Corporate India: A glimpse. New Delhi: Response Books.

13. Budhwar, P. S., Saini, D. S., & Bhatnagar, J. (2005, June). Women in management in the new economic environment: The case of India. Asia Pacific Business Review, 11(2), 179-193.

14. Gupta, A., Koshal, M., & Koshal R. K. (2006). Women managers in India: Challenges and opportunities. In H. J. Davis, S. R. Chatterjee & M. Heuer (Eds.), Management in India (pp. 285-312). New Delhi: Response Books.

15. Budhwar, P. S., Saini, D. S., & Bhatnagar, J. (2005, June). Women in management in the new economic environment: The case of India. Asia Pacific Business Review, 11(2), 179-193.

20

Working Conditions of Female Domestic Workers in Delhi

Gender has been playing a very important role in deciding the participation of men and women in various activities. Gender as a category of analysis has not figured research, analysis, policy making etc prior 1980. But gender cannot be ignored anymore given the gender consciousness and increasing participation of men and women in labour market operations, decision making and administrative positions including political participation. This could be possible only due to change in power relations and social and cultural change realised in the society. However, developing countries like India still continue to be resisting to social change preventing women to participate like men in all fields. Cultural and social practices and customs, traditional beliefs and lack of gender sensitive outlook, resistance to gender mainstreaming and lack of acceptance of women in various positions which were occupied by men, lack of vision to view everything with gender lens are the major issues standing as hurdles for women's participation in outside the household participation.

A large number of urban centers have emerged all round the world in the process of industrialization and urbanization. It has brought similar impact in different parts of India. Both the processes involve heavy construction work. Factory buildings, accessory and ancillary buildings, government offices, roads, railway tracks and Entire Township need to be erected and constructed. Construction works require various kinds of skilled and unskilled workers like kulis, beldars, rajmistris, painters, badhais, bandhanis, sanitary workers, plumber etc. These workers are spread across the width and length of the country; however, they are drawn in large numbers, through pull and push factors to the emerging and flourishing industrial and urban centers. So, these centers have huge concentration of construction workers.

In the era of liberalization and globalization, due to higher rate of economic growth, the construction sector too has got a boost. Irrespective of occasional slumps in the economy or in construction works, the sector is going through a faster growth. Apart from old / traditional urban/ industrial centers, new industrial/urban centers have appeared on the map where construction works are going on large scale. Expanding and fast growing construction sector and, in general, lack of greater employment opportunity elsewhere has drawn large number of workers in this sector. There are more than 20 million of construction workers in India at present. Cities, like Delhi alone have around more than 600 thousand of them. Apart from metros other cities, like Jamnagar in Gujarat, Guwahati & Shillong in the NorthEast are also expanding at fast rate.

Gender has been playing a very important role in deciding the participation of men and women in various activities. Gender as a category of analysis has not figured research, analysis, policy making etc prior 1980. But gender cannot be ignored anymore given the gender consciousness and increasing participation of men and women in labour market operations, decision making and administrative positions including political participation. This could be possible only due to change in power relations and social and cultural change realised in the society. However, developing countries like India, still continues to be resisting to social change preventing women to participate like men in all fields. Cultural and social practices and customs, traditional beliefs and lack of gender sensitive outlook, resistance to gender mainstreaming and lack of acceptance of women in various positions which were occupied by men, lack of vision to view everything with gender lens are the major issues standing as hurdles for women's participation in outside the household participation.

The constitution of India, via articles 325 and 326, guarantees political equality to all men and women. However, women have not benefited from their right. The representation of women in Parliament and State Assemblies is extremely low in India. In spite of registered voting population of 1040 million, in the last General Elections [2004], the total number of women candidates contesting elections from all recognised political parties was just 176, out of which only 45 women were elected. This is just 8.2% of the total strength of the Lower House of Parliament. The average percentage of elected women in 14 State Assembly elections held in 2004, 2005 and 2006 is 6.62%. This is equally true in the 2009 parliament elections too wherein only a few women will be in the Cabinet and less than 10 percent as Member of Parliament.

There are number of issues for lack of participation of women in politics which are related to socio-cultural factors which are evidenced by the primary survey conducted by the researcher and also from the literature survey. It is an opportunity for women to participate in decision making and promote gender friendly policies which are hitherto absent with the participation of lack of gender sensitive men. There are number of issues related to the lack of participation of women in politics which may be brought under cultural and social factors. There are only less than 10 per cent of women participating in politics and in certain areas no participation of women or only one or two women for the entire state. Moreover, it is also evidenced that a few women elected and serving the society through politics are gender sensitive and recommend to policies which are women friendly. They are also products of the patriarchy and surrounded by men ministers and failed to make a dent or influence the men or get the support from women or likeminded men due to poor representation to influence gender friendly policies. This does not mean that having women elected members may not bring women friendly policies, but it needs strength and only when there are more women, the need will be felt and the demand and lobby will be heard and real sanction would be there.

Given the Constitutional guarantee and the signatory of India on various UN Declarations of committing towards promoting and ensuring gender equality, it is necessary that women must equally be encouraged to participate, offered capacity building programmes to enhance the skills to participate in public life and sensitize them to make the people accept the women candidates as contestants. It is observed in almost all elections be it State Assembly elections, or Parliament Elections, or the local body elections, there is a resistance among the voters to vote of women candidates, which is evidenced in the recent elections held in May 2009 where taking Tamil Nadu alone, which is a little progressive state with a contributions of social reformers and feminist leaders like Thanthai Periyar, who was a radical social reformers worked for the women's liberation and freedom from the women's reproductive responsibilities, etc and accordingly very poor representation and acceptance of women in Politics was realised.

A study has been conducted already by the Researcher on the constraints for women to participate in politics taking the experience of the women already in power and also future contestants. The preliminary findings revealed that the women in politics need three important pre requisites.

[i] Family background in which any other member either father, husband or brothers were in politics

[ii] Money backing to spend on entering into politics

[iii] good rapport and relationship with the party as it is very important to affiliate with a political party which is a leading party in the region or nation and the candidate must be in the good books of the leaders of the party.

If they lack these qualifications, it is very difficult to get into politics. There are very rare cases where in women have proved themselves by serving at the grass root and earned a name and sustain in politics. Ms. Balabharathi of CPI [M], Member of Legislative Assembly, in Tamil Nadu where the study has been conducted, is one such case who had started her career as a nutritious meals scheme staff of State Government and slowly worked with people and earned and won the good will. Now she gained power as MLA for the three successive terms. Hence it is necessary to have the background or work for the people, gain significance by getting the good will among the people to get into politics.

Now the question is to how long these pre-requisites will help the women to get into politics, is it not possible for women without such background to contest in election, how to ensure the constitutional guarantee of equal rights to women. These are questions to be probed into in future to make more women to participate in elections and bring a change in power.

In a study conducted invariably revealed in the preliminary survey and the intensive survey done with some candidates who are in power revealed that they have to qualify the above requirements. In addition if they happen to be women, they are expected to be flexible and sometimes sexual favours may also be demanded and failing which may not bring prospects to the women or it is possible for women to participate in politics.

In general there has been a lack of confidence of women leadership in politics among both men and women, which may be attributed to the kind of performance of the women's who had so far in power either at the National or regional or local body levels. It is very rare to see distinctly performing women who would be role models for other women to enter into politics.

India has a three tier system of parliament, legislative assembly and local body. In the local body election of grass root governance, there are a few women who proved successful and also serve as a role model for others. But they failed to influence others due to various due to internal politics and lack of co-operation among the women in different parties. Yes women as such need to come together to fight for their right but unfortunately women who are represented thinly in different parties are so loyal to the party and not for their own women community in getting and delivering the goods.

There is a challenge now to bring more women to mainstream gender in politics and also influence polices with a gender perceptive focus and addresses the gender needs. There is a desperate need to bring more women to politics from the non-political background community and family which is absent till date. Similarly there is a need to strength the grass root governance by bringing the women from different strata including the Dalit community who are the poor among the entire pyramid of distribution of population both economically and socially.

All these need to be seriously looked into and it is critical to enhance the capacity of the women to fight elections, reduce or remove the preventive barriers and to introduce new affirmative steps, such as quotas, that can enhance the participation of women in State and National parliaments. There is a strong need for lobbying for passage of 33% reservation of Seats for Women in Parliament bill which has been pending for two decades or so. It is necessary that the existing networks, which are working on the issue of gender parity in politics, need to be strengthened to support and help sustain women in politics.

Visiting Fellowship period at IDS will be in finalising the report of the study undertaken and also infer the future action to be taken to improve the participation of women in Politics thereby bring about a change in power structure and social change.

It is a universally observed that in a society which is characterized by gender segregation and social stratification, certain sections unfortunately occupy a subordinate position. Indian constitution guarantees democracy and confers the right of equality to all strata. But the reality is that this guarantee and right of equality have not reached many lower sections of society. It is those people who struggle, are impoverished, alienated and concerned with basics for survival. The case of the domestic workers is evidence to the fact that despite the guaranteed constitutional rights their struggle for equality and survival continues.

In the recent past the trend shows that all big cities of country have become the centers to recruit poor women as domestic workers, Delhi being no exception. The non-availability of job in rural or tribal areas facilitates continuous supply of women workers to Delhi and other cities. A major reason for this being a sharp increase of middle class women in employment. These middle class employed women have shifted their household workload to the poor working women as their "maids". In some cases it is seen that the middle and upper classes in order to keep their upward mobility and status symbol have withdrawn themselves from household duties.

The increasing demand of domestic workers in Delhi has played a major role in migration of women from far flung rural or tribal areas. Most of the women who migrate to Delhi are from poor families and are illiterate. Their lack of education and skill make their choice very limited and when they come to big cities such as Delhi they have to face number of problems and because of their inexperience and lack of skill they become easy victim of exploitation.

The existing problems of domestic workers have been studied by many researchers, social activists and voluntary organizations at different levels. But they have not succeeded in providing a feasible solution to the problem. Perhaps lack of a common perspective in this area is a main cause for it. Since the problems of women domestic workers are multifaceted, it should be studied holistically covering economic, legal, social, physical and psychological aspects. For this, it is immensely needed to have an integrated approach to understand the issue and it is also important to develop a collective programme to improve their social status and working condition. Keeping this in view a one-day seminar was jointly organized by Deshkal and FES on "Working conditions, coping strategy and legal status of Female Domestic workers" in Delhi on 12th October, 2002. This was attended by many researchers, members of voluntary organization, social activists and some domestic workers of Delhi.

This book comes as a collection of papers presented in this seminar. The papers included in this book focus our attention on various issues that are of considerable significance in understanding the problems of domestic workers in Delhi. Each paper represents a distinct approach to this issue yet share a common concern for the domestic workers.

In the first chapter Sanjay Kumar has sketched the outline of the seminar and has discussed basic issue involved in this whole problem. He suggests four focal points to deal with the problem such as:

1. Provision of registration
2. Inclusion of the minimum wages
3. collaboration and networking and
4. Collective bargaining.

Leela Kasturi in her paper discusses the issue of migration related to female domestic workers of Delhi. She has argued that migration among the poor domestic workers is sought as a 'coping strategy' for the survival of the families. The paper also tells about the mental trauma faced by migrant women. The paper highlights their social economic and psychological aspect of the problem in a detailed and effective manner.

Pravin Sinha in his paper meticulously discusses total employment scenario of women in India. He mentions many reasons of urban migration most important being the mass poverty and high level of illiteracy. He also suggests 'empowerment of domestic women' and 'skill development as a two important remedial measures to deal with the problem'.

Alex Ekka's paper focuses mainly on the migration of tribal women to the urban centers. The paper mentions various problems faced by these women in Delhi. He suggests ameliorative measures in the interest of domestic workers and action plan for the future. Neetha N's paper talks about two important aspects – 'social networking' and 'identity formation'. Social Networking takes place both before and after the migration. After the migration, social networking plays a major role in overcoming their social and psychological insecurities and low socio economic status. Two other papers by Smita Snehi and representatives of ANKUR respectively discuss various problems being faced by women domestic workers who are displaced to the new resettlement colonies of Delhi.

The real life experience of some women domestic workers quoted in these two papers makes it easier for us to comprehend their difficulties. It also gives a deeper understanding of their lives. It is agreed by all the authors of the papers that a major hurdle in providing a solution to the problem is because of absence of a legal protection system. Seema Durrani's paper is useful to know the legal rights available to the women domestic workers.

Plight of Construction Labourers in North-East

A large number of urban centers have emerged all round the world in the process of industrialization and urbanization. It has brought similar impact in different parts of India. Both the processes involve heavy construction work. Factory buildings, accessory and ancillary buildings, government offices, roads, railway tracks and Entire Township need to be erected and constructed. Construction works require various kinds of skilled and unskilled workers like *kulis, beldars, rajmistris, painters, badhais, bandhanis, sanitary workers, plumber etc.* These workers are spread across the width and length of the country; however, they are drawn in large numbers, through pull and push factors to the emerging and flourishing industrial and urban centers. So, these centers have huge concentration of construction workers.

These construction workers may or may not be migrant workers but they have maximum mobility because of the nature of their occupation. They are always on move from one work-site to another after the construction work at a site is over. These workers also migrate from backward/small industrial, urban and commercial centers to develop and big industrial, urban and commercial centers. The development of a particular urban centre also depends on its political importance. Political importance boosts up industrial, infrastructure development process, this in turn boosts up construction works.

Though they are part and parcel of the large streams of workers, their problems and woes are, in fact, continuation of the problems and woes faced by the workers of other sectors. However, the nature of work, problems and disposition of construction workers are quite different in degree and quality. This is because of various reasons.

These workers fall in the category of unorganized sector. Though this predicament is not exclusive to them, however, highly disorganized and fragmented state hamper their bargaining power and fight against injustice. Neither their job nor their work at a particular site is permanent or of a perennial nature. When construction starts at any place, these workers are hired on daily or monthly or may be on contract basis.

Being part of *unorganized sector of labourers*, they lose in bargaining for fair wages. They are not paid minimum wages; even the agreed wages are not paid in time. Even after the construction work is over, substantial due remains with the builders or the contractors, who are always on the look for devouring these due wages. Moreover, their working time and hours are not well regulated. They do not get overtime rates for excess work.

They work under very hazardous conditions. The working conditions and the facilities provided at the sites are far from satisfactory. Safety conditions and measurers are hardly met. In case of accident, there is, in general, no provision for financial and medical aid. It is up to the workers themselves to arrange for the treatment. There is no scheme like ESI coverage for them. In the extreme cases like death, no body owns the responsibility. Apart from these, there is no recreational facilities, no availability of drinking water, toilets, canteens etc. In big cities, like Delhi, they face another big problem of commuting from one place to other. They have to commute on their own. Travelling from the place of living to the work site and then back to the living place eat much into their time, money and energy. The commutation is not even smooth. Therefore they have much of leisure to spend with family, and less of money and energy to cater the needs of family members.

If the workers are female, the problems at work site and while commuting gets compounded and multiplied. More so if they are pregnant or having small children. There is no system at all to take care of these children at work site. And they just cannot take leave out of work during this period lest they would face extreme financial problems.

Then, living conditions are no way better than the working conditions. It will not be entirely wrong to say that the situation is still worse. They are destined to live in slums where one does not get proper (at all) civic amenities. The surroundings are totally unhygienic. There are no proper facilities for drainage, toilet, potable water, electricity, recreation etc. There are no local medical facilities, hospital, school and fair price shop. They need to struggle quite a lot to get ration cards, they hardly avail the facility of banking services, for postal services they have to travel to far away localities. For all these reasons, it is very difficult for them to maintain healthy community life. Most of the time construction workers are forced to live nearby or at the work site. At these sites living conditions/lack of civic and other facilities are even more appalling.

In the era of liberalization and globalization, due to higher rate of economic growth, the construction sector too has got a boost. Irrespective of occasional slumps in the economy or in construction works, the sector is going through a faster growth. Apart from old / traditional urban/ industrial centers, new industrial/urban centers have appeared on the map where construction works are going on large scale. Expanding and fast growing construction sector and, in general, lack of greater employment opportunity elsewhere has drawn large number of workers in this sector. There are more than 20 million of construction workers in India at present. Cities, like Delhi alone have around more than 600 thousand of them. Apart from metros other cities, like Jamnagar in Gujarat, Guwahati & Shillong in the NorthEast are also expanding at fast rate.

This is not to undermine the problem if we say, under this situation it is really difficult to implement benefits like maternity leave. However, nowadays the construction workers are rising to the occasion and are organizing themselves and agitating to get all these benefits. They are becoming aware of their overdue rights and benefits. The attention of the government has also been drawn towards their plights and it is doing its own bit, albeit at a very slow pace. Recently, in 1996, the central government has enacted a few laws for construction workers in order to ameliorate their situation. However, this is just an initial and small step.

Conclusion and Recommendation

Imphal

A thorough analysis of primary level data revealed that in Imphal more than two third of the construction workers belonged to the home state of Manipur. Majority of construction workers was of Maiteis community, who was the inhabitants of plain land of Manipur, popularly called Imphal Valley. Maiteis' main occupation is agriculture and allied activities. There was hardly any social hierarchy among Maitei societies. As a result agrarian labour it is still a rare phenomenon all over Manipur. Every peasant is a worker and every woman is a weaver as well in the state. Wages labour was still not taken in high spirit in Manipur Society. Handicrafts and its related activities was an important occupation after agriculture in Manipur.

Over the years the above two sectors of economic activities faced severe challenges from large-scale production and as a result its scope shrunk day by day. Closure of Imphal Yarn bank and failure of co-operative movement aggravated this problem. As a result it became uneconomic and compelled a large number of women to search for other jobs. A good number of men were already thrown out of agriculture due to lack of infrastructure facilities as well as steep growth of population. Therefore a large number of people came to construction work because it was the only employment generation field other than rickshaw pulling which, was almost monopolized by Muslim Community of the Valley.

These construction workers were facing a lot of problems. Basic question for them was the question of social dignity. As wage labourship is considered to be against dignity among Maiteis no construction worker dare to be recognized as wage labour. At many occasions, if they were at any public place they covered their faces with cloth to hide their recognition. It weakens their bargaining capacity. Hence, they were bound to work on lower wages.

Itanagar

It was found that in Itanagar most of the migrant workers especially interstate migrants were living in rented houses or jhuggi-jhopari constructed by them on government land. The relationship among migrant workers was quite friendly and harmonious. But this was not so with local workers. Local workers were not taking the work seriously and honestly and at many a time their visit at work-site was for merely attendance sake. They were used to get their wages by muscle flexing or by threatening to the officers/officials.

Hindi language is frequently used by workers to interact among themselves and even with local people. None of them participated in local festivals and hardly anybody knew local language. However, they agreed that tribals had no interest in manual labour so there was no question of any acrimony between the local and outsiders. The availability of infrastructure and services related to sanitation and health were measurably missing at work-sites and in such a situation female workers were the real sufferers. It was found that no worker was member any Political Party. But they agreed that most of them were members of Arunachal Pradesh PWD Workers Union. However, they complained those casual ones.

Workers were aware of some of their rights related to their work. Almost all the workers had their ration cards, but few of them answered in affirmative regarding their names in the Union pays more attention to regular employees rather than the voter list. They complained that most of the workers had their names included in the voter's list but it was struck off due to some unknown reasons. No proper toilet facility was provided at the work-site. Drinking water was available at the work-site through taps. About 20% of the workers were female, but no extra facility was available to them. Contractor did not like pregnant women and retrenched them ruthlessly. Threat of molestation was reported by many of them.

None of the workers was involved in political or trade union activities. None of the workers was found aware of his right as a construction worker. Most of them reported that their economic condition had been changing positively but they were not assured of better future because of working opportunity shrinking. None of them were provided skill promotion training, which they anticipated from government side with regularization of work and availability of all facilities available to permanent government employee of his category.

None help was available to the workers for education of their children or for the health measures of their family members. All the workers were sending their children to government schools and spending 5-15% of their income over it. For health measures of their family members, they were spending a handsome amount.

Guwahati

Most of the construction workers in Guwahati at both the construction sites i.e. Indian Oil Building and KVIC were not aware about the aspects of workers' rights. At both the working sites it was differential wages rate for skilled and unskilled workers. Unskilled workers were paid rupees 60-70 and skilled workers rupees 100-110 a day. No Weekly leave was provided to than however they were allowed to take leave at their will but no payment was made for the leave.

The workers reported that the working relation with contractor and other staffs was good and congenial. The wages were paid in time and nobody was forced to do extra work. He paid the full amount of treatment in case of minor injuries and sickness but no payment was made for the leave. In the name of toilet and related infrastructure, very little facility was available. A few *Katcha* latrines were made for them in a corner of the work-site. A hand pump was installed very near to the hut and its water was used for all purposes.

Electricity was available to the work-site. The work-site was fenced with high brick walls but no security arrangement was available there. There was no display of board at the work-site. Workers were not given any wages slip and they had not even seen any Master roll Register. The contractor denied showing us this register too. Workers had no membership with any Trade Union or Political Party. Bengali workers did not know Assamese but Assamese itself is so close to Bengali that they need no other medium to interact. Their culture was also very similar and they had no barrier except religion to mix-up with each other.

Majority of the workers, who were new to this profession, reported their economic condition better over years due to joining construction work. Almost all of the workers reported their children reading in government school and no aid was being availed by the employer in this context. They were not getting any material help for health purposes of the family as well. They were spending 5-10% of their income on education of their children and rupees 500-2500 on health measures of the family. The workers living away from the family sent almost all the saving to their family and they had no local Bank or Post Office Accounts.

Two Trade Unions viz. Refinery Thekedari Mazdoor Union and Refinery Thekedari Sharmik Union were active among workers with almost equal strength of membership. Approximately 50% of the workers were members of these two Unions. The workers gave the credit of weekly, casual and medical leave provisions as Tiffin Allowance provided to them. They reported the Mazdoor Union members were more honest and sincere than its counterpart.

Shillong

The construction workers at both the sites viz. University Site and Secretariat belonged to different socio-economic and religious group. A section of these workers were also coming from several neighbouring states. Most of them inhabited near the site where wire fencing existed to protect building material. No female worker was employed. The accommodation for the workers was made of straw walls and roofing. Tap water was supplied there during one-hour morning and one-hour evening. Electric bulbs were available in their rooms. Nothing was charged for these facilities. Here again wages differentials were existing for different category of workers- for skilled workers the daily wages was rupees 100-110 and for unskilled workers it was rupees 60-70. No weekly holiday was rewarded to them and no overtime was payable for their half an hour work.

The respondents explained the ever-increasing gap and divide with local tribes especially Khasi as they feel that these outsiders were encroaching their rights in day to day activities. In the opinion of these workers they live here under great fear because Khasi people, who are natives of this area do not like then and try to drive them away from work. Most of the workers accepted that they came to work at Shillong due to lack of sufficient works in their area and also due to better rate of wages at Shillong. And above all the climate of Shillong is very favorable for work. Workers accepted that most of the time they were paid wages in time on weekly basis.

No display board was available at the site. It also came to notice that workers were not given any wages slip and no muster role book was available at the site office. It was also observed that the workers did not know even ABC of their rights as construction workers. Nobody was active member of any Trade Union or any political party. Indeed, some of the youngsters were active in cultural activities. Most of the workers agreed that their economic condition has been improved after coming to Shillong but they were not assured of their better future. None of the workers was involved in political or Trade Union activities. Indeed all the Scheduled Tribes workers and most of the youngsters were active in cultural activities such as dance, music and songs.

Recommendations

It is true that there are various reasons behind the plight of construction workers especially in NE-India but it is not impossible to overcome these problems. Deshkal recommends some important suggestions to be carried out for the amelioration of economic condition of construction workers in Northeast. These are listed below.

1. Every construction worker should be registered with labour department and this department should have all necessary information related to them.
2. Constitution and functioning of 'Workers Welfare Board' should be time bound as any delay in its formation directly goes against the interest of workers.
3. Special groups should be formed to conduct skill enhancing and awareness generation campaign and they should be made responsible to contact all the registered workers. If possible, a permanent institute should be set in each district and compact classes should be organized to provide the workers theoretical knowledge as well as their rights with concerning laws and acts.
4. Formation of Trade Union should not only be the rights of regular workers but it should be made for those constructions workers where certain numbers of them were supposed to work for certain period.
5. Revision of wages rate for casual workers should be made time bound and proper dearness allowance should be fixed to avoid any decrease in their earnings. States should be instructed not to fix minimum rate of wages lower than the Central Government fixation.
6. As makeshift arrangements for workers stay in and around the work site render them vulnerable to all sorts of problems, there is pressing need to arrange for their alternative accommodation.
7. Construction workers should be provided land with concession rate and subsidized building materials to construct their own accommodation.
8. NGO's or other Social Institutions should be encouraged to conduct social awareness programmes to establish the dignity of manual labour in the societies.

9. Some specific rules should be introduced to avoid tension between local and outside workers.
10. Make serious efforts to sensitize the engineering wing to the need for labour welfare, as they are the closest governmental representative to the construction labourers at the worksites.

Conclusions and Recommendations

Conclusions

Security through private guards has become a common phenomenon especially in urban part of India. Similarly it is very common in mega city like Delhi. One can easily spot a private security at all nook and corners of Delhi in their variety of colourful uniforms. In the last decade the number of such guards and agencies employing them had grown with an accelerated pace. Delhi is no exception to that.

The information collected with the help of owners and officials of different security agencies, newspapers, magazines, views of the experts and academicians engaged in the study of unorganized sector workers reveal that there are more than 3,500 registered and un-registered security agencies in Delhi engaging more than 50,000 security guards. Apart from providing security to multinational companies, consulates, corporate offices, industrial units, residential apartments and VIP residences, they also engage themselves in areas of fire protection, surveillance services, cash van services, training services, security audits, housekeeping services, utility services etc.

Security guards in their uniform with the nonexistent power creates a false notion about them as belonging to formal sector/ organized sector of labour category but the fact seems to be that working and living conditions of majority of these working class are even worse than a daily wages labour. Survival and livelihood of security guards in Delhi still revolves around the minimum wages prescribed by the Delhi Government that is rupees 2592 per month. But many of them are getting lesser salary of the minimum wages prescribed by Delhi Government.

If one see the number of security agencies and security guards and their role in providing security to different section of society, it is astonishing that there is no specific government department to register, provide direction and regulate these agencies for better working environment. There is hardly any act or ordinance to safeguard their interest. A big majority of these guards are migrant. They come from all sections of society and a good number of them having educational degree as graduate to post graduate. A section of these working communities also come from retired defence officials.

Recommendations

Based on the above statement regarding the status of private security guards some important recommendations are being put forward to bring necessary improvement for a better and sustainable working environment for this working community. It is as follows:

i. There is urgent need of a viable act and legislation to safeguard the right and bring improvement in the working environment of these security guards. This will provide a shield to them so that they put forward their grievances at a suitable platform.
ii. A proper directive and guideline should be given to all the security agencies employing these guards so that any discrimination may be avoided.
iii. Seeing the mammoth growth in the size and number of these private security guards and the agencies employing them, there should provision for their stay and living facility.
iv. There should a compulsory provision so that all the private security guards should get a minimum salary as prescribe and enacted by the government of Delhi. Although, this act is in force but a few security agencies are following it.

21

Women With Society Development

Indian society is a developing society. It is passing through a transitional stage. The transition has brought out a drastic change in the value system of the society and altered the grim scenario of women folk. Especially, the status of women in India has been changing as a result to growing industrialization and urbanization, spasmodic mobility and social legislation. Over the years, more and more women are going in for higher education, technical and professional education and their proportion in the workforce has also been increased. These changes have led to the emergence of new concepts and patterns of life for all. Particularly, the responsibility of women in the family and society has taken up the new stride. As a consequence, there was a change in the attitude, outlook, attributes and the role of women .Women's emancipation thus has opened new vista in social structural issues of women. The ever rising economic needs have led women to work outside the families and to financially support their families. In the process, women are trying hard to establish themselves as most sensible entrepreneurs despite of challenging constraints they faced both in the home and business front. Women's shift from the kitchen, handicrafts and traditional cottage industries to non-traditional higher levels of activities was facilitated by the government both by training them to start their own ventures and by starting special cells in the financial institutions to assist women entrepreneurs. Especially, the institutions such as Small Industries Service Institutes (SISIs), National Institute of Entre-preneurship and Small Business Development (NIESBUD) and National Small Industries Corporation (NSIC) have contributed much for the promotion of entre-preneurship among women. This has boomerang the women entrepreneurs on the economic scene in the recent years and paved for social development of the society too as quoted by the then prime Minister Pandit Jawaharlal Nehru as "When women moves forward, the family moves, the village moves and the nation moves.

CONCEPT OF WOMEN ENTREPRENEUR

Women entrepreneurs are the women or a group of Women who initiate, organize and operate a business enterprise. The Government of India can notes women entrepreneur as "an enterprise owned and controlled: by a woman having minimum financial in-terest of 51 per cent of the capital and giving at least 51 per cent -of the employment generated in the enterprise to women". However, this been severely criticized on condi-tion of giving employment to more than 50 per cent of the tot at work force to women.

NEED FOR WOMEN ENTREPRENEURSHIP

Women have put into untold sufferings from the time immemorial in our society. Her involvement in economic activities is marked by low work participation rates, excessive concentration in the unorganised sector of the economy and that too in low skill jobs. There is a greater dynamism in the rate of growth of female employment. How-ever, in rural areas, perhaps the agriculture has provided much more employment for women. Their literacy rate, which itself is the cause for low economic status, creates a vicious circle of low social and economic status. In 1991, the rural female literacy rate was 30.4 per cent, whereas the rural male literacy rate was 57.8 per cent. It is in this specific context, that the emergence of women entrepreneurs is to be viewed as a socio-economic emancipation of women.

The status of women in India is an illustration of a paradox. At the micro level she has equal, if not greater, positions in the family as 'Ardhangini' and she is the pivot of the socio-economic fabric of the family as a mother. The scriptures and mythologies give her even the status: of Goddess and many women are remembered even today for their freedom struggle. However, over the period the position of women at the macro level of the society has been downgraded, so much that she is the most abused person of the Indian society.

The women in India have been neglected a lot. They have not been actively involved in the mainstream of development even though they repre-sent a bulk of the population and labour force. Primarily women are the means of survival of their families, but are generally unrecognised and under-valued, being placed at the bottom of the pile. Ideologically as well as in prac-tice women are considered completely inferior to males. Thus, the inequalities inherent in our traditional social struc-ture, based on caste, community and class, have a significant influence on the low status of woman in different spheres. Thus, the main issue which is still being debated is the kind of strategy to be evolved for raising their status and participation in the process of development. Hence, the emergence of women as entrereprenurs in India should be seen as a resurgence of the rightfully respectable socio-economic status of women. However, a society constrained by the suppressive socio-economic factors cannot generate the much needed women entrepreneurs on its own.

Education in India had been the prerogative of men over the centuries. The condition 'has been such that women were not given required scope for education. Besides this, the existing pattern of education in the country is not geared towards instilling of entrepreneurial instincts in young minds in general and women in par-ticular. The higher levels of education too, especially commerce and manage-ment education are not directed towards generating entrepreneurship. Entrepreneurship as a subject is not a part of the curricula in many universities and vocationalisation of education is probably still a dream in our country. The politicians and policy makers are always talk about introduc-tion and development of vocational education at +2 stage and graduation level. But in many a states, vocational courses are not running systematically. The government has not taken any in-itiative in this regard.

Private initiative directed towards the growth of entrepreneurs as existing in U.S.A. and U.K., is not wide spread in our country. Consequently, the governmental policy directions and the performance of commercial banks, financial institutions and training institu-tions engaged in promoting and developing the women entrepreneur-ship become very crucial for the country.

In the 60 years' of independence, an emphasis on the socialistic pattern of the society and the role assigned to the. Public sector, limited the scope for the growth of private entrepreneurship. The liberalization policy of the government has thrown open a vast area of the, economy for private entrepreneurship. Under such circumstances, special efforts to develop women entrepreneur-ship are more keenly felt.

CULTURE AND ENTREPRENEURSHIP

Many factors influence the existence, and the proportion, of individuals with entrepreneurial traits within a population, not least of them the culture of the population itself. Indeed, we believe that one of the main factors defining environmental conditions towards entrepreneurship is the cultural background which establishes behavioural rules for any given group. In fact, culture gives the individuals their set of values and represents their behavioural code; culture is part of the *'mental programming'* which characterizes an individual (Hofstede, 1980).

As such it is in part uniquely personal and in part common and shared with other individuals. One of the levels of this mental programming is the *collective level* (the other two are the universal and the personal levels). This level refers to language and social behaviour and is common to a number of individuals, belonging to the same group. The exclusive sharing of this code is what makes the group different from any other. Culture is situated at this level and can be defined as the collective mental programming distinguishing the members of a human group from those of another (Hofstede, 1980). Indeed, the culture of a population determines its predominant characteristics in terms of behaviour, aspirations, and ways to tackle problems and so on (Konen, 1986).

The cultural characteristics of a given nation or ethnic group thus help to cause a stronger or weaker diffusion of *'grassroots entrepreneurship'* (Trevisan Matuella, 1995) within a given population. Stronger, if a group's culture predisposes the individuals belonging to it towards starting their own independent activity when the occasion presents itself (or to create such an occasion); weaker, if a group's culture creates obstacles to the development of entrepreneurial activities of its members. Culture is not only typical of a nation or an ethnic group, it is something pertaining every group into which a population is divided. One of the levels of culture then is that of the gender: it is generally accepted that culturally determined values and behaviours tend to differ according to gender (Maddock, Parkin, 1994).

CHARACTERISTICS OF THE ENTREPRENEUR

Entrepreneur has been variously regarded by various authors. Some writers identified entrepreneurship with the function of uncertainty, others with the coordination of productive resources, others with the introduction of innovations, and still others with the provision of capital (Hoselitz, 1952). But in general, it has been delineated as an *enterprising* person, who can act in an *innovative* way, has *organising* and *leadership* capacity and who is *willing to take risks*.

We are the happy, then, to go along with the definition of the entrepreneur as an innovator or developer who is capable of identifying opportunities, exploiting them and turning them into viable and marketable ideas in the process of listing the characteristics of the entrepreneur. One who adds value in the form of time, money, effort or skills, accepts the risks of the competitive market with regard to the implementation of ideas or the exploitation of opportunities, and who ultimately reaps the rewards of his or her efforts (Kuratko, Hodgetts, 1992).

According to many authors, entrepreneurs have indeed some traits in common (Low and Macmillan, 1988). Indeed, to be able to carry out his activity, an entrepreneur needs to have some specific personal traits. Some of these traits are widespread among a population while some others are much less common. Individuals who possess the right combination of these traits are better placed than the rest of the population to become entrepreneurs and to develop their activity successfully.

In the literature, there is some disagreement about which specific traits should be included in an 'entrepreneur's profile' (nor there is agreement on the fact that traits should be used as identifying criterion for entrepreneurs). This is to be expected since it is rather difficult to define an individual's profile in a few words. Thus, reviewing the literature (Carland, Hoy, Boulton and Carland, 1984; Gartner, 1989), one finds long lists of widely different characteristics associated with entrepreneurs, with the result that it is practically impossible to provide a precise exposition of the qualities that are of crucial importance for being an entrepreneur and essential for successful entrepreneurship.

The characteristics mentioned in those lists, however, can be divided into three groups: the first relates to the entrepreneur's personality, the second to the entrepreneur's skills and the third to the entrepreneur's background and experience (Ray, 1993). Furthermore, many of the various factors mentioned in those lists are basically different facets of the same few main characteristics and can, therefore, be consolidated into a much smaller set of profile dimensions (Kuratko and Hodgetts, 1992).

Indeed, at the price of a certain degree of simplification, it is possible to whittle down the number of traits which should characterize an individual, in order for him/her to be deemed 'entrepreneur grade.

Limiting ourselves to traits related to the entrepreneur's personality and basically following (Timmons, 1990), were identified as follows: commitment and determination; creativity; attitude towards risks; independence and leadership; long term orientation, motivation to progress; and obsession with opportunity.

Although other characteristics are mentioned by other authors, most of them agree in naming these seven traits among the distinctive characteristics of the entrepreneur. They should belong to any entrepreneur, wherever he lives and whatever his origin.

The emergence of women entrepreneurs in a society depends to a great extends on the economic, religious, cultural, social, psychological and other factors. To developing countries like India, the presence of entrepreneurs, that too women entrepreneurs is of vital necessity, to achieve a rapid, all round and regionally and socially balanced economic growth through industrialization. It also helps in tapping the inherent talent prevailing among them and acts as a panacea for many problems faced by them, such as dowry death, low recognition in society, poverty, unemployment and excessive dependence on male members.

TYPOLOGY OF WOMEN ENTREPRENEURS IN INDIA

Goffee and Scace (1985) have developed a typology of women entrepreneurs based on two sets of factors: women's attachment to entrepreneurial ideals and women's acceptance of conventionally defined gender roles. Alternatively. Carter and Can-non (1992) hypothesized that women could be differentiated on the basis of the behavioral and motivational factors in their desire to start a business. Yet, it would seem that conventionally defined gender roles would depend on the unique cultural context within which these conventions are defined, just as would motivational factors and behaviors (Berger, 1991). Our focus here is the unique cultural context of India, and how different types of women entrepreneurs might face different barriers to growth.

In moving towards a typology that is growth, gender, and context-relevant, it is helpful to consider some of the conceptual building blocks in the entrepreneurial growth literature. Two key building blocks are the stages of growth model and conceptualizations of the entrepreneurial process.

Let us consider the widely cited Churchill and Lewis (1983) 'stages of growth model. In this model, firms evolve through as many as five stages, but are thought to make a choice once they are established between a limited growth or 'disen-gagement' track, or a more aggressive growth track. Thus, small and table businesses would travel a trajectory until the 'success-disengage' stage, while growth oriented firms would move from success to a takeoff stage characterized by ongoing entrepreneurship, aggressive development, and the achievement of scope and scale.

Stages are distinguished from one other in terms of the relative importance of both enterprise-related factors (e.g., resources such as: financial, personnel, systems, and business) and owner-related factors (e.g., abilities such as: operational, managerial, and strategic). What has been ignored here is the specific gender-sensitive issues, such as relational support factors, desire to be of the opposite sex, having an heir, or family responsibilities.

Another conceptual framework that could be adapted to reflect gender-relevant issues for the purposes of explaining growth is the entrepreneurial process. Ac-cording to Saraswathy (1998) the entrepreneurial process involves the selection/ creation of combinations that transform an idea into a firm. Selection/ creation processes occur through sets of entrepreneurial decisions, and these decisions arise out of four interconnected decision domains: resources (non-human), stakeholders, environment, and the entrepreneur. For women-run firms, each of these decision domains will have to include additional aspects that impact the approach to growth.

RESOURCES

Decisions arising out of this domain lead to the selection of relevant inputs. A key issue for women entrepreneurs is not only whether their firms can, in theory, find these resources, but whether the entrepreneur believes that she can gain access to them, given gender as a variable and what influences this belief. Presence of discriminatory markets for resources would influence the resources considered available and therefore the decisions on their use.

STAKEHOLDERS

Stakeholders, both internal and external to the firm, are those whose interests are considered by the entrepreneur in making decisions. Decisions arising out of these domains, according to Saraswathy (1998), lead to the creation of a set of feasible contracts between stakeholders within the firm, as well as the firm's cultural and social responsibility. For women entrepreneurs, this domain should be expanded beyond traditional stakeholders to include specifically mentors, family members, network support members, etc.

ENVIRONMENT

This domain concerns the interface between the firm and the various components of its external environment. Decisions arising out of this domain typically lead to the development of the firm's core competencies, market identification, positioning and strategy development. For women entrepreneurs, there is a need to investigate whether they incorporate gender as a variable in interpreting the external environment. Is the market positioning of the firm responsive to her gender concerns regarding home-work tradeoff, family support, lack of successors, and so forth? How does strategy get affected by these variables?

ENTREPRENEUR

This domain brings in issues of leadership, vision and subjective theories of the entrepreneur. Issues of firm diversity, differentiation and the future trajectory of the firm, including exit strategies for the entrepreneur and other stakeholders, are relevant issues that arise here. Different types of women entrepreneurs will view and plan for growth differently, and it is these differences that need to be inves-tigated and incorporated into our understanding of women- run firms. There is a need to allow for the many subjective issues focused on in contemporary gender studies.

Given the above, taxonomy is submitted that acknowledges the tendency of women entrepreneurs to vary along a number of key dimensions. Thus, we propose that relational support factors represent a key differentiator among entrepreneurial types (Rajivan, 1997; Shabbir & PiGregorio, 1996). Further, given Landa's (1991) extension of the relational concept beyond the family or small group context to the larger networked connectivity context, it was determined that the perceived im-portance of network resources and contacts in government support agencies rep-resent important potential cla3sifiers. Attachment to conventionally defined gender roles might be gauged by the entrepreneur's desire to be of the opposite sex and the time available after satisfying family demands. To be consistent with the growth stages literature, the importance attached to key resource variables (technical, financial, market and human) represent an additional classifier. Further, since studies on women entrepreneurs have underlined the importance of previous business experience and scope for succession in motivating women businesses; these are also proposed as classifiers. The size of the business and the strategic focus of the entrepreneur are also expected to have marked effects on the entre-preneur's desire for growth. This review also shows that in the Indian business environment, the presence or absence of a family business background is important.

Classification of Women Entrepreneurs in India

The proposed classification recognizes four types of entrepreneurs, which have been tentatively named young achiever entrepreneurs, block factor entrepreneurs, family-driven entrepreneurs, and financial need entrepreneurs. These categories are outlined in Table I and summarized below, along with their expected pattern of growth.

Young Achiever Entrepreneurs

Since they typically start enterprises at the age of' 25 or so, directly out of college, by the time they are 30 (if they have survived) they could go in for the second round of entrepreneurship and by 45 could emerge in charge of growing businesses. The work-home conflicts would peak during the success-growth stage, but since by then owner's operational ability is not a critical factor, the firm could grow in a way as to leave the entrepreneur a certain level of flexibility. The owner's managerial and strategic abilities are the critical factors at this stage. The Churchill model suggests that business resources decrease in importance as the firm progresses along the lifecycle. However, this may not be the case if the owner's networks are crucial to the future growth of the firm.

Block Factor Entrepreneurs

Entrepreneurs of this type opted for business either because they could not get promotions fast enough, because of low satisfaction in their jobs (glass ceiling factors), or because they could not get jobs commensurate with their skills, due (o late entry into the workforce for gender reasons (mommy track compulsions).

They could be early drifters who end up self-employed, because of' lack of suitable opportunities in the work place. They are most likely to persist in business until they reach the success-disengage stage given their low-commitment to entre-preneurial ideals. They either choose to spend jeater time on family and home related activities, keeping their businesses small and stable, or opt out and join the formal workforce if that offers a better equilibrium in terms of their personal, financial, family and community related goals. Lack of resources at the startup stage often locks them into low potential ventures and firms that would typically exhibit a low growth potential.

The career women who opt out of the formal workplace, either because of glass ceiling experiences or because of greater need for flexibility to manage work-home conflicts, would typically start ventures when in the 35-40 age group. Relevant career experience may enable them to jump-start and reach the second round of entrepreneurship by the time they are 45. If relational support systems are robust, their success in managing work home conflicts during the grueling subsistence and survival stage would allow us to posit a greater optimism in them being able to steer the firm through the success-growth stage up to resource maturity. The critical factors here would be the owner's managerial abilities, strategic abilities, network-ing capabilities, and the initial choice of a high potential venture.

Family-Driven Entrepreneurs

For these entrepreneurs, business choices and decisions are substantially influenced by family considerations. Business comes after family and is run more like a hobby for self-fulfillment. Given a strong relational support structure, entrepreneurs in this group would typically start ventures in the 35-40 age groups when work-home conflicts have tapered off. Once again, a low commitment to entrepreneurial ideals would see the enterprise being run as a hobby by largely home-based women entrepreneurs and the business would rest at a success-disengage level. In certain cases, especially where the women come from family business backgrounds and if the relational support can provide enough finances and personnel to support growth, the firm may move further up the stages of growth. However, this would depend on the synergies possible with the mainline family business, and at this stage the woman is likely to be aided substantially by others in the network.

Financial Need/Additional Income (-Driven Entrepreneurs

For these women, entrepreneurship is a necessity, not a choice. They could be resource-poor because they are from low income groups or because they have experienced a trauma-the death of husband or a divorce, which reduces their monetary status. Given the high importance of conventionally defined gender roles in this segment, women who start their businesses in their middle age would carry high levels of work-home conflict throu6h the initial subsistence and survival stages of their business. Given also their resource-poor status, low relational support base and their general unprepared ness for entrepreneurship, the likelihood of their being locked into low potential ventures would be great. Once their firms reach success, these entrepreneurs would most likely disengage and opt for• small and stable businesses. Their financial need levels may also make them more risk averse and these entrepreneurs would be more likely to keep the enterprises running so as to provide for their needs or at best to keep the enterprises alive until the next generation can take over.

WOMEN ENTREPRENEURS IN INDIA

Becoming an entrepreneur did arouse a little dilemma in many women who have the potentialities for becoming one. However, to earn quick money was the basic reason for women to start entrepreneurship. They had a deep-seated need for a sense of independence along with a desire to do something meaningful with their time and to have their own identity instead of remaining closeted behind their husband's nameplate. Women with high education view at entrepreneurship as a challenge, while for women with no education background find entrepreneur merely a means for earning money. These women needed little 'pull' and 'push' for venturing ahead as their circumstances forced them. On other hand, women, coming from good financial background need 'pull' and 'push' as at times they themselves were not aware of their own inner strengths and resources and wanted their husbands/family members to decide the ways it should be utilized. Also the women of the upper crust society were hesitating to put forth the idea of taking up a non-traditional role.

It is also found that compared to men, women were less concerned with making money and often choose business proprietorship as a result of career dissatisfaction. Secondly, women find entrepreneurship as a tool of meeting their career needs and childcare role. However, there are drastic differences in the way the men and women-owned enterprise views their activities.

Most women business owners in Indian organization were either housewives or fresh graduates with no previous experience of running a business. These women business owners were in traditionally women - oriented business like garments, beauty care, and fashion designing, which either do not require any formalized training or developed from a hobby or an interest into a business.

Women, who had started out their own business without any mentor or legacy had created their own plateau and also earned many feats. Women on other hand, who inherited a small business from the family, had taken their small business to a greater extent and turned it out into a large organization. While there are also some women who have inherited from the large organization, taken the organization to a much higher plateau. What motivate these women to venture out in the no man's land? The primary motive is for engaging in some economically gainful activity is: (1)Making money/making more money to support the family (2) and a desire for gainful time structuring.

The first motive is found at the lower end of the socio-economic scale. However. the factors that initiate a women to take the plunge are usually environmental, for example, failure of husband business, sudden death of a father in a women only household like in case of Komal Chabbaria, daughter of Late Manu Chabbaria or husband' inability or unwillingness to shoulder the responsibility of the family, and many other similar reasons.

What have been the processes of change for women in the context of the tapestry being woven globally and nationally? Let us look at some of the key changes for women over the last five decades.

WOMEN ENTREPRENEURS OF THE FIFTIES

These women fall into two categories. One set took to creating and managing an entrepreneurial activity where there was no income generating male. The woman gave up her education and any other aspirations for herself and became the income generator for the rest of the family.

The second category was the one who lived by social roles and woke up one day to find that either she took charge of the enterprise the husband had left or she and her own family would be the losers. For both this sets of women, it took enormous courage to break, through the social maps and coding.

However, such women in the fifties were few. For many others the businesses were taken away by relatives and the women and their families lived their lives as dependants while they had the resources or did not have the resources.

WOMEN ENTREPRENEURS OF THE SIXTIES

Sixties were the decade when many women educated in schools and colleges began to have aspirations. These were largely unarticulated. Women accepted the social coding of the socio-cultural traditions and married. But soon they took small steps to start small one-woman enterprises at home and from home. These were still activities for self-occupation and engagement but behind these were the seeds of aspirations to discover a meaning for the self and economic choices. This was still not for economic autonomy or economic self-sufficiency.

WOMEN ENTREPRENEURS OF THE SEVENTIES

This was the decade when a critical mass of women completed their education and entered the work force as professionals. The women in this decade opened up new frontiers. These women were unlike their mothers and had not only aspirations but also ambitions. The opted for self-employment be the enterprise a one woman enterprise or who employed several others. This was an active step swimming upstream and walking uphill. This choice was not out of compulsions or helplessness. It was an active choice to take charge of one's' life. For many this choice began in their parental family and continued in their own personal homes.

1) Women regarded work as an integral aspect of their life space.
2) Income generation and a career choice where both the social system and occupation were equally significant
3) Educated and qualified the women aspired for a different role and life vis-a-vis their mothers and grandmothers.
4) The women wanted homes, marriage and children as well an occupation.
5) The women accepted the social traditional role behaviour from the older generation but from their husbands, colleagues and children they expected understanding and

support in their occupation choice. They looked for redefinition of systems and redesigned interfaces across the systems and institutions they worked with.

6) In entrepreneurial roles the women were willing to carry their share of the work responsibilities and also wanted the enterprise to grow and succeed. They wanted their voices to be heard as leaders to employees and as managers of the enterprise to the outside business environment.

WOMEN ENTREPRENEURS OF THE EIGHTIES

The women entrepreneurs of 50's and 60's, and 70's had accepted both their social an occupational roles. They played the two roles and tried to balance both. However, by the time eighties came around, the women were educated in highly sophisticated technological and professional education. Many had medical, engineering and similar other degrees and diplomas. Many entered their fathers or husbands industry as equally contributing partners. Women in other spheres opened their own clinics and nursing homes and many more opened up small boutiques, small enterprises of manufacturing and entered garment exports. This was the decade of the breakthrough for women in many fields and many frontiers. Women made personal choices, stood up for their convictions and had the courage to make new beginnings. However, all these choices and beginnings was a not smooth sailing. For many, the society was hostile, the family was opposing and non-supportive and the woman carried the guilt of not playing the traditional and appropriate social roles viz. that of being a good mother.

WOMEN ENTREPRENEURS OF THE NINETIES

The women entrepreneurs of the nineties were qualitatively a different breed of women. These women already had a role model in the two earlier generations of women.

The women of the nineties were capable, competent, confident and assertive women. They knew what choices to make, they were clear as to what they wanted to do and they went ahead and did it. The nineties have thrown Lip many names of women who initiated an enterprise, fostered it and nurtured it to grow. There were many others who entered the big enterprises of their fathers and husbands and contributed it with their competencies and capabilities. Sometimes they outshone the names of their fathers and husbands.

This was the first time the concept of 'the best' rather than a 'male heir' began to be talked about. The fathers thought of 'inheritance' or a 'legacy' to a 'daughter' than just a son who may have been incapable and incompetent. Women in the nineties have often questioned their traditional coding of their roles and have become conscious of the voice of their own identity. With economic independence, women have acquired a high self-esteem and have also discovered that they are able to deal with situations single-handedly. In situations of mis-match in marriages, physical violence, demands for dowry, pushing the women into socially confirming roles and other forms of social psychological harassment women do stand tip to make their statements and make difficult choices. Today's women are fearless and have learnt to live alone, travel alone, and rear children alone when failures in marriage and life partnerships occur. Some women have preferred to remain single, are leading happy and contended lives and are successful in their work. . Many couples today, opt for leading a life without children, and prefer to focus on work, relationships, and the joy of experiencing freedom. Many and more and more women in nineties have made up their minds to have a single child in order to meet the demands of home and work and have very well been able to integrate their multiple roles in multiple systems.

THE WOMEN ENTREPRENEURS OF THE 21st CENTURY

This is the century of telecom, IT and financial institutions. Women's expertise in all these industries is beginning to emerge and women are emerging as a force to reckon with.

Many of these new industries are headed and guided by women who are seen as pioneers and mavericks. The loci of power have shifted away from traditional venues such as Old boys Clubs, Golf courses and Cigar smoking rooms to power now being vested with energetic new upstarts working out of their homes or on their computer terminals from homes. This new cauldron of opportunity can become the proverbial melting pot for professionally trained and enterprising women. Here there are fewer barriers to overcome, less pre-conceived notions, fewer well-entrenched assumptions and rules and lesser gender agenda in the secondary environment.

The transition to the next millennium is where the women will create new paradigms of being a daughter who takes the responsibility of her parents, is a wife who wishes to create a home and a family, a mother who takes charge of the children to make them the children of the new millennium. She is also the entrepreneur who builds an enterprise and discovers her relevance and meaning of her life in herself. She accepts the uniqueness of her identity and is willing to share the space. Simultaneously with all the dreams of togetherness she searches for Mutuality, dignity and respect. She is also open to a life without marriage and a parenting without a father.

Women of today have a new avatar in the free rolling 90's. She the Jill of all trades and her children are tickled by their supermom. Infect, many sons unhesitatingly describe themselves as 'Mamma's boys', which in the 90's is no longer considered to be 'Sissy' but 'Savvy'. The children, especially their sons have decided to break the age old tradition of following the father's shoes. Instead, the children of 90's opt to follow in their mother's shoes. For example, Sharmila Tagore inspired her son Saif to follow her to Bollywood rather than husband Pataudi to Lords. Similarly, the queen of the chef world, Tarla Dalai's son Sanjay Dalai, an MBA degree holder, decides to make his mom's cooking as a career rather than to join his father's industrial equipment business.

This mother-son combination shows that women have been successful in inspiring their son to follow in their path, where earlier the son was prescribed to ride in their father's way. However, the next millennium offers a space beyond the present horizon where, instead of hope there is active engagement with the world, instead of dreams there are commitments, instead of aspirations there are choices, instead of ideals there are convictions and instead of searching for bestowal's and affirmation there is the acknowledgement of one's own uniqueness of identity. It is in this discovery that she can create and build an industrial empire from the first steps that she would have taken.

In the next millennium, Indian women would have to cross a major threshold and enter an unknown land. They will have to walk a path where none existed with a sense to discover. They will have to encounter and live with excitement and enthusiasm as well as threat, fears, anxieties and terror. It is the trust in the self, of the resource to be generated, of the courage to journey forth in a new land; to live through the terrains of uncharted land that the women of today will shape the new identity. They will discover the voice, which has been silenced for centuries to sing the songs of life and living and to discover the joys of experiencing the beauty around.

PROBLEMS OF WOMEN ENTREPRENEURS

The greatest deterrent to women entrepreneurs is that they are woman, male chauvinism is the order of the day, and therefore women have a tendency to keep away from high flying activities which are supposedly regarded as a domain of men. As such, the key problems which are being faced by the women entrepreneurs in India are plenty.

Need for achievement, independence and autonomy are the basic ingredients required for entrepreneur. Such requirements are either absent or found in negligible quantities in a woman as they are protected by male through her life either by parents in her childhood and husband in her adulthood and son on her old age by accepting a subordinate status. Therefore, she has no confidence to bear the risk alone as a result they lack confidence of their own capabilities. Even at home, family members do not have much faith in women possessing the abilities of decision-making

Low female literacy is very obvious in India. This causes ignorance among the women anent technological development, marketing trends political skill etc. even among educated, the bookish knowledge gathered by them is not sufficient to face the challenges in the business field.

In the present social setup, a woman is expected to look after her children and family members. As such, her family involvement significantly restricts her economic involvement. Gender discrimination in the family and social level restricts the women in the business field by receiving hostile reactions from her male colleagues of the family. The male superiority, ego, complex creates a barrier in the path way of success. This situation is found even between husband and wife.

Women always suffer from inadequate financial resources as they lack access to external funds (i.e. from banks and financial institutions) due to their inability in providing the security as most of the women have no property on their names. Lack of information needed to achieve entrepreneurial success, inefficient arrangements for marketing the products produced by women entrepreneurs, lack of infrastructure, low mobility characters and inferiority complex also can easily disheartened the women .

Corruption, unnecessary delay, humiliation etc. at the government level (i.e. in government offices, banks etc.) make entrepreneurial life miserable for women. The cases of dropping out the business idea due to such difficulties are not uncommon in India.

SOCIO-CULTURAL BARRIERS

Woman has to perform multiple roles be it familial or social irrespective of her career as working woman or an entrepreneur. In our society, more importance is being given to male child as compared to female child. This mindset results in lack of schooling and necessary training for women. As a result, there is an impediment in the progress of women and handicap them in the world of work.

However, the women of today will touch the magic of enlivening themselves and say, “this far I have traveled, there are distances to travel but there are moments here and now where I can be”. In this statement the past, present and future will emerge to create that space where movement and stability, where noise and silence, where light and darkness, and chaos and tranquility lose their absolutism to create a new rhythm and unfolding.

It is in these new beginnings women will create a legacy and a heritage and pass it their wards. An empire which was built with determination, courage and resilience rise again and again. A world created from nothing to an institution with values anchored in growth, excellence and human sensitivity of people. It is only then the girl child of tomorrow will say that ‘once upon a time there used to be my mother, or grandmother or a great grandmother, who lived in a time and today I am proud to follow her footsteps and add my landmark to her footsteps in the sands of time.

Women need to ask themselves whether they are aspiring for a job, a career, or a ‘higher calling’ in life, since leaders are motivated from the inside out. Their drive comes from within and is exhibited by their outward behavior. Although a very few women may be privileged to achieve congruity between the ‘calling’ and their career, since many economically deprived women are forced to earn their livelihood. Nonetheless, the point is well taken, if one follows one’s heart, if one is flying with a tail wind, propelled forward by inner urge and passion. We believe that counseling / career planning opportunities if available to young women at an early age could go along way towards incubating the leaders of tomorrow.

Women are experienced in managing one of the most complex organizations imaginable the household, with its many human interfaces and interplay between the sexes, different age groups and different stakeholders. Women have learnt over the centuries the art of negotiation and reconciliation and qualities of patience and understanding, along with an inherent quality of emotional intelligence. All these transferable skills can be brought to bear upon the workplace making it the richer, from these valuable experiences.

Women are working in this multifaceted world. The organization scenario changes like a kaleidoscope with every responsibility, accountability and multiple pulls and pushes, which women have faced and came out with success.

In the new order, women will put down roots of a family and discover the freedom of sailing in the open seas. The women will visualize a new horizon and identify directions and make tough decisions. In the cacophony of sounds echoing of the past the women will cross the threshold to listen to their own voices. The silence of centuries will find the first voice, which will beckon women to sail into the unknown and unchartered land to lay the foundations of their growth to contribute to a partnership

FUNCTIONS OF WOMEN ENTREPRENEURS

In developing countries like India, where male and female population ratio is almost equal, the presence of women entrepreneurs has great importance. Otherwise, it amounts to non-utilization of entrepreneurial -talent prevailing in them. According to Berma the develop-ing countries do not necessarily require innovative entrepreneurs of the Schumpeterian type. Limitating entrepreneurs are sufficient to accelerate the pace of industrialization of such countries. As such, a women entrepreneur is ex-pected to perform the- following impor-tant functions.

1. Imitation of successful entrepreneurs.
2. Introduction of new innovations.
3. Explore the prospects of commenc-ing new projects.
4. Assumption of risk and uncertainty bearing.
5. Take decision as to the nature and type of goods to be produced.
6. Managerial functions such as, for-mulation of production plan, arran-gement of finance, purchase of raw materials, organising the sales and personnel management

Factors influencing the women entrepreneurship

The general observation and several studies reveal that two factors influence the women entrepreneurs in India:

1. **Pull Factors:** Pull factors imply' the factors which encourage women to become entrepreneurs. They include desire to do something new in life, need for independence; availability of finance, concessions and subsidies.
2. **Push Factors:** Push factors are those which compel women to become. entrepreneurs: They. include financial difficulties, responsibility in the family, unfortunate family circumstances We death of the husband or father, divorce etc. However, the influence d this fac-tor on women in becoming, entrepreneurs is low than the former factor.

Institutional Network

Entrepreneurship among women is an important avenue through which women cart overcome their subordina-tion within the family and the society as a whole: Therefore, development of entrepreneurship' among: women has received special attention of the policy makers. In this direction a special chap-ter in the seventh plan has covered the integration, of women in economic development. The new industrial policy has stressed the need for conducting special EDPs for women. Besides this, today a network of institution exists in the country to promote woman entrepreneurship. The commercial banks and the financial institutions are an integral part of this network. Many orgarilsations institutions and associations promote and develop the women entrepreneurship by providing .financial assistance at confessional rates of interest, organise industrial fairs and, exhibitions, conduct Entrepreneurship Development Programmes (EDPs) for women, create entrepreneurial awareness among them.

WOMEN IN BEAUTY PARLOUR INDUSTRY

Women have a good combination of entrepreneurial spirit, ambition, discipline and restrains. All these help them to succeed in these highly volatile markets. There has been an almost 10-15 percent increase in women investors during the last five years in beauty parlour industry. Most of these investors are married. The spurt in women investors started from 1997. Since then markets have been providing an easy opportunity to make fast money. Education levels among women are also going up. Women are endowed with a spirit of entrepreneurship, common sense, empowered trade and financial support of their family. A women entrepreneur is a person, who is an enterprising individual with an eye for opportunities and an uncanny vision, commercial acumen, with tremendous perseverance and above all a person, who is willing to take risks with the unknown because of the adventurous spirit she possess (Medha, 1997). Women entrepreneurs represent a group of women who have been broken away from the beaten track for exploring new avenues of economic participation (Gopalan, 1981).

THE PROFILE OF BEAUTY PARLOUR INDUSTRY

The beauty parlour industry in our country is contributing about Rs.5000 crores (2005). It generates employment opportunities to 1 million of our population per annum. It consists of six broad categories, namely, Skin preparation, Hair preparation, Shaving preparation, Dental Preparation, Toilet soap preparation and fragrance preparation. There are about 40 big companies and 500 small scale units. The term cosmetics apply to all substances which are intended to promote the attractiveness, appearance and to impart a mixed feeling of beauty, glamour and liveliness. The field of cosmetics is very wide and extensive. It includes aerosols, colour, perfume formations, pharmacology and toxicology. Notwithstanding the fact that today's, women are much more interested and spending their time and most of the income in Beauty Parlour industry. In classifying cosmetics, the texture, consultancy, colour, odor, packaging and general appearance are far more important than the chemical properties of the ingredients on the finished product. Cosmetics are generally classified on two basis; 1. On the basis of end-use and 2. On the basis of their physical characteristics.

Women are increasingly seeking entrepreneurship as an avenue for economic growth. The government and the self-help groups (SHG) are playing an important role in mobilizing women to become entrepreneurs through different programs. Setting up of an enterprise is in itself a great task for women entrepreneurs but running the same successfully is an uphill task. Running the enterprise successfully is a Herculean task for the women entrepreneurial capability as it determines the profitability and survival of the unit (Renukadevi, 2005). Women got exposed to new ideas through media about their personalities, roles and rights. Women have to perform multiple roles as per the level of their education and professional expectations. They try their best to cope up with these multiple role of expectations and prove themselves worthy of success. Emotional incompatibility with husband, in-laws and relatives, explosive habits of men at work place and antagonistic attitudes, generation gap and gender discrimination create role conflicts on women even now and then. In general, women are positioned themselves to pay the price for the benefits of economic independence, equal status and position of self-respect.

CONCLUSION

The saying entrepreneurs are born and not made has little sense today. A host of evidences shows that they are successfully made. In order to make women entrepreneurship movement, a success, Government and non-Govern-ment agencies have to play a vital role. There is an acute need to re-orient several things right from the grassroots level viz.: increasing the number of vocational courses exclusively for women, including entrepreneurship studies in social science syllabi etc.

Women entrepreneurs in backward areas need special assistance and incentive from the government and financial institutions. The government shall setup marketing agencies to ensure the timely marketing of the goods produced by women entrepreneurs.

Besides organizing a short term EDPs for women, continuous training in all management areas should be given to them.

Separate industrial estates may be setup for women setup for women entrepreneurs to create altogether a special environment At the national level and state level, there is a need to set up WOMEN INDUSTRIAL DEVELOPMENT BANK In the existing banks and financial institutions, it is ad-visable to start a separate call called Women Entrepreneurs Guidance Cell' to promote and guide the women entrepreneurs. Such an attempts al-ready made by Karnataka State Financial Corporation, a premier money lending institution, in Karnataka, More 'and more research is to be conducted to identify the problems which are being faced by them. The new entrants may be' encouraged by organising the im-plant-visit of successful women entrepreneurs. Besides this, to promote and develop the rural women entrepreneurship, efforts shall be made to get the active involvement of Mahlia Samal as' or Women's organizations by launching village adoption schemes.

In recent years, there has been a heightened global awareness regarding the contribution which 'women can make to the process of economic development. Although it is still in the growth stage, there is unquestionably a business revolution in the' works across the nation - and women are a major part of it. The efforts are on to uplift the social and economic status of women. The development of women as entrepreneurs will generate multi-faceted socio-economic benefits to the country.

22

Role of Commercial Banks and Education in the Development of Weaker Section in India

Introduction

Now we are living in the Scientific, Technological and Modern world. A lot of changes are occurring in the day to day life of human beings. India is a developing country. Majority people occupation is agriculture. The Planning Commission made a survey for finding out the number of persons below poverty line and estimated that 18.96% of the total peoples live below poverty line as of the year 1993-94. As per 2001 census the literacy rate of Scheduled Castes and Scheduled Tribes was 54.69% and 47.10% respectively. It is necessary to take care about poor and illiteracy. Banks have an eminent role in the development of weaker sections in the society.

History of Banks in India

Banking in India originated in the first decade of 18th century with The General Bank of India coming into existence in 1786.

This was followed by Bank of Hindustan. Both these banks are now defunct. The oldest bank in existence in India is the State Bank of India being established as "The Bank of Bengal" in Calcutta in June 1806. A couple of decades later, foreign banks like Credit Lyonnais started their Calcutta operations in the 1850s. At that point of time, Calcutta was the most active trading port, mainly due to the trade of the British Empire, and due to which banking activity took roots there and prospered. The first fully Indian owned bank was the Allahabad Bank, which was established in 1865.

By the 1900s, the market expanded with the establishment of banks such as Punjab National Bank, in 1895 in Lahore and Bank of India, in 1906, in Mumbai - both of which were founded under private ownership. The Reserve Bank of India formally took on the responsibility of regulating the Indian banking sector from 1935. After India's independence in 1947, the Reserve Bank was nationalized and given broader powers.

Current Situation of Banks

Currently (2008), banking in India is generally fairly mature in terms of supply, product range and reach-even though reach in rural India still remains a challenge for the private sector and foreign banks. In terms of quality of assets and capital adequacy, Indian banks are considered to have clean, strong and transparent balance sheets relative to other banks in comparable economies in its region. The Reserve Bank of India is an autonomous body, with minimal pressure from the government. The stated policy of the Bank on the Indian Rupee is to manage volatility but without any fixed exchange rate-and this has mostly been true.

With the growth in the Indian economy expected to be strong for quite some time-especially in its services sector-the demand for banking services, especially retail banking, mortgages and investment services are expected to be strong.

In March 2006, the Reserve Bank of India allowed Warburg Pincus to increase its stake in Kotak Mahindra Bank (a private sector bank) to 10%. This is the first time an investor has been allowed to hold more than 5% in a private sector bank since the RBI announced norms in 2005 that any stake exceeding 5% in the private sector banks would need to be vetted by them.

Currently, India has 88 scheduled commercial banks (SCBs) - 28 public sector banks (that is with the Government of India holding a stake), 29 private banks (these do not have government stake; they may be publicly listed and traded on stock exchanges) and 31 foreign banks. They have a combined network of over 53,000 branches and 17,000 ATMs. According to a report by ICRA Limited, a rating agency, the public sector banks hold over 75 percent of total assets of the banking industry, with the private and foreign banks holding 18.2% and 6.5% respectively.

List of Banks in India

Public sector banks

SBI group

State Bank of India, with its seven associate banks commands the largest banking resources in India. SBI and its associate banks are:

- State Bank of India
- State Bank of Bikaner & Jaipur
- State Bank of Hyderabad
- State Bank of Indore
- State Bank of Mysore
- State Bank of Patiala
- State Bank of Saurashtra
- State Bank of Travancore

After the amalgamation of New Bank of India with Punjab National Bank, currently there are 19 nationalised banks in India:

- Allahabad bank
- Andhra Bank
- Bank of Baroda

- Bank of India
- Bank of Maharashtra
- Canara Bank
- Central Bank of India
- Corporation Bank
- Dena Bank
- Indian Bank
- Indian Overseas Bank
- Oriental Bank of Commerce
- Punjab & Sind Bank
- Punjab National Bank
- Syndicate Bank
- Union Bank of India
- United Bank of India
- UCO Bank
- Vijaya Bank

Private Sector Banks

- Axis Bank (formerly UTI Bank)
- Bank of Rajasthan
- Bharat Overseas Bank
- Catholic Syrian Bank
- Centurion Bank of Punjab (Merged with HDFC bank)
- City Union Bank
- Development Credit Bank
- Dhanalakshmi Bank
- Federal Bank
- Kumfu Blade Bank
- Ganesh Bank of Kurundwad
- HDFC Bank
- ICICI Bank
- IDBI Bank

- IndusInd Bank
- ING Vysya Bank
- Jammu & Kashmir Bank
- Karnataka Bank Limited.
- Karur Vysya Bank
- Kotak Mahindra Bank
- Lakshmi Vilas Bank
- Lord Krishna Bank (now Centurion Bank of Punjab)
- Nainital Bank
- Ratnakar Bank
- Rupee Bank
- Saraswat Bank
- SBI Commercial and International Bank
- South Indian Bank
- Tamilnad Mercantile Bank Ltd.
- Thane Janata Sahakari Bank
- Bassein Catholic Bank
- United Western Bank(now IDBI Bank)]]
- YES Bank
- IDBI Bank

Foreign Banks

- ABN AMRO Bank N.V.
- Abu Dhabi Commercial Bank Ltd
- American Express Bank
- Antwerp Diamond Bank
- Arab Bangladesh Bank
- Bank International Indonesia
- Bank of America
- Bank of Bahrain & Kuwait
- Bank of Ceylon
- Bank of Nova Scotia

- Bank of Tokyo Mitsubishi UFJ
- Barclays Bank
- BNP Paribas
- Calyon Bank
- ChinaTrust Commercial Bank
- Cho Hung Bank
- Citibank
- DBS Bank
- Deutsche Bank
- HSBC (Hongkong & Shanghai Banking Corporation)
- JPMorgan Chase Bank
- Krung Thai Bank
- Mashreq Bank
- Mizuho Corporate Bank
- Oman International Bank
- Société Générale
- Standard Chartered Bank
- State Bank of Mauritius
- Scotia
- Taib Bank

Regional Banks

- Adhiyaman Grama Bank
- Alaknanda Gramin Bank
- Aligarh Gramin Bank
- Avadh Gramin Bank
- Balasore Gramya Bank
- Ballia Kshetriya Gramin Bank
- Banaskantha Mehsana Gramin Bank
- Bareilly Kshetriya Gramin Bank
- Bijapur Grameena Bank
- Bilaspur-Raipur Kshetriya Gramin Bank

- Bolangir Anchalik Gramya Bank
- Bundelkhand Kshetriya Gramin Bank
- BundiChittorgarh KshetriyaGraminBank
- Cauvery Grameena Bank
- Chaitanya Grameena Bank
- Chambal Kshetriya Gramin Bank
- Champaran Kshetriya Gramin Bank
- Chhatrasal Gramin Bank
- ChhindwaraSeoniKshetriyaGraminBank
- Chitradurga Gramin Bank
- Cuttack Gramya Bank
- Damoh Panna Sagar Kshetriya Gramin Bank
- Devipatan Kshetriya Gramin Bank
- Dhenkanal Gramya Bank
- Dungarpur Banswara Kshetriya Gramin Bank
- Ellaquai Dehati Bank
- Farrukhabad Gramin Bank
- Gaur Gramin Bank
- Gurgaon Gramin Bank
- Hadoti Kshetriya Gramin Bank
- Himachal Gramin Bank
- Hissar-Sirsa Kshetriya Gramin Bank
- Indore Ujjain Kshetriya Gramin Bank
- Jaipur Nagaur Aanchalik Gramin Bank
- Jamnagar Rajkot Gramin Bank
- Jamuna Gramin Bank
- Jhabua-Dhar Kshetriya Gramin Bank
- Kakathiya Grameena Bank
- Kalpatharu Grameena Bank
- Kamraz Rural Bank
- Kanpur Kshetriya Gramin Bank

- Kapurthala Ferozpur Kshetriya Gramin Bank
- Kashi Gramin Bank
- Kisan Gramin Bank,Budaun
- Kolar Gramin Bank
- Krishna Grameena Bank
- Kshetriya Gramin Bank, Hoshangabad
- Kutch Grameen Bank
- Malaprabha Grameena Bank
- Mandla Balaghat Kshetriya Gramin Bank
- Manjira Grameena Bank
- Marwar Ganganagar Bikaner Gramin Bank (Previously: Marwar Gramin Bank)
- Mewar Aanchalik Gramin Bank
- Nagarjuna Grameena Bank
- Netravati Grameena Bank
- Nimar Kshetriya Gramin Bank
- North Malabar Gramin Bank
- Panchmahal Vadodara Gramin Bank
- Pandyan Grama Bank
- Pinakini Grameena Bank
- Pragjyotish Gaonlia Bank
- Prathama Bank
- Raigarh Kshetriya Gramin Bank
- Rani Lakshmi Bai Kshetriya Gramin Bank
- Ratlam Mandsaur Kshetriya Gramin Bank
- Rayalaseema Grameena Bank
- Rewa-Sidhi Gramin Bank
- Sahyadri Gramin Bank
- Samyut Kshetriya Gramin Bank
- Sangameshwara Grameena Bank
- Shahjahanpur Kshetriya Gramin Bank

- Shivpuri Guna Kshetriya Gramin Bank
- South Malabar Gramin Bank
- Sree Anantha Grameena Bank
- Sri Saraswati Grameena Bank
- Sri Visakha Grameena Bank
- Surat Bharuch Gramin Bank
- Thar Aanchalik Gramin Bank
- Tripura Gramin Bank
- Tungabhadra Gramin Bank
- Vidur Gramin Bank

Weaker Sections in India

In a fresh twist to the controversy over the proportion of OBCs in India's population, a government survey released 1st September 2007 indicated that backward castes formed about 41% of the populace.

A survey by the National Sample Survey Organisation (NSSO) put the OBC population in the country at 40.94%, the SC population at 19.59%, ST population at 8.63% and the rest at 30.80%.

According to the survey, 91.4% of STs, 79.8% of SCs and 78.0% of OBCs were in rural areas. Conversely, 8.6% of STs, 20.2% of SCs and 22% of OBCs were in urban areas, while 37.7% of 'others' lived in India's towns and cities.

The booming economic growth seems to be reflecting in the expenditure of urban India, which is spending nearly double the amount on an average compared to the rural areas. The per capita monthly expenditure of people living in urban areas was Rs. 1,052.36 a month as against Rs 558.78 of those in rural areas.

With minor exceptions, the general level of spending of SCs and STs was lower than OBCs and the others, while that of OBCs in turn was lower than that of the others. According to the NSSO survey, the all India average spending by rural STs was the lowest at Rs. 426.19, followed by rural SCs at Rs. 474.72, OBCs Rs.

556.72 and others Rs. 685.31. In urban India, STs spent Rs. 857.46, SCs 758.38, OBCs Rs. 870.93 and others Rs. 1,306.10 in a month on an average.

The survey highlights the fact that in rural India, 64.3% of the population continues to be dependent on agriculture as a major source of livelihood, either through self-employment in agriculture (39.4%) or as agricultural labour (24.9%). In this sector, the population dependent on self-employment (agriculture and non-agriculture) was reported to be 49.0% for ST, 36.6% for SC, 60.7% for OBC and 66.4% for others and that dependent on rural (agricultural or non-agricultural) labour was 56.4% for SC, 45.2% for ST, 30.7% for OBC and 21.8% for others.

In urban India, the proportion of population located in regular wage/salary earning households was almost the same (42.0% to 42.9%) for all social groups except OBCs (34.3%). Dependence on self-employment was more prevalent among OBCs (46.4%) as well as the residual class (45.3%) than the SCs (30.9%) and STs (27.4%).

In economically backward states like Bihar, Rajasthan, Madhya Pradesh and Orissa, SCs and STs were spending between Rs 344 to Rs. 527. However, in the educationally advanced state of Kerala, SCs were spending over Rs 750 a month, much higher than the national average.

Literacy of SC/ST

- As per 2001 census the literacy rate of Scheduled Castes and Scheduled Tribes was 54.69% and 47.10% respectively.
- Literacy rate of SC females compared to general population was much lower in the states of Bihar (15.58%), Jharkhand (22.55%), Uttar Pradesh (30.50%) and Rajasthan (33.87%).
- Literacy rate of ST females is extremely low in Bihar (15.54%).
- As per 2001 census the literacy rate was lowest for SCs in Bihar (28.47%) and highest in Mizoram (89.20%) and for STs, it was lowest in Bihar (28.17%) and highest in Mizoram (89.34%).

- o Literacy rate of STs was more than the SCs in the states of Jharkhand, Meghalaya, Mizoram and Sikkim.
- o In general the SCs were ahead of the STs in literacy. But in urban areas the STs are ahead of SCs.
- o The percentage of learners of SCs and STs under literacy Campaigns are 23% and 12% respectively.
- o The share of expenditure in implementation of literacy campaigns between the centre and states in tribal areas is 4:1 instead 2:1 in other areas.

Economy of India

The economy of India, when measured in USD exchange-rate terms, is the twelfth largest in the world, with a GDP of US $1.25 trillion (2008). It is the third largest in terms of purchasing power parity. India is the second fastest growing major economy in the world, with a GDP growth rate of 9.4% for the fiscal year 2006–2007. However, India's huge population has a per capita income of $4,542 at PPP and $1,089 in nominal terms (revised 2007 estimate).The World Bank classifies India as a low-income economy.

India's economy is diverse, encompassing agriculture, handicrafts, textile, manufacturing, and a multitude of services. Although two-thirds of the Indian workforces still earn their livelihood directly or indirectly through agriculture, services are a growing sector and play an increasingly important role of India's economy. The advent of the digital age, and the large number of young and educated populace fluent in English, is gradually transforming India as an important 'back office' destination for global outsourcing of customer services and technical support. India is a major exporter of highly-skilled workers in software and financial services, and software engineering. Other sectors like manufacturing, pharmaceuticals, biotechnology, nanotechnology, telecommunication, shipbuilding, aviation and tourism are showing strong potentials with higher growth rates.

India followed a socialist-inspired approach for most of its independent history, with strict government control over private sector participation, foreign trade, and foreign direct investment. However, since the early 1990s, India has gradually opened up its markets through economic reforms by reducing government controls on foreign trade and investment. The privatisation of publicly owned industries and the opening up of certain sectors to private and foreign interests has proceeded slowly amid political debate.

India faces a fast-growing population and the challenge of reducing economic and social inequality. Poverty remains a serious problem, although it has declined significantly since independence. Official surveys estimated that in the year 2004-2005, 27% of Indians were poor.

SC/ST Role in Indian Economy

While the United Progressive Alliance government wants to spread the spectacular gains made by India Inc in the last few years to scheduled castes and scheduled tribes, there are no reliable data on their participation in business, either as employees or as employers. The government, industry and civil society groups agree they have no data, which they admit are the building blocks for any action for inclusive growth.

They, however, agree on one thing — that the participation of scheduled castes and scheduled tribes in business is low, zero in large enterprises, and slightly more in small enterprises. The representation in states like Jharkhand, where their population is high, could be slightly higher.

According to Economic Census, 1998, enterprise distribution under the social group of 'Owner' is 7.7 per cent for scheduled castes, 4 per cent for scheduled tribes and 33.1 per cent for other backward castes. Not only is the data almost a decade old, it is hotly contested by social activists.

"We completely disagree with these numbers. Dalits are being denied ownership in all fields. Even in kirana stores, their proportion is absolutely nil," said Paul Diwakar, convener, National Campaign for Dalit Human Rights.

Rosemary Vishwanath, a Bangalore-based consultant who works on issues confronting the socially weaker sections, said, "I do not understand what they mean by an entrepreneur. I don't know whether we can term a roadside cobbler an entrepreneur." Ashok Bharati, convener, National Conference of Dalit Organisations, said, "Their entrepreneurship is almost negligible."

Milind Kamble of Pune-based 125-member Dalit Indian Chamber of Commerce and Industry, said, "If the proportion of scheduled castes and scheduled tribes in business was so high, what was the need for us to protest the economic imbalance all this while?"

However, Diwakar conceded there had been an improvement in the last three decades. "Some pockets of South India have seen a positive change, with Dalits entering fields like tourist services and prawn culture," he said.

There are other indications too. The Confederation of Indian Industry has been running an entrepreneurship development programme for young people from the economically weaker sections for several years.

"We now realise that most of them belong to scheduled castes and scheduled tribes. Several of them have done well and employ a large number of people," said a functionary of the industry association.

The situation is not so good when it comes to estimating the number of scheduled caste and scheduled tribe employees in the private sector. While members of the Federation of Indian Chambers of Commerce and Industry are averse to doing such a count, only 96 of CII's over 7,000 members have given such figures.

"The spread of such employees is between 5 per cent and 82 per cent. There are no trends in the data, except that their participation is more in areas where their population proportion is higher," said a CII functionary.

Role of Commercial Banks and Educational Institutions in Development of Weaker Sections

The 'Profitability Productivity syndrome' in the banking sector has recently turned out to be a topic of hot and perplexing debate. In the academic circle, however, most of the studies confine themselves to the narrow interpretation of the profitability and productivity. Role of Commercial Banks' Lending to Priority Sector is not related to only service but also with the profit. These studies prove the deterioration in profitability and productivity of Indian Commercial Banks, but more often than not, fail to interlink and analyze some crucial aspects of the problem. There are two distinct characteristics of post nationalization banking development in India. First, since nationalization commercial banks have made great and rapid strides in several spheres such as branch expansion, resource mobilization and credit deployment etc. Consequently, the total number of offices, deposits and advances has stepped up considerably. What is important in the success story of commercial banks is that it involves several structural changes in favour of rural and priority sector. The nationalization 14 + 6 major commercial banks in 1969 & 1980 altered the ownership pattern in favour of public sector and provided wide ranging powers to the Government to influence the banking policy and orientation. At the time of nationalization the socio-economic objectives were explicitly laid down and the banks were asked to contribute to the maximum possible extent towards economic and social development of the country. It was realized that the traditional banking ethics were not compatible with the needs of economic development and that balanced development was not possible without strengthening the hold of commercial banks in the backward and neglected areas.

New policy measures suitable to the rural lot were introduced and a massive thrust into the rural area thus started. Since then, the commercial banks have traversed a long way revealing a process of transformation from a position of petty dealers of debts to the rank of pioneers of economic development. Secondly, amidst the spectacular progress, however attractive it is, there are some discomforting features accompanied in advertently in the process of banking development. These features have helped in building up' strains and stresses' in the system thereby leading the banks gradually towards a difficult situation. The repercussions of these features can be seen in term of deterioration in profitability productivity and overall efficiency of commercial banks.

Role of Banks

- o Bank staff may help the poor borrowers in filling up the forms and completing other formalities so that they are able to get credit facility within a stipulated period from the date of receipt of applications.
- o In order to encourage SC/ST borrowers to take advantage of credit facilities, greater awareness among them about various schemes formulated by banks will have to be created. As a majority of the eligible borrowers would be illiterate persons, publicity through brochures, other literature, etc. will be of limited utility. The more desirable method would be for the field staff of banks to contact such borrowers and explain to them the salient features of the schemes as also the advantages that will accrue. Banks should advise their branches to organize meetings more frequently exclusively for SC/ST beneficiaries to understand their credit needs and to incorporate the same in the credit plan.
- o Bank should keep Application Register/ Deposit Register, Complaint Register in desired order and maintain relevant documents and pass book in local language too, besides in Hindi and English.
- o Circulars issued by RBI/NABARD should be circulated among the staff for compliance.
- o Banks should not insist on deposits while considering loan applications under Government sponsored poverty alleviation schemes/self-employment programmes from borrowers belonging to SCs /STs.It should also be ensured that applicable subsidy is not held back while releasing the loan component till the full repayment of bank dues.

Non release of subsidy upfront amounts to under-financing and hampers asset creation/ income generation.

- A National SC/ST Finance and Development Corporation have been set up under the administrative control of Ministry of Welfare. Banks should advise their branches/ controlling offices to render all the necessary institutional support to enable the institution to achieve the desired objectives.
- Advances sanctioned to State sponsored organizations of SC/ST, for the specific purpose of purchase and supply of inputs to and/or the marketing of outputs of the beneficiaries viz. artisans, village and cottage industries of these organizations, should be treated as priority sector advances, subject to the condition that the relative advances are exclusively for the purpose of purchase and supply of inputs to and/or marketing of the outputs of beneficiaries of these organizations.

Reservations for SC/ST beneficiaries under major centrally Sponsored Schemes

Swarnjayanti Gram Swarozgar Yojana (SGSY)

Under Swarnjayanti Gram Swarozgar Yojana (SGSY) Scheme, which is a major poverty alleviation scheme in rural / semi urban areas, not less than 50 percent of the families assisted should belong to SCs/STs.

Prime Minister's Rozgar Yojana

The Prime Minister's Rozgar Yojana (PMRY) has been designed to provide credit to educated unemployed youth for setting up of the self-employment ventures in industries, services and business sectors. A reservation of 22.5 percent has been provided for SCs/ STs in the scheme.

Swarna Jayanti Sahari Rozgar Yojana

Under Swarna Jayanti Shahari Rozgar Yojana (SJSRY), which is a poverty alleviation scheme in urban areas, advances should be extended to SCs/STs to the extent of their strength in the local population.

Differential Rate of Interest Scheme

Under the DRI scheme, banks provide finance up to Rs.6, 500/ - at a concessional rate of interest of 4% p.a to the weaker sections of the community for engaging in productive and gainful activities. In order to ensure that persons belonging to SCs/STs also derive adequate benefit under the Differential Rate of Interest (DRI) scheme, banks have been advised to grant to eligible borrowers belonging to SCs/STs such advances to the extent of not less than 2/5th (40 percent) of total DRI advances.

Scheme for Liberation and Rehabilitation of Scavengers

The National Scheme for Liberation and Rehabilitation of Scavengers is for liberating the scavengers and their dependents from the existing hereditary and obnoxious occupation of manually removing night soil and filth and to provide them with alternate dignified occupation. The scheme covers primarily all scavengers belonging to the scheduled caste community. Scavengers belonging to other communities are also eligible for assistance.

Relaxations for SC/ST beneficiaries under major centrally sponsored schemes

Under SGSY scheme, beneficiaries belonging to SC/ST are entitled to subsidy of 50% of the project cost with a maximum ceiling of Rs.10,000/- as against the subsidy of 30% of project cost with a maximum ceiling of Rs.7,500/- in case of beneficiaries under general category.

There is 10-year relaxation for the beneficiaries belonging to SCs/STs in the upper age limit to be eligible under PMRY (age limit for general category is 18-35).

Under the DRI scheme, the eligibility criteria that size of land holding should not exceed 1 acre of irrigated land and 2.5 acres of unirrigated land is not applicable to SCs/STs. Moreover, members of SCs/STs satisfying the income criteria of Rs.7, 200/

- under the scheme can also avail of housing loan upto Rs.5, 000/- per beneficiary at a concessional rate of interest of 4% over and above the loan of Rs.6, 500/- available under the scheme.

The main aim of banks is to get profit. They give first priority for profit, then service. The majority of weaker section people are suffering because of banks rules. The banks services are available for only higher (economically) class people in the weaker section. Because of illiteracy the majority of weaker section people are not getting benefits from the governments and from the banks. The corruption is also high in our society when compared to developed countries in the world.

Educational Institutions

Education is the solution for all type of problems in the society. It is necessary to increase number of residential schools and colleges for SC's and ST's. They have no idea about banks. They don't know how to get loan from the banks? It is banks duty to find and give loan to the suitable poor weaker person in the society.

Allotment of funds for SC/ST students in the Budget 2008-09

- Navodaya Vidyalayas to be opened in 20 districts with special focus on regions having SC/ST concentration. Allocation of Rs 130 crore for this purpose.
- Rs.750 crore more to be given for merit scholarship to students up to 10th and 12th class.
- Rs. 85 crore sanctioned for scholarships to students pursuing science education.
- Twenty per cent hike in education budget this year from Rs. 28,674 crore to Rs. 34,400 crore.
- Rs. 75 crore sanctioned for Rajiv Gandhi National Fellowship Programme for SC/ST students pursuing M.Phil.
- SC, ST and minority students to continue to get special attention.
- Rs. 230 crore will be extended as additional equity to developmental organizations looking after the welfare of SC.

National Commission for SC/ST

With a view to provide safeguards against the exploitation of SCs and STs and to promote and protect their social, educational, economic and cultural interest, special provisions were made in the constitution. Due to their social disability and economic backwardness, they were grossly handicapped in getting reasonable share in elected offices, Govt. jobs and educational institution and, therefore it was considered necessary to follow a policy of reservation in favour to ensure their equitable participation in governance. For effective implementation of various safeguards provided in the Constitution for the SCs and STs and various other protective legislations, the Constitution provided for appointment of a Special Officer under Article 338 of the Constitution. The Special Officer who was designated as Commissioner for SC/STs was assigned the duty to investigate all matters relating to the safeguards provided for SCs/STs various statutes and to report to the President upon the working of these safeguards. In order to facilitate effective functioning of the office of the Commissioner for SC/STs 17 regional offices of the Commissioner were set up in different part of the country.

Conclusions

We are living in the Modern and Technological world. We developed in all the fields. But, the position of weaker sections in the society is not good. The poor becoming very poor and the rich becoming very rich. The economic inequalities are very much in between poor and rich in the society. The majority people occupation is agriculture. We are seeing suicide attempts of farmers daily in the news papers. It shows the economic position and problems and farmers in the society. Banks have a prominent role in the development of farmers and other people in the society. The main aim of banks is profit oriented. It is necessary to change the attitude of banks towards weaker sections. Education is a solution for all type of problems. Through education it is possible to change the economic position and inequalities in the society. It is government duty to take necessary steps for the development of weaker section in the society.

Reference

1. Budget 2008-09 - Highlights—India Development Gateway.
2. Census of India, 2001.
3. National Literacy Mission— Literacy Scenario in India—Literacy rates for Total Population, Schedule Caste Population and Schedule Tribe Population by Sex.
4. Reserve Bank of India Report-2007-08.
5. The Evaluation of State Bank of India (Volume III).
6. Times of India, 1st Septembr 2007.

23

Pioneering Institutions in Adult Education – Aicmed, ams, iaea, Literacy House, Rdt, Sevamandir

Introduction

The contribution of the human factor towards progress both in the urban and rural areas, can't be over emphasized, more so in a world of ever-changing social systems and values. Such an endless task – like the development of educational activities for innumerable farmers and workers, illiterate and semi-illiterate adults, men and women, boys and girls – needs a deep involvement of all national forces, government and non-governmental. From even before 1947, voluntary organisations have been playing a significant role in the reconstruction of education and their success has been in no small measure owing to the dedication of social workers and the larger academic and administrative freedom they enjoy to conduct new experiments.

Voluntary organisations are initiating and developing activities and programmes which can be considered to be of relevance to adult education directly or indirectly. This trend needs to be encouraged and supported. Many of them are closely linking their out-of school activities or programmes of social education with other socio-economic or socio-cultural goals which are part of their objectives.

The contribution of voluntary organisations in general has been encouraging, promising and stimulating. It is fervently hoped, that voluntary organisations, both from their headquarters and in the field will expand their interest for adult and youth education, as well as channelise their efforts to common national goals.

The contribution of the following six voluntary agencies to the development of adult education, non-formal education is briefly described.

1. ALL INDIA COUNCIL FOR MASS EDUCATION AND DEVELOPMENT (AICMED), WEST BENGAL.
2. ANDHRA MAHILA SABHA (AMS), HYDERABAD.
3. INDIAN ADULT EDUCATION ASSOCIATION (IAEA), NEW DELHI.
4. LITERACY HOUSE, LUCKNOW
5. RDT, ANATAPUR.

SEVAMANDIR, UDAIPUR.

ALL INDIA COUNCIL FOR MASS EDUCATION AND DEVELOPMENT (AICMED), WEST BENGAL

All India Council for Mass Education and Development (AICMED), established in 1987 (Regn. No. S/56626 1987-88) is a voluntary non - profiteering registered organisation. It is also covered by Foreign Contribution Regulation Act (FCRA) of the Government of India (Regn. No. 147120474).

It had its genesis in the formation, in 1965, of the West Bengal Students' Council to Eradicate Illiteracy, which was the culmination of large-scale mobilisation of students and youth from the colleges and universities of Calcutta to the villages of West Bengal to launch a mass literacy campaign. The vision of the organisation is to develop an enlightened, empowered and self-sustained rural community - both materially and morally. The mission of AICMED is 'enlightenment' and 'empowerment', particularly of the poor and the underprivileged, with special emphasis on women and the tribal people.

Aims and Objectives

- o To encourage and develop adult education programme as a part of the development programme.
- o To encourage and promote voluntary actions in the rural areas in favour of rural development and introduction of advanced technology.
- o To organise workshop and prepare teaching and learning materials for various programmes.
- o To orient adult education functionaries and development activists of different levels so that they can undertake adult education and developmental programmes independently.
- o To undertake research and promotional work to develop and sharpen existing technologies and methodologies of rural development. The structure of the organisation provides opportunities to involve people of different kinds drawn from a wide spectrum of the society.

Activities

In the course of implementing National Adult Education Programme, AICMED has developed people's organisation in 13 of the 17 districts of West Bengal and elsewhere. However, presently it has concentrated activities in several districts of West Bengal, Andhra Pradesh, Jharkhand, Orissa and Tripura in other rural development programmes.

AICMED conducts projects, holds seminars & camps, organises exhibitions, runs awareness and training programmes, and such other activities lead to the empowerment of the poor and the underprivileged of our society.

It has successfully completed, and has been continuing, the projects in the following domains in West Bengal and Tripura.

- **Mass Education Programmes:** Adult Education, women's education, early childhood education and non-formal education.
- **Gender & Health Programmes:** Health & Family Welfare especially mother & child health, Family Planning, awareness and different aspects of women's/men's awareness.
- **Livelihood Generation Programmes:** Training in modern fishery activities, poultry farming, piggery, weaving etc. especially among the rural people.
- **Environment Programme:** Safe drinking water, use of eco-friendly organic fertilisers, smoke-less chulhas etc. among villagers.
- **Herbal Programmes:** Capacity building workshops on Herb therapy, kitchen-gardening of relevant herbs, cottage-scale preparation of herbal products (like spices, pickles, jam), preservation, containerization and micro-marketing of the products.
- **Arsenic Programmes:** Mass awareness generation and mitigation of arsenic pollution through community participation in forty villages of two districts of West Bengal. The mitigation devices include Arsenic Removal Plants, Rainwater Harvesting Units and Domestic Filters.
- **Other Programmes:** AICMED, through its central resource centre in Calcutta (which houses a modest library of relevant books, documents, pamphlets, handbills etc.) continually disseminates useful information among potential users.

ANDHRA MAHILA SABHA (AMS), HYDERABAD

Introduction

Andhra Mahila Sabha, a unique institution dedicated to the up-liftment of women, was established by Padma Vibhushan Dr.(Smt) Durgabai Deshmukh in 1948 as a registered society under Indian Societies Act (XXI) of 1860 and a Trust in the same year. With its Central Office located in Hyderabad, Andhra Mahila

Sabha has 30 units working under its flag – 9 of them in Chennai and rest in the State of Andhra Pradesh. The institutions run by Andhra Mahila Sabha cater to care of Women, Children, Senior Citizens, Disabled, Health and Education.

Aims and Objectives

Andhra Mahila Sabha is a non-profitable voluntary organisation with the specific objective of promoting education and training of women to overcome their socio-economic and political backwardness and empower them to participate in all aspects of national development. It has also established a regional handicraft training institute for the women. AMS runs a hospital and research centre providing various services including outpatient services in eye care, general surgery, orthopedics and in patient services including neo-natal unit and well equipped air conditioned operation theatres. It also runs a vocational training and rehabilitation centre, girls high school and colleges and legal aid centre for women.

Activities

Andhra Mahila Sabha is the premier Women's organization in the country, with around 40 units functioning under its logo. These units focus on education, health care, upliftment, empowerment, old age care of the downtrodden of the society, in particular women, causes dear to Dr Durgabai Deshmukh's legendary figure of 20th Century. The major services provided by the various institutions established under this organization are:

- Education
- Health
- Rehabilitation
- Training
- Women's issues

o Education Provides training and education to women and children and enable them to harness their services for building the nation. Dr Durgabai Deshmukh was inspired by the work done by Welthy H Fisher, a Canadian literacy worker at Lucknow, Uttar Pradesh. This led to the establishment of Literacy house at Andhra Mahila Sabha during 1967.

The Progammes/ Courses under Andhra Mahila Sabha Literacy House

- Computer Courses
- Fabric Painting
- Glass Painting
- Embroidery
- Tailoring and Maggam work
- Basic Art designers Drawing Grade I & II
- Pre Primary Teacher Training
- Hand Writing
- Speed Mathematics
- Concentration & Memory
- Personality Development

Andhra Mahila Sabha has publications to its credit. AMS, Chennai releases a bi-monthly newsletter. AMS, Hyderabad releases a quarterly newsletter.

- o Health Care Outreaches giving free treatment to the needy and dedicated to the rehabilitation and integration of disabled children.
- o Upliftment & Empowerment Spreads literacy among women, counsels them on matrimonial and property matters, conducts training for trainers of teachers and teachers and also in various mass media of communication.
- o Old Age Care Provides shelter and food at affordable price to the needy senior citizens who desired to live the remaining years of respectably.

INDIAN ADULT EDUCATION ASSOCIATION, NEW DELHI

Introduction

Indian Adult Education Association was established on 2nd Dec. 1939, Under the Indian Societies Registration Act. 1860. With unflinching faith in the effective participation of every citizen in social, economic, religious and political life of the country and consequent there to the imperative need for every citizen to have access to the expanding realms of knowledge through adult and life-long education, IAEA is specially committed to ceaselessly work towards raising the literacy level in its overall bid to safeguard the interests of the illiterates, down-trodden and deprived sections of population so as to enable them to take their rightful place in society.

In the beginning, IAEA's major emphasis was on creation of public opinion for a public policy on adult education, besides mobilising support from government and other public institutions for literacy movement. Today, when adult education has been duly recognised as an essential component of national reconstruction, IAEA functions as a federation of some 500 affiliated organisations spread throughout the length and breadth of the country, supporting their activities by bringing them together in its conferences, seminars, workshops and discussion groups. Through its publications, both periodic and otherwise, IAEA disseminates research findings and field experience on adult/non-formal and life-long continuing education to its more than 2500 'life' and yearly individual members coming from its 16 state branches, and others.

Aims and Objectives

1. Spread knowledge among the people of India on all subjects related to their all-round development, welfare and culture in a popular and attractive manner through suitable agencies.
2. Initiate, wherever necessary, adult education activities in cooperation with various organisations and individuals

interested in the work, and to encourage and coordinate local efforts and organisations engaged in promoting the cause of adult education.

3. Serve as a 'Clearing House' for exchange of ideas, information and advice concerning adult education in different States of India.
4. Cooperate with movements aiming at removal of illiteracy and ignorance, and promotion of civic, economic and cultural interests of the people.
5. Serve as a connecting link for inter-State cooperation and coordination among the State Governments and NGOs.
6. Prepare and supply, if necessary, slides, charts, films, booklets, suitable literature, etc., and to undertake publication of bulletins, newsletters and journals. Arrange public lectures, demonstrations, seminars, etc., in furtherance of the objectives of the Association.
7. Organise All India Adult Education Conferences, Zonal, Regional and State level Conferences in furtherance of its objective.
8. Persuade universities, Govt. Depts.; NGOs; colleges and other educational bodies in the country to take up adult education work and to do all other acts that are incidental to fulfillment of the above mentioned aims and objectives of the Association.

Activities

Functions of IAEA are as varied and wide-ranging as its aims and objectives. The following is a brief account of its activities over the years.

As Catalytic Agent

Being a pioneer, promoter, catalyst and leader, IAEA advises Central/ State Governments, Universities, State Resource Centres, Jan Shikshan Sansthans, Zilla Saksharta Samitis (ZSSs), its member-institutions and other organisations on adult, non formal and population education programmes.

As 'Clearing House'

IAEA has been functioning as a 'Clearing House' to disseminate information on growth and development of adult education through its periodicals, books, correspondence, etc., for the benefit of individuals and organisations.

Training

IAEA accords high priority to training of adult education functionaries. Since 1948, it has been organising training for adult education functionaries and public opinion leaders. It organises intra-state and inter-state training for key-level functionaries of Government Departments, NGOs, Universities, Colleges and trade union workers in different parts of the country, including the far flung areas.

IAEA also provides hands-on training in computer and information technology to women. The Association is recognised as a Study Centre of Makhanlal Chaturvedi University, Bhopal for DCA and PGDCA courses and Accredited Vocational Institute of National Institute of Open Schooling (Previously National Open School). The Association has started Library Science and CCA courses.

Research

IAEA accords high priority to research in adult education to strengthen the programme of adult education. It undertakes surveys and research projects on its own as well as in collaboration with other institutions.

Research Methodology Courses

IAEA also organises Research Methodology Courses for budding researchers in collaboration with Jawaharlal Nehru University, Directorate of Adult Education, Government of India and other agencies. So far 10 courses have been organised by the Association.

Research Fellowship

IAEA instituted Mohan Sinha Mehta Research Fellowship in 1986 in honour of its late President Dr. Mohan Sinha Mehta. This fellowship is awarded every year to individuals to carry out research in the field of Adult Education.

Monitoring and Evaluation

IAEA has, over the years, been engaged in monitoring and evaluation of literacy programmes. Empanelled by the National Literacy Mission for this purpose, IAEA has undertaken external evaluation work of the Total Literacy Campaigns/Post Literacy Programmes in about 22 districts in the country.

Other Activities

Under UNFPA-assisted project on Population Education in Adult Literacy Programme, IAEA houses the National Documentation Centre on Literacy and Population Education (DCLPE). Its activities were given below:

- Publication of quarterly Indian Journal of Population Education containing information on health education, adolescent education and gender issues, family welfare and population education in India
- Bringing out quarterly bibliography/accession list of latest acquisitions on population and population education
- Publication of bi-monthly Newsletter on Population Education
- Repackaging and dissemination of information through networking arrangements with various agencies, institutions and persons.
- Acquiring books and periodicals on the subject from national/international organisations.

IAEA has established an International Institute of Adult and Life Long Education. The mission of the Institute is to professionalize adult education by strengthening and promoting it as a distinct but distinguished field of practice and discipline of study.

LITERACY HOUSE, LUCKNOW

'Literacy is an idea whose time has come. Local, national and international programmes – public and private-are hard at work on one of the most stubborn problems facing mankind-the development of an articulate and informed citizenry in a free society'.

—Welthy Honsinger Fisher

Introduction

Literacy House was founded in 1953 by Dr. Welthy H. Fisher. Mahatma Gandhi, Six weeks before his assassination said, "Cities have everything. Our villages have nothing. Go and help the villages". This was the first step shown to Mr. W.H. Fisher. She took the first step in 1953 when she started her literacy work for the villages near Alhabad. At the request of the Governor, the literacy House was moved to Kucknow in 1956 and literacy work began on the present campus. Literacy house is the creation of the Ford Foundation. It is situated six miles from the City on the Luknow-Kanpur Road.

Aims and Objectives

- o To develop through its programmes of education and training, the techniques of communication with the masses.
- o To produce educational materials-books, pamphlets, periodicals and simple audio-visual aids such as flash cards, khaddar graphs, puppets and puppet stages etc. for illiterate and literate adults.
- o To produce professional literature for adult education and literacy workers.
- o To publish books in Hindi, English and other languages dealing with problems such as those of citizenship, cottage industries, folk literature, health and agriculture.

Activities

Illiteracy is strongly linked to poverty, poor health, disadvantage and exclusion, and education is not an issue that stands in isolation from the many challenges that face the poor.

As a result, Literacy House has developed a highly integrated approach to literacy that includes community programs that focus on women's rights, social justice, and health care, access to public services, advocacy, and community building.

Adult Literacy Programme

In UP, according to census 2001 survey, the literacy rate in Male are 68.8% and among adult women literacy rates are 42.98% only. In India the overall literacy rate is 64.8 % (Male: 75.3%; Female: 53.7%). Historically, a variety of factors have been found to be responsible for poor female literate rate,viz gender based inequality, social discrimination and economic exploitation, occupation of girl child in domestic chores, low enrolment of girls in schools and low retention rate and high dropout rate.

Children's Education Programme

In India, only 62% of children reach grade 5 and one-third of all children aged 6 to 14 do not attend school. Presently 62 Balwadi Kendras are running either through literacy house directly or rural NGO partners in 9 districts of eastern UP where over 1600 kids are receiving informal education.

Health Awareness Programme

Major Activities of Health Program are: Clinical Support, House Visit, Immunization, Health Awareness Meeting, Pregnant women check up and distribution of Iron / Folic acid tab, Health awareness Camp, Sterilization and distribution of family planning material, Networking for health facilities, Special Cases, Health Staff Training etc.

Health Awareness Meetings

A combined total of 300 Health awareness meeting were held in the period April 2005 to March 2006.

Social Enterprise Programme

The term 'Social Enterprise' implies a linking of business ventures to achieving social good. 'Social enterprise' program consists of assisting poor women in developing new methods of income generation, especially through small business ventures, in order to improve the income and quality of life of their families.

Advocacy Programme

The advocacy program works to actively engage targeted communities on issues of human rights, women's empowerment, literacy, democratization and good governance. Our goal is to help these people understand the larger issues that affect the quality of their lives, and to enable them to make their voices heard for change.

RDT, ANATAPUR

Introduction

The Rural Development Trust (RDT) is a voluntary organisation working in Anantapur District of Andhra Pradesh, India. Fr. Vincent Ferror was established RDT in the year 1969. Anantapur district is the second most drought prone district in India due to failure of monsoons coupled with untimely and erratic rains and also high wind velocity and extreme heat. The average rainfall in the district is around 520 millimeter per annum, ranging from 120 millimeters in some parts to 650 millimeters in some other parts of the district. Temperatures normally upto 45 degrees centigrade in summer and wind velocity reaches 50 to 60 kilometers per hour during the wind season. The district lies between 13'-40' and 15'-15' northern latitude and 76'-50' and 78'-30' eastern longitude.

Aim and Objective

The main and for most aim and objective of RDT is overall rural development in Anatapur Distcit.

Activities

- Rural Development
- Women empowerment
- Child Education

- Health Facility
- Cultural Development
- Old age Homes

SEVA MANDIR

Introduction

Dr Mohan Singh Mehta a social worker and an educationalist, founded Seva Mandir. Udaipur, in the pre-independence period 1900-1947, was witness to an increasing awareness among educationalists and liberal thinkers of the particular backwardness and political stagnation of Rajasthan. This realisation provoked a move to change, and inspired certain individuals, who had imbibed ideas of voluntarism, to seize the initiative. Dr Mehta, not only played a very important role in founding Seva Mandir in 1966, but also was an inspiration to progressive change throughout Udaipur District. He was a true liberal influenced by the thoughts of Tagore, Gandhi, Dr. Kunzru, and Pandit Madan Mohan Malviya and by tenets of the scout movement. In pre-independence time he served as education minister and Prime Minister of Banswara in the State of Mewar and later as an Ambassador of independent India and as Vice Chancellor of Rajasthan University. He set up Vidya Bhavan at Udaipur in 1931, one of the pioneer co-educational institutions, with the philosophy of treating every child as a unique individual and molding them into citizens with sound moral character and a deep sense of social responsibility.

Aims and Objectives

- To create and strengthen institutions for development (at the village, organization and society levels)
- To enhance people's capabilities for self-development (both at individual and community level); and
- To create sustainable improvements in the livelihoods base; These three objectives form the basis for Seva Mandir's three program sectors.

Activities

- Natural Resources Regeneration
- Non Farm Income Generation
- Education
- Health
- Women's Empowerment
- Child and Youth Development
- Village Institution
- Building
- People's Management School

Each of these programs, in achieving its respective goals, is also designed to build values and social capacities needed to achieve development and democracy for the poor.

Note:

- At present there are 165 Balwadi centers in Seva Mandir's work area, reaching out to a total of 3,806 children.
- Today some 9,307 women have managed to amass a total saving of Rs.6, 172,957 at women's groups.

Conclusions

India is a democratic country. We have freedom to do any type of good work. The literacy rate of India very less when compared to any other developed country or developing in the world. The roles of NGOs' are very important to increase literacy rate. They have a prominent role to do all the activities like literacy improvement, empowerment etc. Education in general, Adult Education in particular gives strength to human beings. Educate all the human beings.

References

1. All India Council for Mass Education and Development (AICMED).
2. Annual Reports. Lucknow, India: Literacy House, 1958, 1959, 1960, 1961, 1962, and 1963.

3. Anuradha Prasad et.al., (2005): "Living in Diversity", External Review.
4. Complete Puppet Kit. A leaflet, Ibid. Undated.
5. "Eleventh Anniversary of Literacy House," National Herald. New York. February 14, 1964.
6. Fisher, Welthy M. To Light A Candle. London: Peter Davies, Ltd. 1963.
7. Go to Ramon Magsaysay Award Foundation Online
8. Grimes, Paul. "Literacy Village near Lucknow Keeps Promise of Aid to Gandhi," New York Times. April 2, 1961.
9. Imprint. Bombay: F & S Distributors Private Ltd. Vol. 3, no. 7, October 1963.
10. Koshy, T. A. Five Year Plan - A Summary. Lucknow India: Literacy House. November 22, 1960
11. Lederer, William J: and Eugene Burdick. "Some Non-Ugly Americans," Life International. New York. March 14, 1960.
12. Lekhak. Lucknow, India: Literacy House, Vol. 2, no. 2, April 1962; Vol. 3, no. 3, 4, January 1964.
13. "Light for the Illiterate," Asia Magazine. Hong Kong. December 3, 1961.
14. Literacy House, The First Decade. Delhi: Publications Division, Indian Cooperative Union. 1963.
15. Messages Received on the 10th Anniversary of the Founding of Literacy House, Lucknow, India. February 15, 1963.
16. News Circle. Delhi: American Women's Club. Vol. 4, no. 9, May 1959.
17. Shah, M. A. Hyder. "The Literacy Village in Lucknow," The Asian Student. San Francisco: Asia Foundation. May 13, 1961.
18. Siddiqi, Abdur Rashid. An Approach to Educating Adults for Functional Literacy in India. A thesis presented to the Faculty of the Graduate School of Cornell University for the Degree of Master of Science, September 1963.

19. Simple Visual Aids on Development Problems. Lucknow, India: Literacy House. Undated.

20. "Teaching People to Teach People to Read and Write," Yojana. India. February 19, 1961.

21. Visit to Literacy House and its field work in the villages. Interviews with persons acquainted with Mrs. Fisher and her work.

22. www.andhramahilasabha.com

23. www.sevamandir.com

24

Role of Ncte, Ncert, Ciet, Scert for the Cause of Teacher Education

According to Sri *Sarvepalli Radha Krishnan,* Teacher is a national builder. Education is a powerful instrument of national development. Education is a solution of all types of problems in the society. Through education we get knowledge, good habits, character, morals and values. We have thousands of years of tradition and culture. In Vedas the teacher was called 'Guru'. According to Indians teacher is third god. We give more respect to teacher after mother and father in the society.

Teacher is a national builder. It is necessary to give importance to teacher education. Today's children are tomorrow's citizens. By taking good steps in the framing of teacher education curriculum, we can give good quality and value based education to the teachers.

National Council for Teacher Education, National Council of Educational Research and Training, Central Institute of Educational Technology, State Council of Educational Research and Training etc. are the institutions for the strengthening the teacher education in India.

National Council for Teacher Education (NCTE)

The National Council for Teacher Education, in its previous status since 1973, was an advisory body for the Central and State Governments on all matters pertaining to teacher education, with its Secretariat in the Department of Teacher Education of the National Council of Educational Research and Training (NCERT). Despite its commendable work in the academic fields, it could not perform essential regulatory functions, to ensure maintenance of standards in teacher education and preventing proliferation of substandard teacher education institutions. The National Policy on Education (NPE), 1986 and the Programme of Action there under, envisaged a National Council for Teacher Education with statutory status and necessary resources as a first step for overhauling the system of teacher education. The National Council for Teacher Education as a statutory body came into existence in pursuance of the National Council for Teacher Education Act, 1993 (No.73 of 1993) on the 17th August,1995.

Objective of NCTE

The main objective of the NCTE is to achieve planned and coordinated development of the teacher education system throughout the country, the regulation and proper maintenance of Norms and Standards in the teacher education system and for matters connected therewith. The mandate given to the NCTE is very broad and covers the whole gamut of teacher education programmes including research and training of persons for equipping them to teach at pre-primary, primary, secondary and senior secondary stages in schools, and non-formal education, part-time education, adult education and distance (correspondence) education courses.

Organizational Structure of NCTE

NCTE has its head quarter at New Delhi and four Regional Committees at Banglore, Bhopal, Bhubaneshwar and Jaipur to look after its statutory responsibilities. In order to enable the NCTE to perform the assigned functions including planned and co-ordinated development and initiating innovations in teacher education, the NCTE in Delhi as well as its four Regional Committees have administrative and academic wings to deal respectively with finance, establishment and legal matters and with research, policy planning, monitoring, curriculum, innovations, co-ordination, library and documentation, in-service programmes. The NCTE Headquarters is headed by the Chairperson, while each Regional Committee is headed by a Regional Director.

All teacher education colleges are under the control of NCTE. There are 24 Government D.Ed. colleges, 324 B.Ed., Government, aided and un-aided colleges, 17 Telugu pandit training colleges, 5 UGDPEd colleges, 7 B.P.Ed. Colleges, 5 Urdu pandit training colleges and 20 M.Ed., colleges under the control of NCTE in Andhra Pradesh. Nearly 50 thousands of trainee teachers are studying in all the above colleges. It is the duty of NCTE to provide quality education in all the above colleges. It is the duty of NCTE to frame curriculum for teacher education.

The Parliament appreciated the role of quality teacher education in providing quality teachers for quality school education and passed an Act in 1993 for setting up of the National Council for Teacher Education (NCTE) as a statutory body. The broad mandate given to the NCTE is to achieve planned and co-ordinated development of the teacher education system throughout the country, the regulation and proper maintenance of norms and standards in the teacher education system and for matters connected therewith.

The NCTE has been conducting orientation programmes on education in human values for teacher educators and repackaging electronically the contributions of the experts and those of the participants. The outcomes of its programmes are distributed to each of its recognized institutions on multimedia CD-ROMs and through the World Wide Web of the Internet. Full texts of publications on value education in easily downloadable form have been made available on the NCTE web site (http://www.ncte-in.org). Titles related to value education available from the NCTE web site are: Education for Character Development; Education for Tomorrow; Report of the Working Group to Review Teachers' Training Programme; Role and Responsibility of Teachers in Building up Modern India; Gandhi on Education; Sri Aurobindo on Education; and Tilak on Education. The titles of the NCTE CD-ROMs on value education are New Education for New India - Integral Education of Sri Aurobindo, Jeevan Vigyan and Teachers as Transformers. A CD-ROM based on the workshop that was organised by the NCTE jointly with the Chinmaya World Centre will be released shortly. Recently, in December 2001 two workshops on value orientation in teacher education for teacher educators of the Southern States were organised by the RIMSE (Ramakrishna Institute for Moral and Spiritual Education).

It may be appreciated that the role of the NCTE in bringing any curricular change in teacher education programme, even providing facilitation in integration of education in human values in it, at best, is that of a catalytic agent. What NCTE is trying is to make available a basketful of resource materials on education in human values to teacher education institutions.

National Counsel of Educational Research and Training (NCERT)

The National Council of Educational Research and Training (NCERT) is an apex resource organisation set up by the Government of India, with headquarters at New Delhi, to assist and advise the Central and State Governments on academic matters related to school education. NCERT doing so many researches to improve the quality of teacher education. The objective of NCERT is to assist and advise the Ministry of Education and Social Welfare in the implementation of its policies and major programmes in the field of education, particularly school education. The NCERT provides academic and technical support for improvement of school education through its various constituents, which are:

- o National Institute of Education, New Delhi
- o Central Institute of Education Technology, New Delhi
- o Pandit Sunderlal Sharma Central Institute of Vocational Education, Bhopal

- o Regional Institute of Education, Ajmer
- o Regional Institute of Education, Bhopal
- o Regional Institute of Education, Bhubaneswar
- o Regional Institute of Education, Mysore.
- o North Eastern-Regional Institute of Education, Shillong

Priorities

Among the top priorities of NCERT are:

- o Implementation of National Curriculum framework
- o Universalization of Elementary Education (UEE)
- o Vocational education
- o Education of groups with special needs
- o Early childhood education
- o Evaluation and examination reform information technology (IT) education
- o Value Education
- o Educational Technology
- o Development of exemplary textbooks/workbooks/teacher's guide/supplementary reading materials
- o Production of the girl child
- o Identification and nurturing of talent
- o Guidance and counselling
- o Improvement in teacher education
- o International relations

By conducting national seminars, workshops and conferences NCERT gives valuable recommendations to teacher education. Now we are living in the technological world.

Programmes and Activities

The NCERT undertakes the following programmes and activities.

Research

Being an apex national body for research in school education, the NCERT performs the important functions of conducting and supporting research and offering training in educational research methodology. The different Departments of the National Institute of Education (NIE), Regional Institutes of Education (RIEs), Central Institute of Educational Technology (CIET) and Pandit Sunderlal Sharma Central Institute of Vocational Education (PSSCIVE) undertake programmes of research related to different aspects of school education, including teacher education.

Besides conducting in-house research, the NCERT supports research programmes of other institutions/organizations by providing financial assistance and academic guidance. Assistance is given to scholars for publication of their Ph.D. theses. Research fellowships are offered to encourage studies in school education to create a research base for developmental, training and extension programmes and to create a pool of competent research workers. It also organizes courses for educational research workers. The NCERT also organizes educational research in the country. It has computer facilities for storing, processing and retrieval of data. It collaborates with international agencies in inter-country research projects.

Development

Developmental activities in school education constitute an important function of the NCERT. The major developmental activities include development and renewal of curricula and instructional materials for various levels of school education and making them relevant to changing needs of children and society. The innovative developmental activities include development of curricula and instructional materials in school education in the area of pre-school education, formal and non-formal education, vocationalisation of education and teacher education. Developmental activities are also undertaken in the domains of educational technology, population education, and education of the disabled and other special groups.

Training

Another important dimension of NCERT's activities is the pre-service and in-service training of teachers at various levels; pre-primary, elementary, secondary and higher secondary, and also in such areas as vocational education, educational technology, guidance and counseling, and special education. The pre-service teacher education programmes at the Regional Institutes of Education (RIEs) incorporate innovative features such as integration of content and methodology of teaching, long-term internship of teacher trainees in the actual classroom setting, and participation of students in community work. The RIEs also undertake the training of key personnel of the states and of state level institutions and training of teacher educators and in-service teachers.

Extension

The NCERT has comprehensive extension programmes in which various Departments of the NIE, RIEs, CIET, PSSCIVE and the offices of the Field Advisers in the states are engaged in various ways. It works in close collaboration with various agencies and institutions in the states and also works extensively with Extension Service Departments and Centers in teacher training colleges and schools with the purpose of providing assistance to various categories of personnel, including teachers, teacher educators, educational administrators, question-paper setters, textbook writers etc. Conferences, seminars, workshops and competitions are organized *as* regular on-going programmes as a part of the extension activities. Several programmes are organized in rural and backward areas in order to reach out to the functionaries in these areas where special problems exist and where special efforts are needed. Special programmes are organized for the education of the disadvantaged sections of the society. The extension programmes cover all States and Union Territories of the country.

Publication and Dissemination

The NCERT publishes textbooks for different school subjects for Classes I to XII. It also brings out workbooks, teachers guides, supplementary readers, research reports, etc. In addition, it publishes instructional materials for the use of teacher educators, teacher trainees and in-service teachers. These instructional materials, produced through research and developmental work, serve as models to various agencies in States and Union Territories. These are made available to state level agencies for adoption and/or adaptation. The textbooks are published in English, Hindi and Urdu.

For dissemination of educational information, or the NCERT publishes six journals: *The Primary Teacher* is published both in English and Hindi and aims at giving meaningful and relevant educational inputs to primary school teachers for direct use in the classroom; *School Science* serves as an open forum for discussion on various aspects of science education; *Journal of Indian Education* provides a forum for encouraging original and critical thinking in education through discussion on current educational issues; *Indian Educational Review* contains research articles and provides a forum for researchers in education; and *Bharatiya Adhunik Shiksha,* published in Hindi, provides a forum for encouraging critical thinking in education on contemporary issues and for dissemination of educational problems and practices. Besides these, a house journal called *NCERT Newsletter* is also published in English and Hindi. The title of the Hindi version of the newsletter is *Shaikshik Darpan.*

Exchange Programmes

The NCERT interacts with international organisations such as UNESCO, UNICEF, UNDP (United Nations Development Progammes), NFPA (National Federation of Paralegal Associations) and the World Bank to study specific educational problems and to arrange training programmes for personnel from developing countries. It is one of the Associated Centers of APEID (Asia-Pacific Programme of Educational Innovation for Development). It also acts as the Secretariat of the National Development Group (NDG) for Educational Innovations. The NCERT has been offering training facilities, usually through attachment programmes and participation in workshops, to educational workers of other countries. The NCERT also acts as a major agency for implementing the Bilateral Cultural Exchange Programmes entered into by the Government of India with the governments of other countries in the fields of school education and teacher education by sending delegations to study specific educational problems relevant to Indian requirements and by arranging training and study visits for scholars from other countries. Educational materials are exchanged with other countries. On request, the faculty members are deputed to participate in international conferences, seminars, workshops, symposia, etc.

Central Institute of Educational Technology (CIET) - India

Central Institute of Educational Technology (CIET) is a constituent unit of the National Council of Educational Research and Training (NCERT), an autonomous organisation under the Ministry of Human Resources Development, Government of India. Established in 1984 with the merger of the Centre of Educational Technology and Department of Teaching Aids. Its chief aim is to promote Educational Technology especially mass media singly or in combinations (multimedia packages) to extend educational opportunities and improve quality of educational processes at the school level.

As a premier institute of Educational Technology at the apex level, major functions of the CIET are:

- To design, develop, try out and disseminate alternative learning systems to achieve the national goal of universalisation of primary education and
- To address various educational problems at micro and macro levels. The broad areas of activities of the CIET are as given below:
- To design and produce media software materials viz., television/ radio (for both broadcast as well as non-broadcast use) film, graphics and other programmes for strengthening the transaction of curricular and co-curricular activities at the school level.

- o To create competencies in development and use of educational software materials mentioned above through training in areas such as script development, media production, media communication, media research, technical operations, setting up studios, repair and maintenance of equipment.
- o To train the faculty of Institutes of Advanced Study in Education/Colleges of Teacher Education and District Institutes of Education and Training in the use of Educational Technology in their teacher education programmes.
- o To undertake research evaluation and monitoring of the systems, programmes and materials with a view to improving the materials and increasing their effectiveness.
- o To document and disseminate information, materials and media programmes for better utilization and to function as a clearing house / agency in the field of Educational Technology.
- o To advise and coordinate the academic and technical programmes and activities of the SIET set up by the MHRD in six states of India.
- o To ensure a continuous progress in the quality of production, various evaluation studies are carried out on a regular basis. Some of the important research programmes undertaken during the year 1997-98 are:

- Monitoring and evaluation of Training
- Analysis of viewer's mail
- Field-testing of media programmes
- Review of research with implications for media production
- A need assessment for media programmes for the middle schools.

Sate Counsel of Educational Research and Training

The State Council of Educational Research and Training (SCERT) Andhra Pradesh was established on 27-07-1967, amalgamating the following institutions:

1. The State Institute of Education.
2. The State Bureau of Education and Vocational Guidance.
3. The State Science Education Unit and
4. The State Evaluation Unit

Objectives

- To organize in – service training for teacher educators and to teachers of Primary, Upper Primary and Secondary Schools.
- To Act as a clearing house for ideas and information to keep the teacher educators and teachers abreast of the latest developments in the field of Education
- To provide academic guidance to the schools through extension services.
- To undertake studies, investigations and surveys relating to educational matters on the appraisal of educational programmes.
- To Undertake and co – ordinate action research projects on instructional practices, Educational problems etc.
- To undertake publication of books, periodicals and other literature necessary for furtherance of knowledge for teachers.
- To undertake evaluation and research studies to find out the impact of educational programmes in the state.

Functions

Based on its objectives as the academic wing of the Department of School Education. The following are the functions of SCERT.

- Preparation of curricula, syllabi, instructional material for Primary, Upper Primary, Secondary and alternative systems of education.
- Department of evaluation procedures and material which are helpful to the practicing teachers.
- Bridging gaps between the methods and techniques advocated in training and the actual classroom practices.

- o Dissemination of knowledge to improved methods and techniques to be followed by educational institutions.
- o Co-ordination with national and international organizations in academic programmes.
- o Organization of orientation programmes for the professional growth of teachers, teacher – education, supervisor's etc.
- o Publication of journals, periodicals, books etc.,
- o Resource support to implement the academic policies lay down by the Government.

Services

Constituent Units

SCERT has some constituent units spread over the entire state. They are:-

- o Institutes or Advances Study in Education (IASEs) Colleges of Teacher Education. (CTEs)
- o District institutes of Education and Training (DIETs)/ Teacher Training institutes (T.T.I.s)
- o Extension Service Departments.
- o Science Teacher's Centers.

Professional Growth

For the professional growth of teachers, SCERT takes up in-service training courses for Primary, Upper – Primary, Secondary teachers and teacher–educators, besides providing sources material like hand books, manuals and other publications. SCERT also organizes seminars. Workshops, conferences involving teachers, teacher - educators, supervisors and administrators.

Research and Evaluation

SCERT undertakes action research, studies, experimental research and evaluation of the programmes implemented by it. It also promotes research and evaluation studies by teacher educators and action research by the practicing teachers.

Co-ordinate Efforts

SCERT co-ordinates various academic programmes of IASE's CTE's. DIETs. TTIs and the Extention Services Departments functioning in IASE, CTEs and DIETs.

Future Vision of the Department

National Policy of Education 1986 and Programme of action lay a lot of stress on the qualitative improvement of education. The Govt. of India has made the State Councils of Education Research and Training as nodal agencies to look into the task of qualitative improvement of Elementary Education at Elementary and Secondary Education levels. Teacher Education Institution like DIETs, IASEs, CTEs etc., co-ordinate and implement UNICEF projects like UGC, EFA (Education For All) and other projects like MLL (Minimum Level of Learning), Distance Education. The institution's major responsibility is to ensure quality in teacher education.

SCERT organizes seminars, workshops, conferences with the help of NCERT, NCTE AND NIEPA to give quality education for teachers.

Conclusion

We know teacher is a national builder. He has a power to change the world. It is necessary to take care about teacher education. NCTE, NCERT, CIET and SCERT have to play prominent role in the development of quality in teacher education. NCTE has major role in framing of teacher education curriculum and establishment of teacher education institutions. We are living in the modern world. It is necessary to use technology. It is necessary to provide computer and technology labs and other type of labs.

Index

D

E

F

G

H

I